"If he had read *Unequal Development and Capitalism*, Napoleon would have exclaimed: 'From the heights of this pyramid, two centuries of economics of the profit rate look down upon developing countries. Highly recommend.'"

Gérard Duménil, *Director of Research at the Centre National de la Recherche Scientifique, Paris*

Unequal Development and Capitalism

Unequal development has been a defining characteristic of capitalism. Throughout history, countries and regions have exhibited differences in labor productivity growth – a key determinant in poverty reduction and development – and although some nations may catch up with the productivity levels or well-being of developed economies at times, others fall behind. This book explores these processes of catching up and falling behind of developing countries from Asia, Latin America, Central and Eastern Europe, and Africa in relation to the US economy from 1970 to 2019.

The research presented in this book integrates a historical interpretation of post-World War II capitalism with economic theory and empirical analysis. By exploring the historical experiences of these countries, the book provides an overview of their economic transformations. The interplay between technical change, profit rate and capital accumulation, on one hand, and institutional change, on the other, are combined to explain the dynamics of catching up or falling behind in labor and capital productivities. Furthermore, the book provides, from the perspective of developing countries, fundamental lessons for the implementation of successful strategies for catching up and development.

This book is a major resource for readers interested in economic growth and development, heterodox macroeconomics, development economics, and related areas.

Adalmir Antonio Marquetti is Professor of Economics at the Pontifícia Universidade Católica do Rio Grande do Sul (PUCRS), Porto Alegre, Brazil.

Alessandro Miebach is Associate Professor of Economics at the Department of Economics, Universidade Federal do Rio Grande do Sul (UFRGS), Porto Alegre, Brazil.

Henrique Morrone is Associate Professor of Economics at the Department of Economics, Universidade Federal do Rio Grande do Sul (UFRGS), Porto Alegre, Brazil.

Routledge Frontiers of Political Economy

Economic Policies of Populist Leaders
A Central and Eastern European Perspective
Edited by István Benczes

Political Economy of the Spanish Miracle
State, Labor and Capital, 1931–1973
Diego Ayala

Heterodox Economics and Global Emergencies
Voices from Around the World
Edited by Ariane Agunsoye, Thoralf Dassler, Eurydice Fotopoulou, and Jon Mulberg

Political Economy of the Firm
Authority, Governance, and Economic Democracy
Helena Lopes and Christophe Clerc

Digital Capitalism and New Institutionalism
Daniil Frolov

What Is Financialization?
Taner Akan and Halil İbrahim Gündüz

Unequal Development and Capitalism
Catching up and Falling behind in the Global Economy
Adalmir Antonio Marquetti, Alessandro Miebach and Henrique Morrone

Economic Growth and Long Cycles
A Classical Political Economy Approach
Nikolaos Chatzarakis, Persefoni Tsaliki, and Lefteris Tsoulfidis

For more information about this series, please visit: www.routledge.com/Routledge-Frontiers-of-Political-Economy/book-series/SE0345

Unequal Development and Capitalism

Catching Up and Falling Behind in the Global Economy

**Adalmir Antonio Marquetti,
Alessandro Miebach and Henrique Morrone**

Routledge
Taylor & Francis Group
LONDON AND NEW YORK

First published 2024
by Routledge
4 Park Square, Milton Park, Abingdon, Oxon OX14 4RN

and by Routledge
605 Third Avenue, New York, NY 10158

Routledge is an imprint of the Taylor & Francis Group, an informa business

British Library Cataloguing-in-Publication Data
A catalogue record for this book is available from the British Library

Library of Congress Cataloging-in-Publication Data
Names: Marquetti, Adalmir Antonio, author. | Miebach, Alessandro, author. | Morrone, Henrique, author.
Title: Unequal development and capitalism : catching up and falling behind in the global economy / Adalmir Antonio Marquetti, Alessandro Miebach and Henrique Morrone.
Description: Abingdon, Oxon ; New York, NY : Routldge, 2024. |
Series: Routledge frontiers of political economy | Includes bibliographical references and index. |
Identifiers: LCCN 2023055438 | ISBN 9781032121642 (hardback) | ISBN 9781003223382 (ebook)
Subjects: LCSH: Economic development--Developing countries. | Capitalism--Developing countries. | Developing countries--Economic policy.
Classification: LCC HC59.7 .M5124 2024 |
DDC 338.9009172/4--dc23/eng/20231214
LC record available at https://lccn.loc.gov/2023055438

ISBN: 978-1-032-12164-2 (hbk)
ISBN: 978-1-032-12166-6 (pbk)
ISBN: 978-1-003-22338-2 (ebk)

DOI: 10.4324/9781003223382

The Open Access version of this book was funded by Knowledge Unlatched.

An electronic version of this book is freely available, thanks to the support of libraries working with Knowledge Unlatched (KU). KU is a collaborative initiative designed to make high quality books Open Access for the public good. The Open Access ISBN for this book is 9781003223382. More information about the initiative and links to the Open Access version can be found at www.knowledgeunlatched.org

This book is dedicated to our teachers and our students.

Contents

Figures and tables

Figures

Tables

Acknowledgments

This book results from a long journey of learning and contributions from numerous individuals. Among the many people we have learned from, we would like to thank the invaluable insights of Eduardo Maldonado Filho, Zander Navarro, Duílio Berni, André Scherer, Duncan Foley, Gérard Duménil, Álvaro Magalhães, Carlos Pinkusfeld Bastos, Frederico Gonzaga Jayme Junior, Luiz Niemeyer, Anwar Shaikh, Eleutério Prado, José Oreiro, Gabriel Mendonza Pichardo, Ignacio Perrotini, Claudio Putty, Michael Roberts, Fernando Rugitsky, Airton Valada, Raul Assumpção Bastos, Augusto Alvim, Naphon Phumma, Gustavo de Moraes, Adelar Fochezatto, Deepankar Basu, André Contri, Kellen Fraga da Silva, Sergio Cámara Izquierdo, Fabian Balardini, Eduardo Calliari, Victor Isidro Luna, Praopan Pratoomchat, Matias Vernengo, Eduardo da Motta e Albuquerque, Leonardo da Costa Ribeiro, Rudiger von Arnim, Alfredo Gugliano, Pedro Fonseca, João Rogério Sanson, David Fields, Al Campbell, Minqi Li, Maria Lourdes Mollo, Daniel Jeziorny, Valter Stulp, Guilherme de Oliveira, Marcelo Milan, Andrés Ferrari Haines, Carlos Henrique Horn, Codrina Rada, Éder Henriqson, Korkut Erturk, Robert Gordon (in memoriam), Carlos Nelson dos Reis, Eduardo Calliari, Thomas Palley, Fernando Mattos, and many others whom we could cite. A special expression of gratitude goes to Luiz Eduardo Ourique for helping with the mathematical aspects of our model.

We are also profoundly grateful for the institutional support provided by the Pontifícia Universidade Católica do Rio Grande do Sul (PUCRS) and the Universidade Federal do Rio Grande do Sul (UFRGS). Without their institutional support, the writing of this book would have been a far more challenging endeavor. We extend our appreciation to Newcastle University for hosting Adalmir Antonio Marquetti during the final stages of this book's preparation, and we wish to express our gratitude to Stephen Elstub, who kindly facilitated this.

We would also like to acknowledge the financial support provided by Brazilian research institutions Coordenação de Aperfeiçoamento de Pessoal de Nível Superior, CAPES, and Conselho Nacional de Desenvolvimento Científico e Tecnológico, CNPq, during the writing of this book.

Lastly, our thanks go to our families who often had to endure our absence during the book's elaboration. We express our gratitude to Silvana Zardo Pacheco, Luís Gabriel Pacheco Marquetti, Natália Pacheco Marquetti, Dilva Marquetti,

Denico Marquetti (in memoriam), Ronaldo Marquetti, Valter Marquetti, Márcia Marquetti, Nicolas Marquetti, Antonio Cézar Marquetti, Daniel Knijnik Morrone, Roberto Knijnik Morrone, Adriane Vieira, João Juergen Clemente Miebach (in memoriam), and Maria Angela Donadio Miebach (in memoriam) for their understanding and support.

Introduction

Capitalist transformations and unequal development

Unequal development is one of the main features of capitalism. Countries and world regions have exhibited differences in their productivity and growth performances throughout history. Although some nations manage to catch up with the labor productivity and the well-being of developed economies, many fell behind. An enduring challenge for political economy is to comprehend the mechanisms underlying the phenomena of nations either catching up or falling behind. In the nineteenth century, capitalist development was almost exclusively confined to European countries and the United States; however, the scenario changed in the second half of the twentieth century.

After World War II, numerous nation-states emerged due to the process of decolonization. The weakening position of colonial powers, the increasing economic and political strength of the colonies, and changing international conditions propelled the waves of decolonization. The year 1945 marked the establishment of the United Nations, when 51 countries, four from Africa, eight from Asia, and 11 from Europe, signed the United Nations Charter. Over the decades, the successful decolonization movement led to an increase in the number of sovereign nations, there was an expansion of the United Nations members to 193 and two permanent observers.

One of the primary objectives of most countries is to foster development through higher economic growth. Economic growth is fundamental to expand labor productivity, promote better-paid employment, and reduce poverty. However, achieving these goals poses many challenges for developing nations.

The quest for economic growth and development is contingent upon three crucial conditions. These are necessary but not sufficient conditions. Firstly, a country must have a functioning state governance. Secondly, it must be protected from external aggression. Lastly, it should be able to maintain internal stability by averting intense disputes and civil conflicts. These are vital conditions for a country to implement a national development project.

The book investigates the processes of catching up and falling behind in developing countries in relation to the United States from 1970 to 2019. The analysis encompasses the Golden Age crisis and the era of neoliberalism. The research approach combines a historical interpretation of post-World War II capitalism with economic theory and empirical analysis of a large dataset. The primary goal is to shed light

DOI: 10.4324/9781003223382-1

on the conditions under which a country may experience catching up or falling behind. Mechanization, achieved through industrialization, raising labor productivity and capital-labor ratio, and reducing capital productivity, was the typical pattern of technical change observed in the successful follower countries during catching up.

In the book, we study the question of what determines the increase in the wealth of nations in developing countries, where most of the world's population lives. Before delving into the analysis, we will first review key topics related to economic theory, the historical transformation of capitalism, the relationship between technical change, profit rate and the dynamics of catching and falling behind, and some issues posed by population growth, environment, and inequality.

Economic thinking

In his influential work, "The Wealth of Nations," Adam Smith comprehensively explains the nature and causes of economic growth in a capitalist society. Central to this explanation is the division of labor, which involves breaking down the labor process into smaller parts. The division of labor contributes to economic growth through three primary mechanisms. First, it reduces the time workers spend transitioning between different tasks. Second, it allows workers to develop expertise in specific areas, enhancing overall efficiency. Third, it facilitates the introduction of machinery into production.

The division of labor enables firms to specialize in various economic activities, increasing the complexity of economies. It also allows countries to specialize in producing certain commodities, giving rise to an international labor division.

The size of markets determines the extent of the division of labor in society. Population growth, increased income, and advancements in transportation and communications contribute to expanding the market size. A larger market enables a rise in sales and further division of labor, leading to higher labor productivity and reduced production costs. This, in turn, expands the market even further. As a result, a self-reinforcing mechanism exists between the division of labor, market extension, and capital accumulation.

However, Smith argues that appropriate institutional arrangements are crucial for this mechanism to work properly. He believed the market's invisible hand would translate self-interest into collective social benefits. The state's role is to provide national security against external threats, ensure justice and internal order, and provide essential public goods, like basic education. The state must refrain from adopting stimulus measures, such as industrial policy directed toward the private sector. Such interventions could distort investment incentives, favoring sectors with lower profitability than the average rate, and ultimately diminish national wealth in the long run.

Economic growth stems from within the economic system, being endogenous. According to Smith, adopting capitalism with the appropriate institutional framework fosters economic growth and development. However, for him, there is a secular tendency for the profit rate to decline as capital becomes abundant and competition intensifies.

Ricardo's ideas expressed in the "Principles of Political Economy and Taxation" present a pessimistic outlook on the future of capitalism. Ricardo considers three social classes defined according to their property. The capitalist class, the owners of the productive capital, receives profit as the surplus over the production cost, saving and reinvesting most of it. The landlords are the land's owners, referred to as natural resources in modern language. They receive rent by allowing capitalists to utilize their properties productively. Rents are easily spent to bolster and maintain their political power in a rapidly changing capitalist society. The workers, who own nothing besides their own labor power, receive wages in exchange for labor provided in production.

Capital accumulation leads to population growth, which in turn increases the demand for lower-quality land, resulting in a decline in the surplus product from marginal lands. Meanwhile, capitalists engage in competitive bidding to secure the use of better-quality land, leading to increased rent associated with these areas. As capital accumulation progresses, the profitability of marginal land, which defines the general profit rate through competition, declines. Eventually, this process culminates in the stationary state, where the profit rate declined to zero, with no further capital accumulation.

There are two interesting aspects of Ricardo's analysis. First, raising rents reduce profitability, the main class struggle is between capitalists and landlords. Second, nature impose limits on the economic growth of capitalist societies.

Ricardo proposed two ways to delay the stationary state. Firstly, he emphasized that Britain would postpone the stationary state by increasing international trade, exporting industrial and importing agricultural commodities. Secondly, the technical change could also delay the stationary state, raising labor productivity through the employment of machinery. However, unlike Smith and Marx, Ricardo failed to see technical change as an inherent feature of the capitalist system.

The Ricardian theory of comparative advantage in international trade advocates for a division of labor between trading partners. The core idea is that by specializing in producing a commodity that requires relatively less labor time, both countries can save on labor time compared to autarky, exporting the commodity in which each one has a comparative advantage. His theory aligns with the principle of "laissez-faire," which orthodox economics has fully embraced over the last two centuries. However, constructing comparative advantages outside the market, breaking with the international labor division, is a central question for developing countries, an issue raised by the critics of the theory of comparative advantage.

In the third edition of his work, Ricardo explores the impact of machinery on income distribution. The capitalists would substitute labor for machinery, especially when wages exert pressure on overall costs. The substitution raises labor productivity and reduces production costs, thereby increasing profits. Landlords also benefit, as the reduced production costs translate into lower prices for luxury commodities. The introduction of machinery would be detrimental to the interest of workers. The decline in labor demand resulting from increased mechanization may lead to a rise in unemployment, making part of the population redundant and deteriorating the life condition of the working class.

Marx developed his analysis of the capitalist economy through a critical reinterpretation of the political economy, particularly the works of Adam Smith and David Ricardo. In his seminal work "Capital: A Critique of Political Economy," Marx aimed to demonstrate that capitalism is a class-based society characterized by exploitation, where capitalists appropriate the social surplus generated by the working class during production. To display capitalism as a class society, Marx considers two classes in his analysis. Capitalist owns the means of production, while workers are free of properties, except by their labor force.

In capitalism, workers sell their labor power in exchange for a wage. However, the labor performed by workers during production adds a value greater than their wages. The surplus value is the basis of profits and other rents in capitalist society. The proportion of value added that accrues to wages, the wage share, is typical greater than zero and lower than one. The capitalist class organizes production and controls the social surplus, making crucial decisions regarding savings, and investment, production technique, and employment. These decisions shape the economic growth and capitalist trajectory. The investment decisions are based on expected profitability. Currently, managers participate in the social organization of production.

Marx disagreed with Ricardo's explanation of the falling rate of profit, which attributed it to declining labor productivity and raising rents due to the scarcity of natural resources. Ricardo disregarded the powerful incentives for technical progress inherent in the capitalist mode of production. Marx viewed capitalist economies as dynamic systems that consistently fostered technical advancements to counter the diminishing returns of scarce factors of production.

Marx argued that individual capitalists forced by competition would actively pursue and adopt technical innovations that reduced production costs at the current real wages. These technical changes, known as "viable" technical changes in modern theory, allowed capitalists to continue selling their outputs at prices determined by less technologically advanced competitors, thereby reaping "super-profits." The pursuit of profit is the fundamental driving force of capitalism.

In Marx's view, this process served as a potent catalyst for the continuous revolution of capitalist production methods. However, a crucial aspect of this dynamic is that if real wages increase in proportion to the rise in labor productivity, corresponding to a stable wage share in national income, the mechanization process can result in a decline in the rate of profit.

Okishio (1961) emphasized that viable technical changes can decrease the rate of profit only with a simultaneous increase in real wages. Marx encapsulated this vision of the long-term development of the capitalist mode of production in his theories of relative surplus value and the falling rate of profit. These theories shed light on the intricate relationship between technological progress, labor productivity, wage dynamics, and the overall profitability of the capitalist system.

According to Marx, the struggle between capitalists and workers over the value-added creates a powerful incentive for technical change to follow a labor-saving, capital-using pattern, where the use of machinery and equipment replaces the living labor. Mechanization is the typical pattern of technical change in capitalist development. Foley and Michl (1999) dubbed Marx-biased this pattern of technical change.

From this perspective, two factors determine the profit rate in a capitalist economy, the pattern of technical change, and the evolution of the wage share in value added. The Marx-biased technical change with a constant or slowly falling wage share in income may lead to a falling profit rate.

The Marx-biased pattern of technical progress with a stable wage share results in the following long-run trends:

- i rising labor productivity, falling capital productivity, and increasing capital intensity per worker;
- ii declining profit rate while the wage share remains relatively stable;
- iii rising real wages;
- iv declining capital accumulation;
- v rising output at declining growth rates.

Marx called attention to the countertendencies to the falling profit rate. Among them are the increase in exploitation; the reduction of wages below their value; the cheapening of the price of capital goods; the relative surplus population, pressure down wages; the increase in share capital; foreign trade; and investment in less developed countries. Concerning this last contra tendency, Marx (1991, p. 345) pointed out that "capital invested in the colonies … is generally higher there on account of the lower degree of development." Marx considers that a less developed country has lower labor productivity and higher capital productivity than the developed one.

For Keynes in the "General Theory," laissez-faire capitalism would fail to maintain full employment due to a lack of aggregate demand, generating unemployment. The laissez-faire should give place to government intervention in the markets, using fiscal and monetary policies to promote full employment through capital accumulation.

As the scarcity of productive capital was eliminated by the proper administration of the effective demand, the marginal product of capital would approximate zero, with the profit rate and interest rate declining to low levels. The "euthanasia of the rentier" would reduce the profit share in total income. As the profit rate falls, it is necessary to increase the social control over investment. Keynes proposed a socialization of investment to ensure social progress and the maintenance of full employment.

Capitalist transformation

Capitalism is a dynamic system that displays long-term phases characterized by different combinations between institutions and technology. Each phase exhibits a distinct institutional framework that articulates the roles of the market and the state in organizing the productive system. Moreover, the institutional framework influences the power relationships and income distribution between and within social classes, as well as the power relations between the countries and the transfer of income from underdeveloped nations to the leading countries.

Changes in income distribution and increased capital intensification impact the profit rate, thereby affecting capital accumulation and the allocation of savings between productive and financial investments. The different phases of capitalism exhibit varying patterns of capital accumulation and economic growth, resulting in distinct impacts on countries and regions, ultimately contributing to unequal development. Moreover, a country may grow faster in one phase and lower in another.

The institutional organization can activate the countertendencies against the declining trend of the profit rate. Structural crises arise when the existing institutional organization and technology fail to sustain capital profitability. A fresh wave of technical innovations and a revised institutional framework must emerge to increase and maintain the profit rate.

In industrial capitalism in the late XVIII Century, the United Kingdom was the dominant economic power. Classical capitalism saw the rise of the industrial bourgeoisie class, who owned and managed the means of production. At the same time, the laborers moved from rural areas to work in mechanized factories in cities. The United Kingdom, advocating for free trade and the international export of its capital, expanded its colonial empire and economic ties with many regions to access cheap raw materials from around the world.

During the late 19th Century, capitalism underwent a notable transformation characterized by the concentration and centralization of capital within large enterprises under the control of the financial sector. As capitalism became the dominant form of organizing the economies of Western Europe, the international competition intensified as France, Germany, and the United States advanced their industrial capabilities. This shift led to the emergence of large corporations, giving rise to a distinct division of labor that separated the owners and managers of these enterprises. As a result, capitalism began to evolve, according to some analysis, into a three-class society, with distinct roles occupied by capitalists, managers, and workers.

The rising power struggle among capitalist nations triggered a significant geopolitical consequence, leading to the division of Africa, Asia, and Oceania between European countries and the United States, emerging a new era of imperialism. The escalating tensions culminated in the outbreak of the First World War, a conflict that reshaped political boundaries and catalyzed transformative events such as the establishment of the Soviet Union in 1917. Additionally, the war paved the way for the rise of the United States, solidifying its position as the leading capitalist country.

The Great Depression of the 1930s marked the failure of liberalism as a guiding principle for modern capitalism, leading to the conception that the system should be organized under some type of administered capitalism. The effects of the 1930s crisis accentuated the international tensions unleashed by imperialism, which World War I failed to solve. The culmination of this process was World War II.

In the post-war period, the capitalist economies, under the shadow of socialist countries, implemented labor market regulations that, along with rapid economic growth, strengthened the bargaining power of workers (Maddison, 1995). Consequently, the working classes, especially in advanced countries, experienced improvements in their living standards (Armstrong et al., 1991). The period from

1945 to 1973, the Golden Age, was marked by rapid capital accumulation, economic growth, low unemployment, and the widespread adoption of Keynesian macroeconomic policies.

Keynesianism propelled the role of the state within capitalism, resulting in an expansion in the control of investments by state and public enterprises. The Keynesian approach advocated active government intervention to stabilize the economy, promoting fiscal and monetary policies aimed at controlling the aggregate demand. With the state assuming a prominent function, public bureaucracy played a crucial role in managing the capitalist economy.

After the World War II, with the economic fragility of the European countries, a wave of decolonization occurred in Africa and Asia. This also opened space for more nationalist policies aimed at fostering development in Latin American countries. Both contributed to the emergence of development economics as an academic branch of economics.

Eastern Europe ended up under the influence of the Soviet Union. Decolonization was a heterogeneous political process. Some cases involved violent conflicts and wars between colonial powers and the independence movements, while some nations witnessed a peaceful power change. In certain countries, conflicts associated with the disputes of the Cold War emerged after independence.

The newly independent nations, along with the developmental impetus in Latin America solidified developmentalism as the predominant model in what is now referred to as developing countries. Under the influence of the then-dominant Keynesianism, the Import Substitution Strategy became the model adopted in the developing nations during the Golden Age. A minority of countries aligned themselves closely with the Soviet Union.

By the late 1960s, there were signs of exhaustion of the Golden Age and that a profitability crisis was underway. The decline in capital productivity and the rise in wages caused a fall in the profit rate. The crisis of the Golden Age manifested in developing countries in the late 1970s, as the neoliberal turn took shape in the United States and the United Kingdom. Through neoliberal reforms, it was necessary to restore the power of capitalists. Neoliberalism was imposed in advanced countries in the late 1970s and early 1980s. After the restoration of capitalist power, there was an increase in the profit rate in developed economies (Duménil and Lévy, 2011). However, the accumulation rates failed to increase at the same speed due to the expansion of finance.

A central moment in the transition to neoliberalism was the interest rate hikes in the United States between 1979 and 1980. These hikes triggered the debt crisis in the developing world in the 1980s, leading to the abandonment of developmentalism. While a few countries in Asia were able to adapt to the neoliberal turn and sustain their catching-up process, most Latin American, African, and Western Asian countries fell behind during neoliberalism.

Another critical event was the collapse of the Soviet Union. In a process that combined external and internal factors, the centrally planned countries embarked on reforms that led to the demise of their economic systems. The 1990s marked a period of economic and social regression in what were formerly referred to as real socialist nations as they transitioned their economies to capitalism. For most developing countries, neoliberalism marked the end of the catching-up observed during the Golden Age.

A common element in developed and developing countries was the growing relevance and international integration of the financial sector under neoliberalism. At the same time, the developed and developing economies also integrated into the global supply chains, with globalization reshaping the dynamics of production.

The profitability of the financial sector requires new spaces of appreciation to convert capital assets into financial assets. This movement generated innovations and speculative bubbles in many countries. Driven by defaults on subprime mortgage loans, the 2007 financial crisis hit the global financial system, negatively impacting the productive sector. The 2010s were characterized by reduced accumulation and growth rates in developed countries (Kotz and Basu, 2019).

The financial crisis marked the beginning of a gestation period for a new institutional and technical structure poised to replace neoliberalism. The structural capitalist crises result in institutional and technical changes in the hegemonic country with effects on the global economy. These changes play a central role in the processes of catching up and falling behind.

The post-financial crisis era has raised two fundamental questions. Firstly, what will be the emerging institutional framework following the crisis of neoliberalism? Secondly, for the first time in the history of capitalism, the dominance of a Western country is being challenged. In the year 2000, the combined GDP of Brazil, India, China, and South Africa, collectively known as the BRICS and measured in terms of purchasing power parity, accounted for 44.3 percent of the GDP of G7 countries, which include Canada, France, Germany, Italy, Japan, the United Kingdom, and the United States. By 2019, this figure had expanded to 93.3 percent. Traditionally, Western Europe and the United States have responded to hegemonic disputes with economic sanctions and wars.

The upward trend fueled by the rapid rise of China and the gradual expansion of India, along with the deepening of their economic connections with other developing countries, holds the potential to reshape the global economic and political landscape in the coming years. Whether this trend of catching up will continue, eventually leading to China leapfrogging the United States, and whether the conflicts arising from this change will be resolved peacefully or in confrontations remains uncertain.

Profit rate and capital accumulation

The relationship between profit rate and capital accumulation is crucial in explaining the historical processes of catching up and falling behind. We develop a model in the classical-Marxian tradition to describe this relationship, highlighting capital accumulation as central to boosting economic growth. Capital accumulation also functions as a measure of a country's effort to catch up, reflecting the capability of the institutional organization of society in controlling investment, an essential point in both Marxian and Keynesian traditions. A higher accumulation rate may result from a higher profit rate and the social control of the investment.

The book presents an economic growth model in which profit, saving and investment rates drive productive investment and capital accumulation. Differences in capital accumulation between the follower and the leader play a central role in catching up and falling behind. While the leader has to develop new production techniques, the follower has to copy the techniques employed by the leader through capital accumulation. The leader uses techniques with high labor productivity and lower capital productivity than the follower. Then, for a similar wage share, the follower country's profit rate is higher than the leader's. Gerschenkron (1962) pointed out that the greater the gap, the larger the growth possibilities of the follower countries. We interpret the advantage of backwardness as the higher profit rate in the follower countries in relation to the leader. There are, in reality, two gaps, one in labor productivity and the other in capital productivity.

The classical tradition assumes that technological change stems from a historical process in which a country can either develop new production methods or benefit from the transfer of techniques employed in other countries. The new techniques are not a public good. They have a diffusion cost and demand time to be adopted in backward countries. Their successful adoption requires access to machinery and equipment, workforce education, and a period of apprenticeship for firms and workers. Nonetheless, it is relatively easier and faster for countries to adopt techniques already employed in the leading country than discovering new ones.

Following Schumpeter, new techniques were developed and adopted in the successive industrial revolutions or technological waves. The technical innovations that comprise these waves have a life cycle with effects on the long-term trajectory of labor and capital productivities, especially when combined with changes in the institutional framework. During periods of structural crisis and transition between technological waves, there is the possibility that a well-defined developmentalist strategy with high capital accumulation may result in an accelerated rise in production, thereby opening opportunities for rapid increases in labor productivity in follower countries. In these periods, follower countries have a window of opportunity to catch up with developed nations. For an analysis of technological waves and the windows of opportunity available to underdeveloped countries, see Freeman and Soete (1997).

In our analysis, we consider the United States as the leader country. There are four reasons for employing the US economy as the benchmark. First, the US economy presented the highest labor productivity in the period of analysis. Second, other developed countries had labor and capital productivity similar to the United States. Third, the United States and its financial institutions occupy the epicenter of global finance. Third, for the policymakers and international institutions, such as the International Monetary Fund and the World Bank, the institutional framework of the United States provides the right model for economic development.

The interplay between technical change and income distribution determines the profit rate and, through this, the path of capital accumulation. Catching up occurs when the profit rate and capital accumulation are higher in the follower countries. During the catching-up, labor productivity rises while capital productivity and profit rate decline in the follower country. However, an increased capital accumulation in the follower may reduce the capital productivity and the profit rate to a level close to or lower than that in the leading country, putting the process at risk. Then, it is essential to exercise social control over investments to effectively sustain the process of catching up.

The theoretical insights of the model combined with the historical analysis of the concrete development experiences of the follower countries provide a consistent framework to investigate the unequal global capitalist development after the Golden Age.

Environment crisis, population, and personal income distribution

The environmental crisis, population growth, and personal income distribution are relevant economic questions. However, we deliberately decided not to address these topics in the book, and the rationale behind our choice is briefly explained below.

The production process combines labor, capital, and energy. Through this process, a desired output, the gross domestic product, GDP, is generated alongside an undesired output, the emission of anthropogenic greenhouse gases, which are the primary contributor to global warming. Fossil fuel has been the dominant energy source and the main emitter of carbon dioxide since the establishment of industrial capitalism in the late XVIII Century in England. Global warming is perhaps the most pressing environmental problem of our time, but there are many others, such as biodiversity loss, deforestation, water scarcity, and air and plastic pollution.

Expanding capital accumulation as the main driver of economic growth and catching up may imply further greenhouse gas emissions in the present technical conditions. In 2019, the United States, China, and India were responsible for half of the carbon dioxide emissions worldwide. China multiplied its emissions by 13.3 times between 1970 and 2019, India by 14.5, and the United States by 1.2. The individual voluntary definition of the emission targets in the Paris Agreement "resulted in an unequal distribution of the abatement efforts among developing and developed countries ... the reductions in capital accumulation are sharper for developing than developed countries" (Marquetti, Mendoza Pichardo, and Oliveira, 2019, p. 106).

Achieving the decoupling between GDP production and greenhouse gas emissions worldwide is imperative. It necessitates the utilization of public green technologies and socially controlled investment. However, most developing countries have limited resources, and no capacity to achieve an economic growth pattern able to reduce poverty without expanding greenhouse gas emissions. Addressing these complexities requires a novel form of international cooperation that promotes both social justice and environmental sustainability, while facilitating the increase in labor productivity and the development of these countries, bringing them closer to their developed counterparts.

We sympathize with many of the degrowth criticisms of the capitalist economy, particularly the necessity of decommodification of basic services. However, labor productivity growth has been the fundamental determinant of both poverty reduction and lower working hours over the last 200 years. The degrowth as a political platform calls for a profound institutional reform of capitalism, or even its abandonment. A related question is how individual consumers and firms will answer the social goal of reducing growth in a liberal democratic society.

Population dynamics is another critical aspect that the book will not address. In the classical and Marxian traditions, the population growth rate is not a determinant of the economic growth rate and, therefore, of the processes of catching up and falling behind. However, some key statistics provided by the United Nations are worth noting. From 1970 to 2019, according to the United Nations, Department of Economic and Social Affairs, Population Division (2022), the world population was multiplied by 2.1, moving from 3.695 to 7.765 billion inhabitants. During this period, the share of the Asian population expanded from 58.01 to 59.61 percent, the African population from 9.89 to 17,09 percent, the Latin American population from 7.75 to 8.33 percent, Oceania from 0.52 to 0.55 percent, while the share of Europe declined from 17.76 to 9.01 percent, and North America from six to 4.79 percent.

The world regions are currently situated at different stages of their demographic transition, which has significant implications for future populational trends. In the absence of immigration, several European, North American, and many East Asian countries are projected to face population decline in the coming decades. Similarly, although with some delay, Latin America is also expected to witness a decline in population growth. On the other hand, African countries and certain regions of Asia are anticipated to continue experiencing relatively substantial population increases.

While these shifts in population hold important implications, their precise impact on capital accumulation, technical innovation, and societal transformation remains uncertain. The relationship between populational decline and its effects on economic growth and technological progress is complex and multifaceted. Consequently, it is difficult to predict the specific consequences that declining populations may have on the process of catching up and falling behind. However, it is plausible to assume that labor productivity growth will remain essential for improving living standards.

Personal income distribution is also a relevant factor we have not considered in our book. One noteworthy observation, as highlighted by Piketty (2013), is the increasing prominence of the top one percent of income earners in numerous countries worldwide since the rise of neoliberalism in the early 1980s. This phenomenon has been closely associated with the observed decline in wage share, indicating a regressive shift in functional income distribution.

To comprehensively analyze the links between personal income distribution and functional income distribution, it becomes necessary to delve into the relationship between the share of wages, profits, and income of managers. This latter information needs to be included in the future distribution statistics. The links between these dimensions of income distribution would provide insights into the underlying mechanisms influencing economic and political power. In looking at the functional income distribution between wages and profit, we will pose some questions related to the political power of the social classes and their relationship with capital accumulation and economic growth.

The book's structure and how to navigate it

The book is organized into two main blocks. The first block, comprising Chapters 1 and 2, introduces the basic methodological elements used in the economic and historical analysis of the second block.

Chapter 1 introduces the definitions and the data set, the Extended Penn World Tables 7.0 (PWT 7.0), employed to measure economic growth, distribution, technical change, and the dynamics of catching up and falling behind. Moreover, it explores the data set, presenting the stylized facts about economic growth and differences between developed and developing countries.

Chapter 2 develops a classical-Marxian economic model that explains the dynamics of catching up and falling behind. Considering the hypothesis that the follower country exhibits lower labor and higher capital productivity, the model illustrates the possibility of catching up through capital accumulation and mechanization of the productive process.

The second block, comprising Chapters 3 to 7, utilizes the data set and the classical-Marxian model to investigate the historical processes of catching up and falling behind in developing countries. Given that catching up involves comparison to a leader country, the first step is to provide an analysis of this leader. Chapter 3 offers a concise historical analysis of the US economy, the leading country, spanning from the end of the Golden Age to the neoliberal crisis. Institutional and technical changes in leading nations profoundly influence the global dynamics of the economy. The following chapters discuss the developing countries.

Chapter 4 examines the economic growth and the dynamics of catching up for 40 Asian countries. It was the continent with the highest number of successful countries in catching up in the last five decades. It is the largest continent in area and population, with heterogeneous regions in terms of economic history and performance. The chapter examines the main reasons for successfully catching up in most Asian regions.

Chapter 5 analyzes the experiences of 20 Latin American economies. Most countries in the region experienced setbacks during the neoliberal era, following a period of catching up during the Golden Age. The chapter explores the reasons for the reduced economic growth after 1980 and provides insights into how the region may partially regain the lost momentum of higher economic growth.

Chapter 6 investigates 18 Central and Eastern European nations. Neoliberalism was unable to spur economic growth in the transitional countries, with some displaying a trajectory of falling behind. The nations that joined the European Union showed better economic results in raising labor productivity and catching up. The chapter rises some possibilities on how the countries in the region may catch up using its strengths, and abandoning neoliberalism.

Chapter 7 studies 47 African economies and their economic trajectories. The continent was the last to be integrated into the capitalist economy, and still suffers the consequences of decolonization. The chapter explores the links between institutional building and capital accumulation rates, calling the attention for the possibilities of economic growth in the region.

Finally, the conclusion explores the fundamental conditions for generating a trajectory of catching up and development. It discusses whether a national development plan, involving (re)industrialization, can function as a viable path for development. The book ends with a discussion on the imperative of acknowledging backwardness as a global problem, demanding international cooperation to address the critical challenges that humanity faces in the XXI Century.

When navigating the book, readers have multiple options. The primary approach is to read the chapters sequentially. However, the chapters are self-contained and can be read independently. In this case, we suggest starting with the first two sections of Chapter 1 for a better understanding of the definitions and the data set used throughout the book. Nevertheless, each chapter can be read in isolation from the others. Enjoy your reading!

Bibliography

Armstrong, P., Glyn, A., Harrison, J., and Harrison, J. (1991). *Capitalism Since 1945*. Oxford: Basil Blackwell.

Duménil, G., and Lévy, D. (2011). *The Crisis of Neoliberalism*. Cambridge: Harvard University Press, 2011.

Foley, D., and Michl, T. (1999). *Growth and Distribution* Cambridge: Harvard University Press.

Freeman, C., and Soete, L. (1997). *The Economics of Industrial Innovation*. Psychology Press.

Gerschenkron, A. (1962). *Economic Backwardness in Historical Perspective:* a Book of Essays. Cambridge: Belknap Press of Harvard University Press.

Hickel, J. (2021). What does degrowth mean? A few points of clarification. *Globalizations*, 18 (7), pp. 1105–1111.

Kotz, D., and Basu, D. (2019). Stagnation and institutional structures. *Review of Radical Political Economics*, 51(1), pp. 5–30.

Maddison, A. (1995). *Explaining the Economic Performance of Nations*. Cheltenham: Edward Elgar Publishing.

Marquetti, A., Mendoza Pichardo, G., and Oliveira, G. (2019). Are the Paris agreement efforts equally shared? GDP and CO_2 production regularities. *Investigación Económica*, 78(310), pp. 103–136.

Marx, K. (1991). *Capital*: volume III. London: Penguin.

Okishio, N. (1961). Technical change and the rate of profit. *Kobe University Economic Review* 7, pp. 85–99.

Piketty, T. (2013). *Capital in the 21st Century*. Cambridge: President and Fellows, Harvard College.

United Nations, Department of Economic and Social Affairs, Population Division (2022). *World Population Prospects 2022: Data Sources*. New York: UN.

1 Measuring technical change, catching up, and falling behind globally

The system of national accounts, SNA, plays a central role in measuring economic growth and distribution for countries worldwide. It offers a set of guidelines on measuring economic production and how the value added is distributed as wages and profits, which, in turn, are consumed, saved, and invested. The modern SNA framework was developed during the 1930s and 1940s in the context of World War II and the emergence of macroeconomics. The SNA allows for both national and international comparisons of economic growth.

The SNA played a pivotal function in post-World War reconstruction and in the effort of countries to expand their economic growth. Nations at different stages of development have benefited from the information provided by the SNA. However, the SNA and its primary indicator, the gross domestic product (GDP), have been criticized for emphasizing the quantitative measurement of the production process while giving minor attention to the measures related to the quality of life and environment.

We utilize the SNA statistics to study the dynamics of catching up and falling behind, looking at the quantitative aspects of economic growth. Catching up requires the follower countries to increase their labor productivity at higher rates than the leader. The rise in labor productivity requires capital accumulation and technical change. The SNA provides the necessary data to measure whether nations are catching up or falling behind. This chapter introduces the accounting framework and the variables employed to investigate the process of economic growth and construct the macroeconomic model.

The chapter is organized into four sections. The first section presents the national accounts from the income and expenditure sides, defining the empirical variables employed throughout the book. The second section outlines the measurement and the representation of technical change over time. The third section introduces the dataset, connecting it with the previously discussed definitions. The fourth section gives a worldwide perspective on distribution, technical change, and capital accumulation, emphasizing the differences between developed and developing countries, and outlining the main stylized facts of economic growth.

DOI: 10.4324/9781003223382-2

Measuring growth and distribution

Social production requires the employment of inputs, labor, capital, energy, and natural resources to generate an output. Gross output measures the market price of the goods and services produced by a country over time. It consists of two primary components: intermediate consumption, including products consumed during production, and gross value added.

The GDP is the gross value added at market price produced within a country's borders in a year. Domestic refers to the production within the territory of a nation, and National refers to production by the means of production owned by a country's residents. The gross national income, GNI, is equal to the GDP plus the income residents receive from abroad minus the income paid to nonresidents. The net domestic product, NDP, is the GDP minus the depreciation or consumption of the fixed capital. Depreciation is the decline in the value of the fixed capital stock over time.

The changes in GDP occur from movements either in quantities produced or in prices due to inflation. The SNA recommends the computation of real GDP by deflating the nominal GDP by an index price, the GDP deflator. For international comparisons, the GDP is converted to a common currency to eliminate the price differences in goods and services between countries, using the purchasing power parity index. We employ the real GDP measured at purchasing power parity to calculate the growth rate and compare countries, expressing it by the symbol X.

It is necessary to employ inputs to produce goods and services. For simplicity, we consider just capital and labor as inputs despite the critical role of energy and natural resources in production. The measurement of capital, the stock of fixed assets in a particular year, involves empirical simplifications and theoretical controversies. The perpetual inventory method is employed to compute the net capital stock. It consists of accumulating gross fixed capital formation flows and deducting the depreciation. The same capital stock may represent different compositions of capital goods, a question raised by the Controversy of Capital (Harcourt, 1972). We use the symbol K for the net fixed capital stock, expressing it in the same unit as GDP. We measure labor by the number of workers without considering the working population's differences in education and skill. We denote labor by the symbol N.

The national accounts are represented graphically by the growth-distribution schedule. It was employed as a mechanism for displaying the national accounts by Foley, Michl and Tavani (2019), Foley and Marquetti (1999), Pichardo (2007), among others. The growth-distribution schedule is based on a generalization of Sraffa's (1959) wage-profit frontier, allowing a visual representation of national accounts.

The GDP measured by expenditure and income sides are central to macroeconomic investigations. To simplify, we consider a closed economy without a government with two economic agents: workers and capitalists. These assumptions allow us to empirically investigate and model the fundamental relationship between technical change, capital accumulation, and distribution. On the expenditure side of national accounts, GDP equals the sum of consumption and gross investment denoted by C and I, resulting in X = C + I. On the income side, GDP is equal to the sum between wages and gross profits, symbolized as W and Z, leading to X = W + Z.

In order to compare countries, it is convenient to express the variables in terms of the number of workers or capital stock; hence x = X/N is output per worker or labor productivity; k = K/N is capital per worker or capital intensity; w = W/N is the average real wage; z = Z/N represents gross profits per worker; c = C/N is the social consumption per worker, including nonworker consumption; and i = I/N is investment per worker. These variables are expressed as purchasing power parity per worker.

Some variables are normalized by the capital stock: a = X/K = x/k is output per unit of capital or capital productivity; v = Z/K is the gross profit rate; d = D/K is the depreciation rate; r = v – d is the net profit rate; and $g_K + d = I/K$ is the capital accumulation, the ratio of gross investment to the capital stock. The unit of measurement of these variables is the inverse of time, like the interest rate. The profit share is π = z/x, and the wage share is (1 – π) = w/x. The profit rate, v = πp, can be calculated as the multiplication between profit share, a distribution variable, and capital productivity, a technological variable. The growth rate of the variables, for example x, is computed as $g_x = \Delta x/x$, then, g_x represents the labor productivity growth rate and g_a the capital productivity growth rate.

The gap in labor productivity between the leader and the follower countries is measured by $\mu = (x^L - x^F)/x^L$, where x^L is the labor productivity of the leader and x^F is the labor productivity of the follower. It indicates the distance in labor productivity between the leader and the follower, it declines with the increase in the follower's labor productivity. For example, a gap in labor productivity of 0.5 indicates that the leader's labor productivity is one hundred percent higher than in the follower country in a given year. The gap in capital productivity is computed by $\xi = (a^L - a^F)/a^L$, where a^L is the leader's capital productivity and a^F is the follower's capital productivity. It expresses the distance in capital productivity between the leader and the follower. In the present case, a gap in capital productivity of minus one indicates that the follower has one hundred percent higher capital productivity than the leader in a certain year.

After dividing the expenditure and income sides of the national accounts by the number of workers and performing a few algebraic manipulations, we arrive at the following expressions:

$$c = x - i = x - (g_K + d)k \tag{1.1}$$

$$w = x - z = x - (r + d)k \tag{1.2}$$

The identity (1.1) represented in Figure 1.1 is the social consumption-growth rate schedule. For a given output, it shows the trade-off between social consumption and capital accumulation. At the capital accumulation, $g_K + d$, the labor productivity is divided into the social consumption per worker, c, and gross investment per worker, i. The maximum capital accumulation is equal to capital productivity, a, when social consumption per worker is equal to zero, c = 0. The maximum consumption per worker occurs when the investment per worker is equal to zero, $g_K + d = 0$, being equal to labor productivity, x.

The identity (1.2) also displayed in Figure 1.1 is the real wage-profit rate schedule. This schedule shows the trade-off between real wage and profit rate for a given output. The labor productivity, x, is divided into the real wage per worker, w, and profits per worker, z = Z/N, at the gross profit rate, r + d. The maximum profit rate corresponds to w = 0, being equal to capital productivity, a. The maximum real wage occurs when r + d = 0, being equal to labor productivity, x.

The growth-distribution schedule in Figure 1.1 illustrates the interdependence between consumption and investment, as well as between wage and profits in the (a, x) space. It is a straight line with the horizontal intercept equal to capital productivity, a, and the vertical intercept equal to labor productivity, x. The capital-labor ratio, k, is the negative slope of this line. The expenditure side shows the trade-off between consumption and capital accumulation. From the income side, it reveals the trade-off between real wage and profit rate.

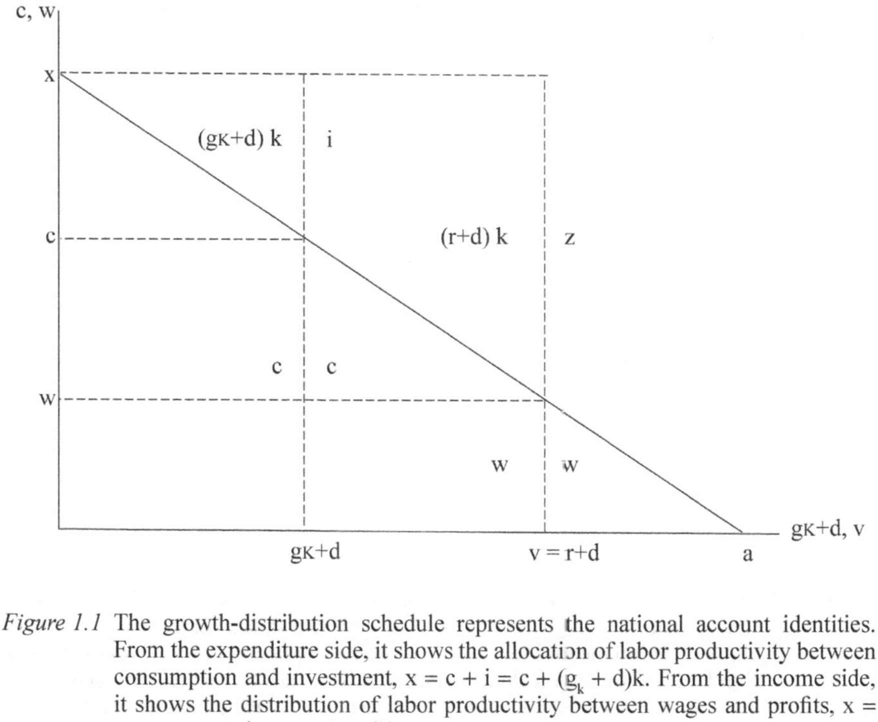

Figure 1.1 The growth-distribution schedule represents the national account identities. From the expenditure side, it shows the allocation of labor productivity between consumption and investment, $x = c + i = c + (g_k + d)k$. From the income side, it shows the distribution of labor productivity between wages and profits, $x = w + z = w + vk = w + (r + d)k$.

Representing technical change

The movements of the growth-distribution schedule over time reveal any pattern of technical change in a real economy. A production technique is described by labor productivity, capital productivity or capital-labor ratio, and the depreciation rate. The technology is the set of all known techniques.

The classification of technical change into neutral and non-neutral in its different conceptions is defined by shifts in the growth-distribution schedule. Harrod-neutral technical change or purely labor-saving corresponds to an increase in labor productivity with constant capital productivity, resulting in a clockwise rotation of the growth-distribution schedule in the horizontal axis intercept from technique A to technique C as shown in Figure 1.2. Solow-neutral technical change or purely capital-saving corresponds to an increase in capital productivity with the labor productivity constant, leading to a counter-clockwise rotation of the growth-distribution schedule in vertical axis intercept from technique A to B in Figure 1.2. Hicks-neutral technical change occurs when the growth rates of labor and capital productivities are equal, causing the growth-distribution schedule to move parallel to itself. Figure 1.2 presents this shift from technique A to technique D.

The fourth movement in Figure 1.2, from techniques B to C, is labor-saving and capital-using, corresponding to a clockwise rotation of the growth-distribution schedule around a point in the positive quadrant. Foley et al. (2019) named this pattern of technical change Marx-biased. It has a positive growth rate of labor productivity and a negative growth rate of capital productivity. The intersection of the new and old growth-distribution schedules represents a real wage at which the two

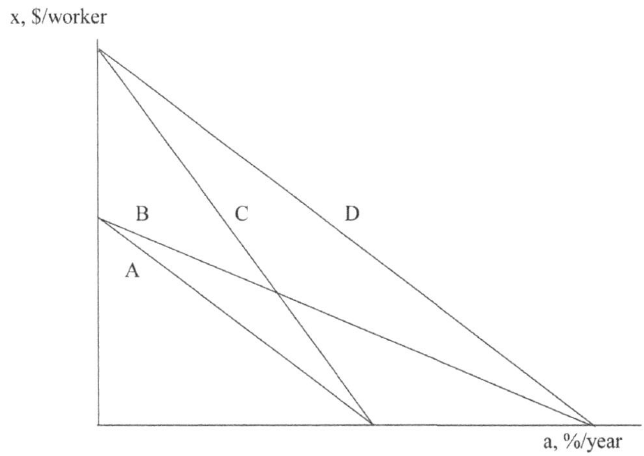

Figure 1.2 The growth-distribution schedule and the definition of neutral technical change. Harrod-neutral technical change corresponds to a shift from technique A to technique C. Solow-neutral technical change corresponds to a shift from technique C to D. Hicks-neutral technical change corresponds to a shift from technique A to D. Marx-biased technical change corresponds to rising labor productivity and declining capital productivity, a transition from technique B to C.

techniques are equally profitable, and it is called the switch point. The combination of Marx-biased technical change with a constant wage share can lead to a falling rate of profit.

The technical regress can also be defined in terms of shifts in the growth-distribution schedule. Technical regress occurs when the opposite movements of the neutral technical change take place. Therefore, Harrod-neutral technical regress or purely labor-using corresponds to a decline in labor productivity with constant capital productivity, a movement from technique C to technique A in Figure 1.2. Solow-neutral technical regress or purely capital-using corresponds to a decline in capital productivity with the labor productivity constant, a change from technique B to A in Figure 1.2. Hicks-neutral technical regress corresponds to an equal decline in labor and capital productivities. A particular case of technical regress is technical stagnation, when labor and capital productivities are constant. Another form of technical regress is the decline in labor productivity and the increase in capital productivity, a movement from techniques C to B in Figure 1.2. It was named reverse Marx-biased technical change by Villanueva and Jiang (2018), while Marquetti and Porsse (2017) called it de-mechanization.

The patterns of technical change can also be observed directly by looking at the plot of the capital and labor productivity growth rates, (ga, gx), in the Cartesian plan represented in Figure 1.3. The Harrod-neutral technical changes are in the

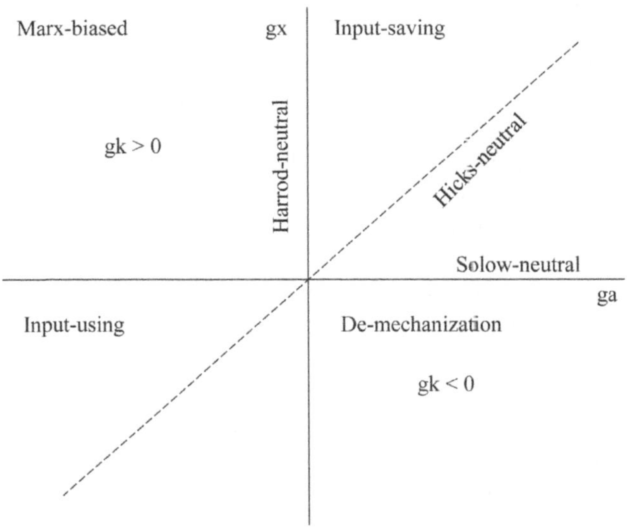

Figure 1.3 Visualizing the representation of technical change in the plan growth rate of capital and labor productivities (g_a, g_x). Harrod-neutral changes are located on the vertical axis, (0, g_x). Solow-neutral technical changes are located on the horizontal axis, (g_a, 0). Hicks-neutral technical changes lie on the dotted line ($g_a = g_x$). Input-saving technical changes are located in the first quadrant. Marx-biased technical changes are located in the second, the input-using technical changes in the third, and the de-mechanization technical changes in the fourth.

vertical axis at the set of points $(0, g_x)$. The Solow-neutral technical changes lie in the horizontal axis at the set of points $(g_a, 0)$. The Hicks-neutral technical changes are located on the dotted line at the set of points where $g_a = g_x$. Marquetti and Porsse (2017) dubbed the cases located in the first quadrant in which $g_x > g_a > 0$ and $g_a > g_x > 0$ as input saving technical change with raising or declining capital intensity. The Marx-biased technical changes are in the second quadrant, where ga < 0 and gx > 0. The input using technical changes with an increase in the capital intensity when $g_a < g_x < 0$ or a decline in capital intensity when $g_x < g_a < 0$, are in the third quadrant. The de-mechanization or reversed Marx-biased technical changes are positioned in the fourth quadrant.

The dataset

The dataset we employ is the Extended Penn World Tables version 7.0, EPWT 7.0. It is an extension of the Penn World Tables version 10.0 (Feenstra, Inklaar and Timmer, 2015), associating the variables in the data set with the growth-distribution schedule. The EPWT 7.0 allows us to investigate the relations between economic growth, capital accumulation, income distribution, and technical change in the processes of catching up and falling behind.

The EPWT 7.0 displays data on 183 countries expressed in 2017 international dollars to correct differences in price levels, allowing for intertemporal comparisons between countries. The EPWT 7.0 also shows data in 2017 constant national prices and current national prices. We added information on energy use, gas carbonic emissions, and we expanded the number of countries with wage share information. We expressed the GDP, the capital stock, and the variables in terms of the number of workers in 2017 international dollars.

The EPWT encompasses the 1950–2019 period, with variations in the starting year of observations among countries. The dataset starts in the 1950s for 75 countries, the 1960s for 39 countries, the 1970s for 43 countries, the 1980s for one country, the 1990s for 23 countries, and the 2000s for two countries. The geographical distribution among continents is as follows: 43 are in America; 50 in Africa; 47 in Asia; 40 in Europe; and three in Oceania.

Table 1.1 gives an overview of the thirty biggest economies in 2019 in comparison with their position in 1970. In 2019, these countries produced 83.3% of the world's GDP, comprising 82.2% of the capital stock, and 76.3% of the labor force. The group composition changed moderately with seven new entrants: South Korea, Egypt, Thailand, Taiwan, Pakistan, Malaysia, and Bangladesh. The countries that have dropped out are Switzerland, South Africa, Sweden, Belgium, Austria, Greece, and Denmark. The developing Asian countries replaced the developed European countries.

There were changes in the GDP ranking. China ascended from fifth to first place, becoming the largest economy in terms of GDP, capital stock, and number of workers in 2019. The United States slipped from first to second place in GDP and capital stock. China became the main challenger of the United States' worldwide economic leadership. India surged from eighth to third place in GDP and from

Table 1.1 The 30 largest economies in 2019 in comparison with 1970

Country	*2019*			*1970*			*Change in*
	X a)	*K a)*	*N b)*	*X a)*	*K a)*	*N b)*	*GDP ranking*
1. China	20572606	81726344	798.81	1085341	2739707	360.96	4
2. United States	20563592	69059072	158.30	5332995	21404618	84.70	−1
3. India	9163052	35423260	497.62	684889	2374540	195.36	5
4. Japan	5099254	26138818	69.98	1601754	5270958	55.02	−1
5. Germany	4314068	20957202	44.80	1682669	7845501	38.10	−3
6. Russia	4052185	19440892	71.67	n.a.	n.a.	n.a.	n.a.
7. Indonesia	3110470	17785758	131.17	195463	769836	34.02	16
8. Brazil	3042119	13716488	93.96	586407	1990087	29.12	2
9. United Kingdom	3016695	15374464	32.98	1031309	5543913	24.70	−1
10. France	2965339	18013436	28.53	1036055	6132885	21.33	−3
11. Italy	2467814	18900204	25.60	1091992	5698253	19.94	−6
12. Mexico	2406410	10934025	54.99	521774	2061189	12.02	0
13. Turkey	2242847	10213821	28.09	261568	573060	11.37	8
14. South Korea	2193132	11198646	26.80	85524	298706	9.66	28
15. Spain	1896315	11733525	19.87	553604	2587869	13.45	−4
16. Canada	1874187	8757840	19.30	508118	1909364	8.16	−3
17. Saudi Arabia	1649509	7117220	13.74	302702	386498	1.17	1
18. Australia	1315734	5913514	12.86	309083	1473596	5.47	−1
19. Egypt	1287589	1837650	26.79	94629	50047	7.66	21
20. Thailand	1229521	5667203	37.54	92786	484189	15.20	21
21. Poland	1214222	3155212	16.16	271562	557488	14.17	−1
22. Taiwan	1127989	4278237	11.50	51190	168897	4.75	28
23. Pakistan	1078573	1723807	63.09	112720	300185	17.25	9
24. Nigeria	1006237	3115442	73.02	171430	628642	21.72	2
25. Iran	1001589	6812133	24.59	358567	883519	7.27	−10
26. Argentina	975569	3399149	20.64	388738	1069101	8.65	−12
27. Netherlands	960771	4748428	9.46	314629	1715089	5.58	−11
28. Philippines	929960	2744660	42.42	122620	283053	11.10	1
29. Malaysia	821183	3603976	15.12	38493	131508	3.55	27
30. Bangladesh	766135	2844180	65.53	95964	149870	20.21	7

Notes: a) In 1,000,000 2017 international dollars. b) In million workers. n.a.: Information not available.

Source: EPWT 7.0.

ninth to third place in capital stock. Japan, the fourth economy, dropped one position. Germany, the sixth economy, fell three positions. Indonesia made substantial gains, advancing 16 positions. Brazil, the United Kingdom, and France completed the list of the top ten largest economies.

Interestingly, most countries classified as industrialized or developed in 1970 experienced downward shifts in the GDP ranking. The negative highlights were the Netherlands, Italy, and Spain, which lost 11, 6, and 4 positions. Some developing countries also faced declines, with Argentina and Iran dropping 12 and 10 positions. Latin American, African, and Western Asia countries displayed mixed results.

As previously mentioned, the developing Asian countries moved up in the ranking. South Korea, Hong Kong, Singapore, and Taiwan transitioned from developing to developed countries.

Distribution, growth, and technical change worldwide: A first look

One of the central questions in political economy is explaining the dynamics of catching up and falling behind among nations. This involves the intricate task of deciphering the interplay between technical change, distribution, and economic growth. The first step consists of examining patterns and identifying stylized facts in the data to reveal the fundamental determinants of economic growth. The countries having less than one million inhabitants in 2019 were removed from our sample.

During economic development, countries display a technical change pattern of rising labor productivity, declining capital productivity, and increasing capital-labor ratio. Figure 1.4 depicts the capital and labor productivities and the linear fit between them for 99 countries in 1970 and 2019. The figure did not include outlier nations with a high oil rent as a percentage of GDP.

The data displays a negative correlation between capital and labor productivities. Countries with lower labor productivity tend to exhibit higher capital productivity, while countries with high labor productivity tend to have lower capital productivity. Moreover, there is a movement of the national economies toward a

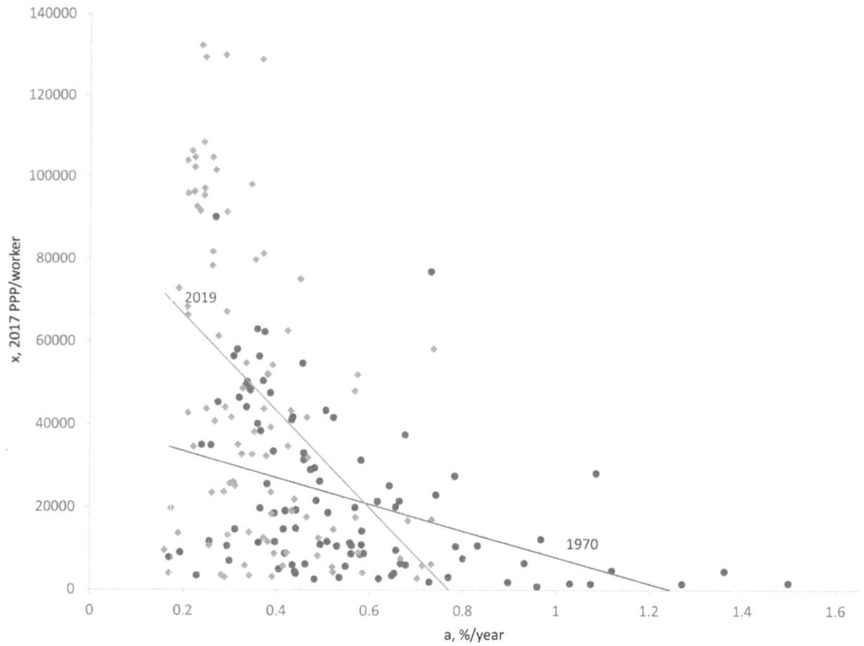

Figure 1.4 The pair capital and labor productivity, (a, x), and their linear fits in 1970 and 2019.

Source: EPWT 7.0.

northwest direction, and the linear fit in 2019 is much steeper than in 1970, revealing a tendency for the technical change to follow a path of falling capital productivity and rising labor productivity. While variations exist in the paths of economic development, the data consistently suggest a movement toward lower capital productivity and higher labor productivity.

Figure 1.5 exhibits data on the pair capital-labor ratio and labor productivity, along with their fits, for 104 countries in 1970 and 2019. The capital-labor ratio and labor productivity have a positive correlation. For countries with low capital-labor ratios, there exists a concave relationship between these variables. Furthermore, the fitted lines illustrate a movement toward the northeast between 1970 and 2019, indicating that countries have been increasing their capital-labor ratios and labor productivity along the path of economic growth.

Figure 1.6 displays the data on the compound growth rate of capital productivity and labor productivity between 1970 and 2019 for 105 countries, organized according to their geographical location. There is a strong tendency for the data points to locate in the second quadrant, corresponding to a negative growth rate of capital productivity and a positive growth rate of labor productivity in all continents. The Marx-biased pattern of technical change, capital-using, and labor-saving occurred in 80 countries. There were a minority of other types of technical change, with 14 countries experiencing capital-using and labor-using technical

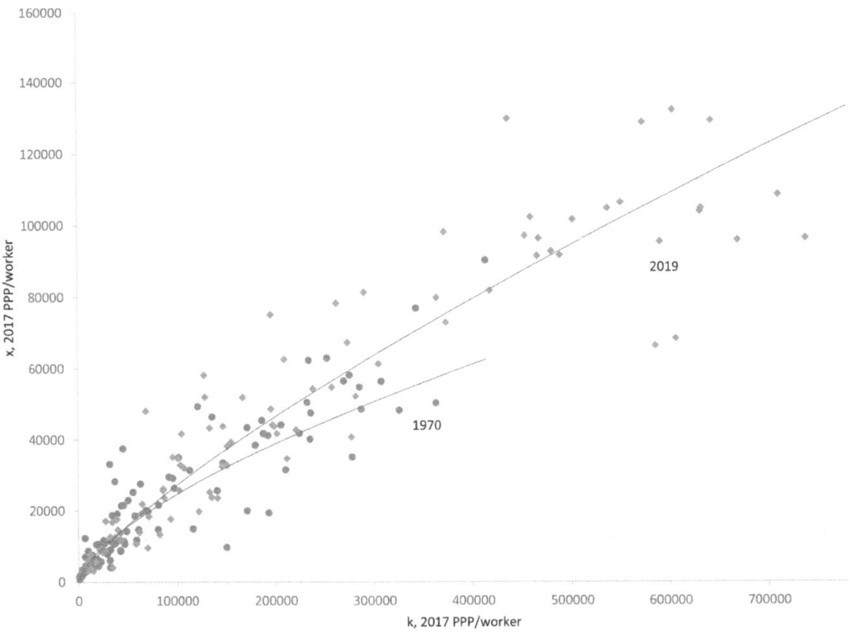

Figure 1.5 The pair capital-labor ratio and labor productivity, (k, x), and their fits in 1970 and 2019.

Source: EPWT 7.0.

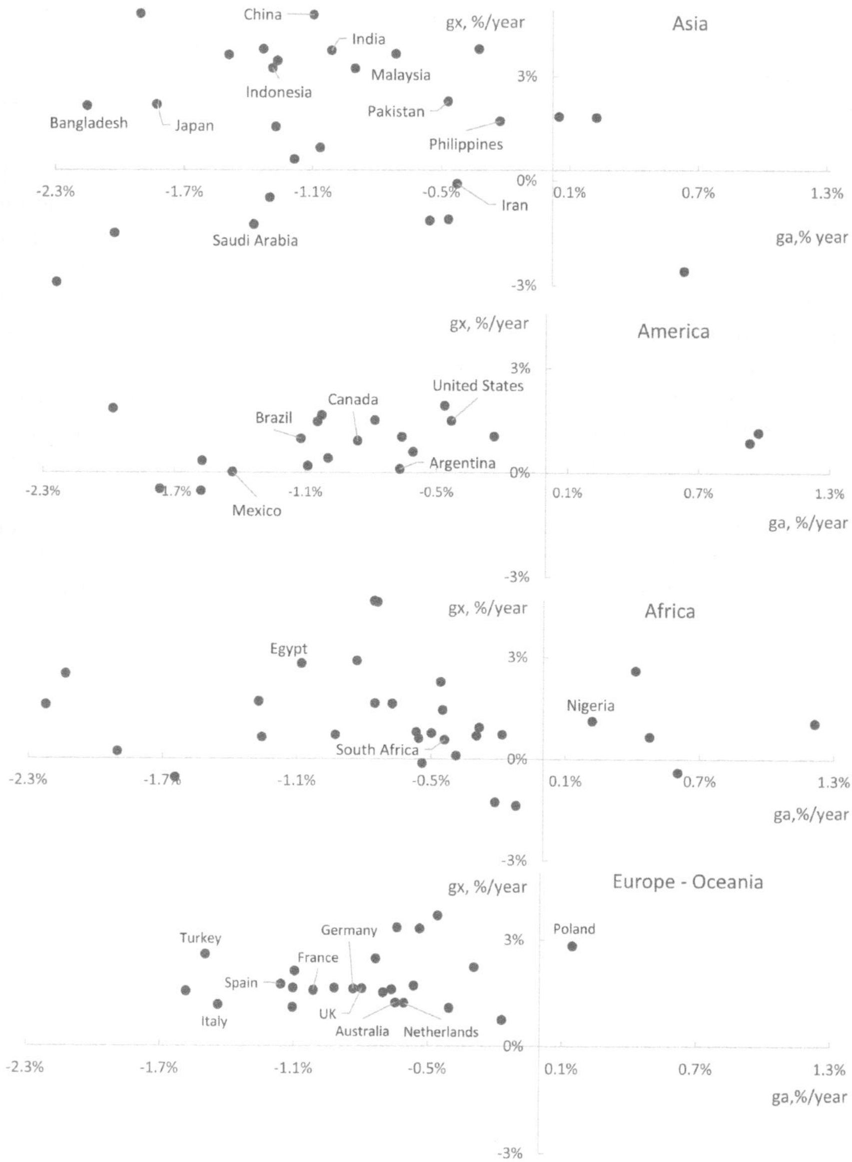

Figure 1.6 The compound growth rates of capital and labor productivities, (ga, gx), between 1970 and 2019.

Source: EPWT 7.0.

change; nine countries undergoing capital-saving and labor-saving; and just two instances of capital-saving and labor-using technical change.

Table 1.2 presents data on economic performance and the types of technical change for 105 countries. The country classifications, categorized as high, medium-high,

Table 1.2 Economic performance and the types of technical change by continent, 1970–2019

Econ. performance	*Technical change*	*Asia*	*America*	*Africa*	*Europe-Oceania*	*Total*
High	ga > 0 and gx > 0	0	0	1	1	2
	ga < 0 and gx > 0	12	0	6	6	24
	ga < 0 and gx < 0	0	0	0	0	0
	ga > 0 and gx < 0	0	0	0	0	0
Medium-high	ga > 0 and gx > 0	2	0	0	0	2
	ga < 0 and gx > 0	3	6	4	11	24
	ga < 0 and gx < 0	0	0	0	0	0
	ga > 0 and gx < 0	0	0	0	0	0
Medium-low	ga > 0 and gx > 0	0	2	3	0	5
	ga < 0 and gx > 0	3	4	8	6	21
	ga < 0 and gx < 0	0	0	0	0	0
	ga > 0 and gx < 0	0	0	0	0	0
Low	ga > 0 and gx > 0	0	0	0	0	0
	ga < 0 and gx > 0	1	6	4	0	11
	ga < 0 and gx < 0	7	2	5	0	14
	ga > 0 and gx < 0	1	0	1	0	2
Total	ga > 0 and gx > 0	2	2	4	1	9
	ga < 0 and gx > 0	19	16	22	23	80
	ga < 0 and gx < 0	7	2	5	0	14
	ga > 0 and gx < 0	1	0	1	0	2

Source: EPWT 7.0.

Note: Economic performance is defined in high, medium-high, medium-low, and low according to the quartile of the labor productivity growth rate between 1970 and 2019.

medium-low, and low economic performance, are based on quartiles computed from the compound labor productivity growth rates between 1970 and 2019. The rise in labor productivity is a fundalmental source of poverty reduction and improvements in the standard of living.

Among the high-performance countries, there were 12 Asian, seven African, and eight European ones, with 24 displaying Marx-biased technical change. In the medium high-performance countries, there were five Asians, six Americans, four Africans, and 11 Europeans, with 24 exhibiting the Marx-biased technical change. The medium-low-performance countries included three from Asia, seven from America, 11 from Africa, and six from Europe, with 21 presenting the Marx-biased technical change. Moreover, five out of nine countries with a capital-saving and labor-saving technical change fell into the medium-low economic performance. In the low-performance group, there were nine from Asia, eight from the Americas, and ten from Africa, with 16 countries experiencing technical regression. Among these, capital-using and labor-using technical change was predominant in 14 countries, while capital-saving and labor-using change occurred in two cases. Interestingly, the Marx-biased technical change was predominantly in the countries with high, medium-high, and medium-low economic performance.

Countries may present different phases of technical change and economic performance over time. The structural changes that occur in catching up and falling behind are associated with different types of technical change. Industrialization and urbanization imply the mechanization of the production process, while deindustrialization tends to be associated with de-mechanization. Adopting communication and information technologies opened up possibilities for organizational technical change after 1980. The phases of technical change will be discussed in Chapters 3–7.

Figure 1.7 illustrates the wage-share and labor productivity relationship for 81 countries in 1970 and 2019 and displays their linear fit. For some countries, there are no observations for the wage share. The data reveals a positive correlation between them in both years: labor productivity increases as the wage share raises. There was a shift toward the northwest direction in the linear fit between labor productivity and wage share in the 1970–2019 period. On average, the wage share declined, and labor productivity increased over these years.

Figure 1.8 presents the profit rate and real wages and their fits for 85 countries in 1970 and 2019. The data reveal a strong negative correlation between profit rate and real wage in the process of economic development. The fitted lines exhibit a concave shape toward the origin, consistent with the claim that economies tend to decline profit rates and raise real wages during economic development.

Figure 1.9 displays the relationship between profit rate and capital accumulation and their nonlinear fit for 85 countries in 1970 and 2019. There was a positive

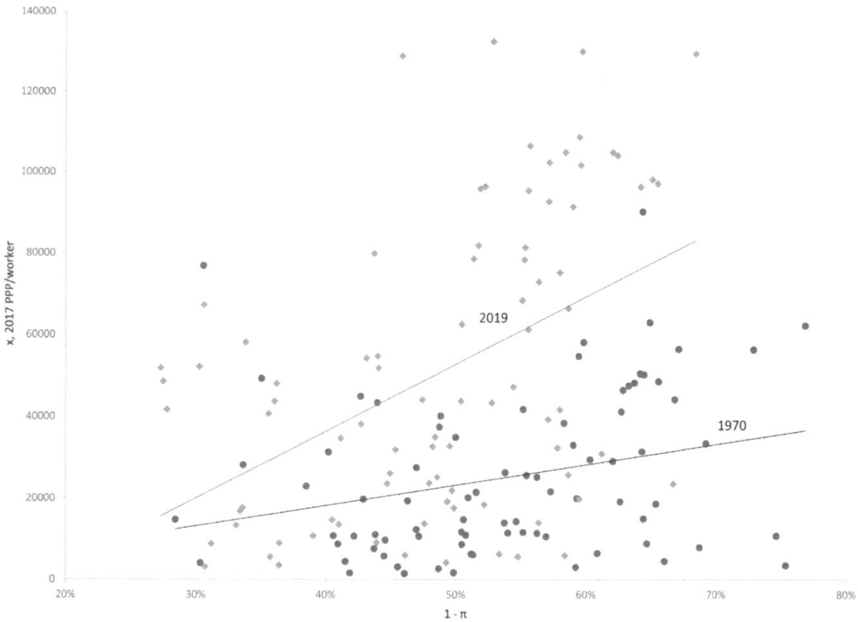

Figure 1.7 The pair wage share and labor productivity, (1-π, x), and their linear fits in 1970 and 2019.

Source: EPWT 7.0.

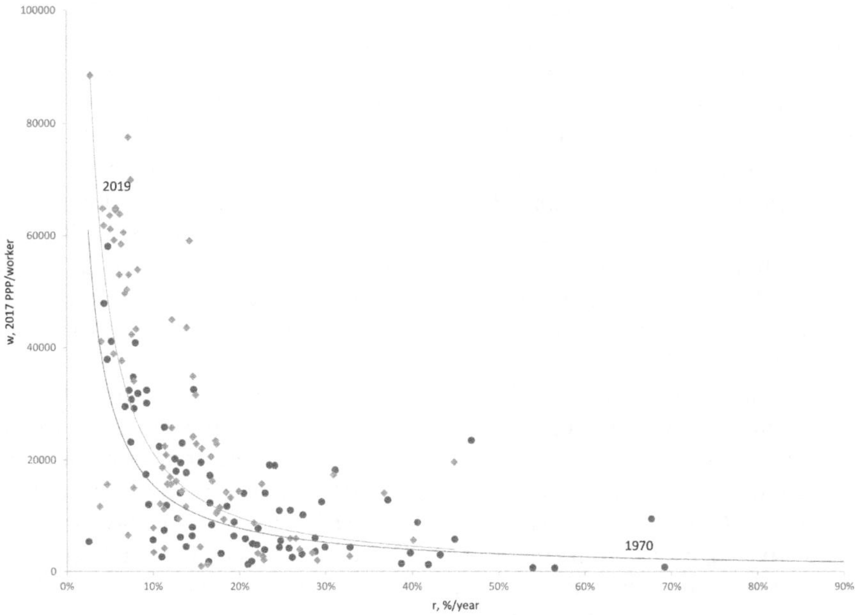

Figure 1.8 The pair profit rate and real wage, (r, w), and their fits in 1970 and 2019.
Source: EPWT 7.0.

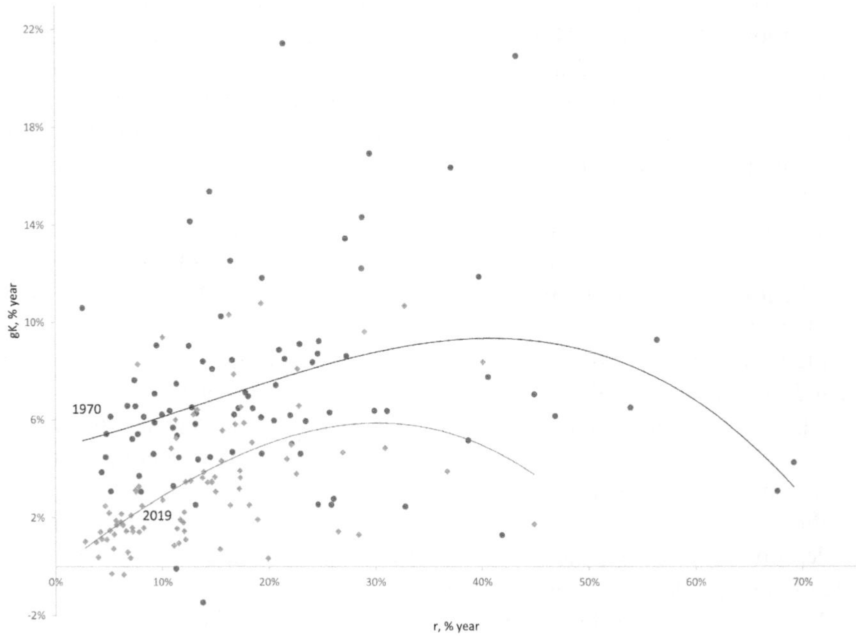

Figure 1.9 The pair profit rate and capital accumulation (r, g_K), and their fits in 1970 and 2019.
Source: EPWT 7.0.

correlation between profit rate and capital accumulation for most countries; then, for higher profit rates, it became negative in both years. Apparently, in the countries with the largest profit rates, the benefits of backwardness did not translate into higher capital accumulation. The institutional framework also plays an important role in the process of economic development.

The observations and the fitted lines moved in the southwestern direction between 1970 and 2019, indicating that, on average, the capital accumulation in 2019 was lower than in 1970 for a similar profit rate. This decline can be attributed to two main factors: a decrease in profit rates driven by diminishing capital productivity and a lower investment rate resulting from neoliberal institutional changes. These changes resulted in a structural break between profit rates and capital accumulation after 1980.

Two fundamental issues are the relationships between capital accumulation and growth rates of labor and capital productivities. Figure 1.10 exhibits the data on the pair capital accumulation and the compound growth rate of labor productivity, (g_K, g_x) for 105 countries between 1970 and 2019 and their estimated linear fit by continents. A positive association exists between capital accumulation and labor productivity growth for all continents. However, the impact of capital accumulation on labor productivity growth differs among continents. The outliers are the oil rent countries located in Western Asia, which have experienced impressive expansion in the number of workers.

Figure 1.11 displays the scatterplot between capital accumulation and the compound growth rate of capital productivity (g_K, ga) for 105 countries in the 1970–2019 period, and their linear fits by continent. There is a linear negative correlation between capital accumulation and capital productivity growth. Interestingly, higher capital accumulation is associated with higher and positive growth in labor productivity and lower and negative growth in capital productivity. These results are consistent with the conception that labor productivity tends to increase while capital productivity declines during the process of development.

There are two other essential questions to investigate. The first is the distance in labor and capital productivities between the followers and the leader. The second is if the followers' countries were able to catch up in both productivities during the 1970–2019 period.

Figure 1.12 presents data on the gap in labor productivity in 1970 and the compound growth rate of labor productivity (μ, gx) between 1970 and 2019 for 95 countries, excluding oil rent countries. The horizontal lines intersect the vertical line at 1.4%, representing the annual compound growth rate of labor productivity of the United States, the leader. Countries to the right of the y-axis had lower labor productivity than the United States in 1970, with only one country exceeding the leader's productivity. Countries above the vertical line exhibited a higher growth rate of labor productivity than the leader.

The countries in the first quadrant had lower labor productivity but managed to catch up with the United States, whereas those in the fourth quadrant increased their distance to the leader. There is no consistent pattern of catching up, about

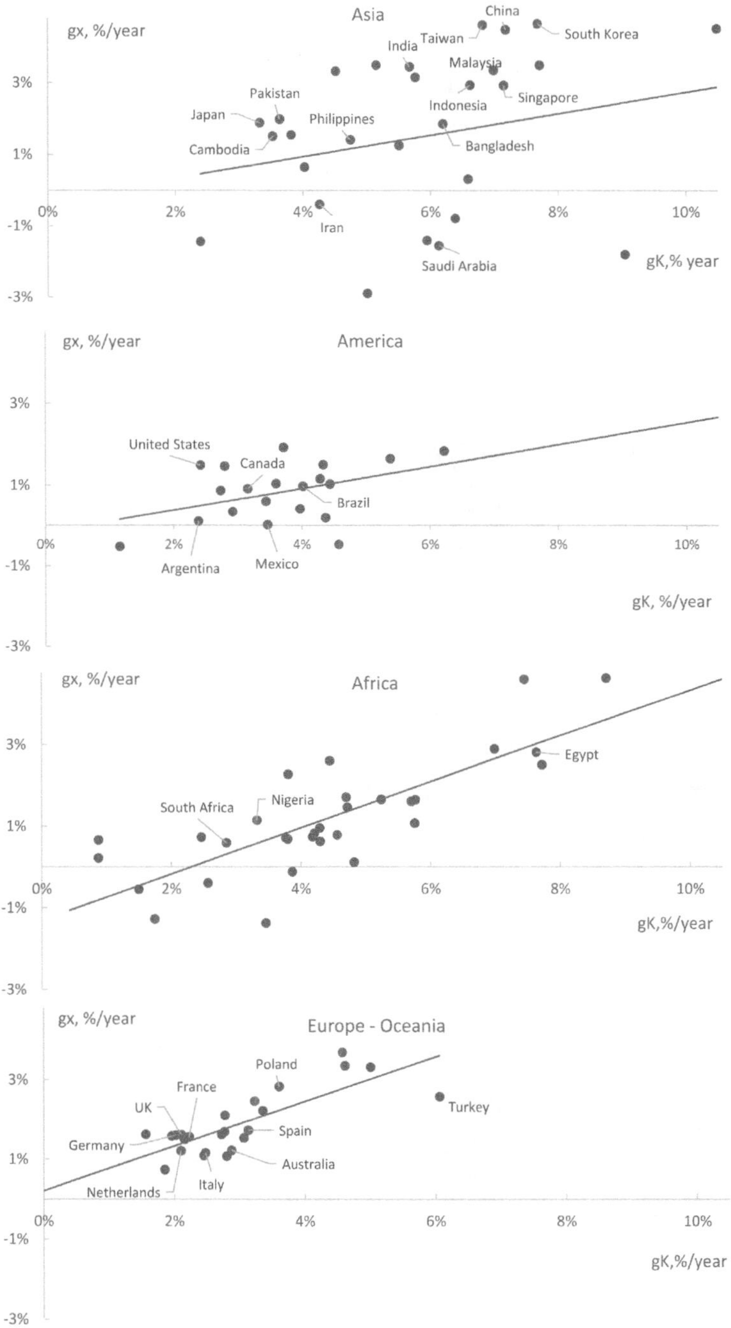

Figure 1.10 The pair capital accumulation and growth rate of labor productivity (g_K, gx), and their linear fit between 1970 and 2019 by continent.

Source: EPWT 7.0.

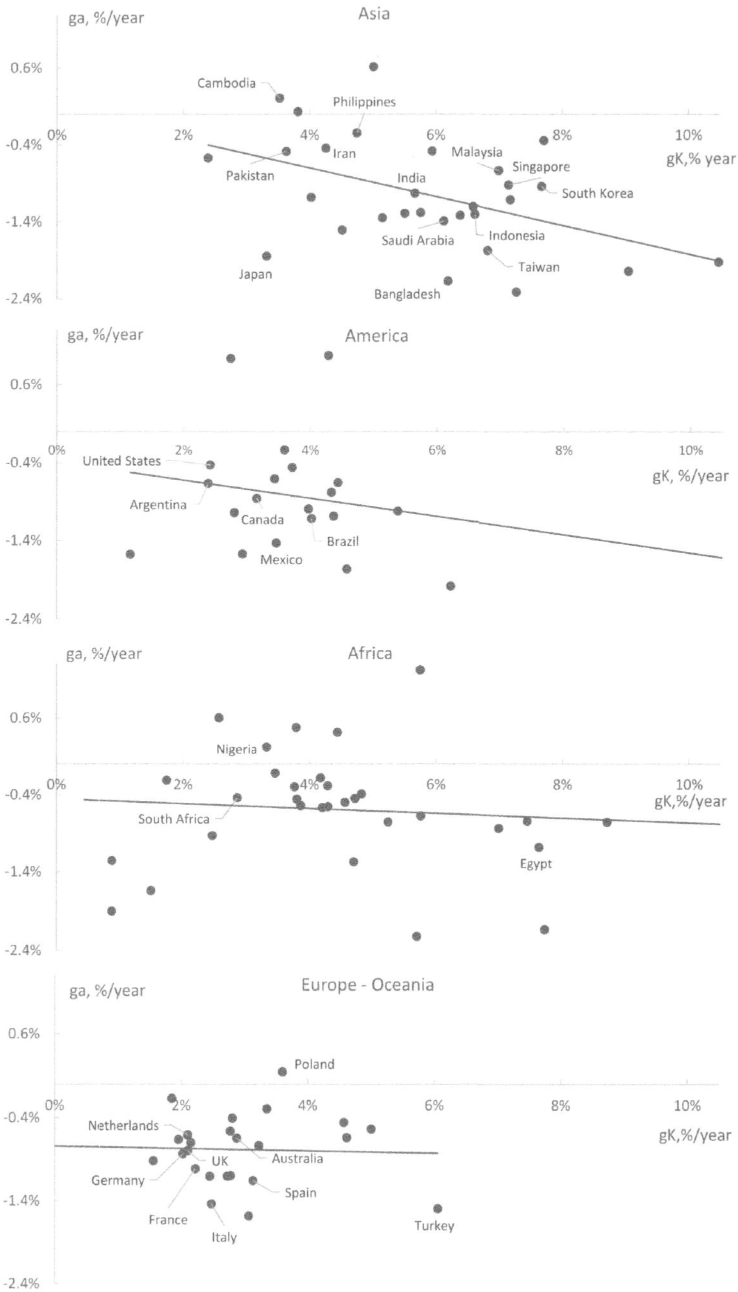

Figure 1.11 The pair capital accumulation and growth rate of capital productivity (g_K, ga), and their linear fit between 1970 and 2019 by continent.

Source: EPWT 7.0.

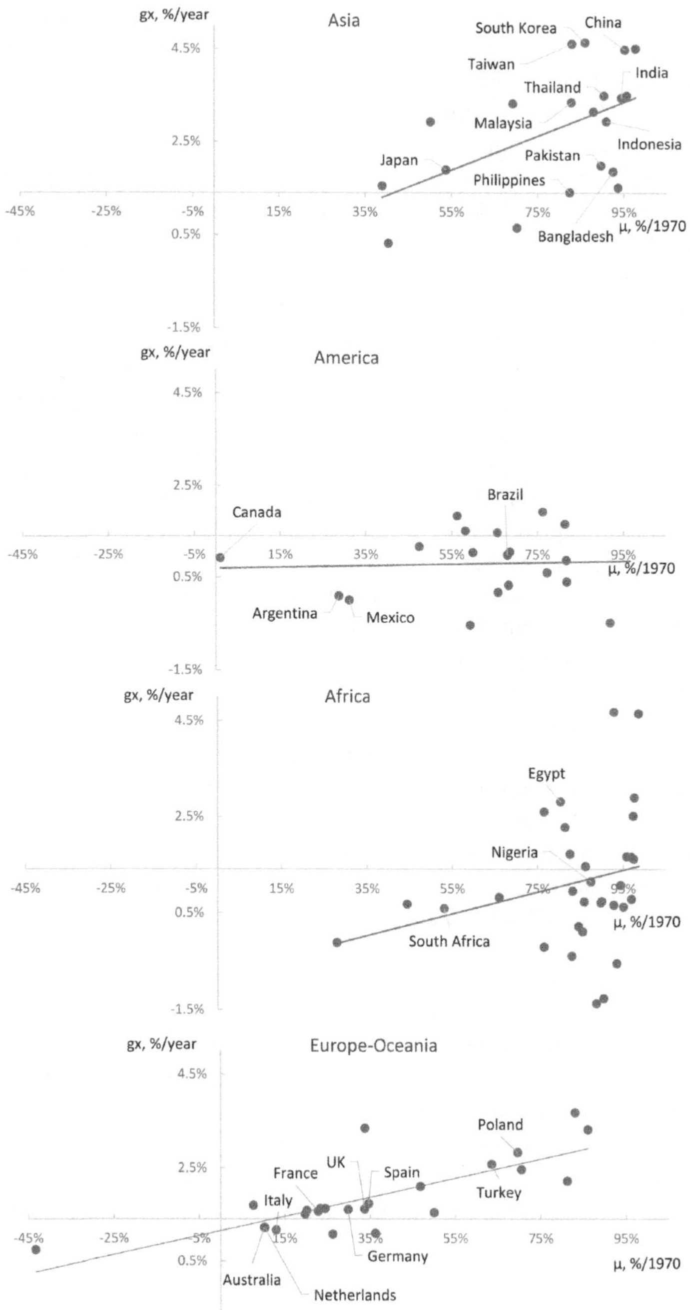

Figure 1.12 The pair labor productivity gap in 1970 and growth rate of labor productivity between 1970 and 2019, (μ, gx), by continent.

Source: EPWT 7.0.

half of the sample fell further behind. The increasing data spread as the labor productivity gap and the distance from the leader expanded suggests that while some countries benefit from their backwardness, others in a similar situation do not take advantage of it. When examining the catching-up process by continent, a pattern emerges. In Africa, 11 countries caught up, while 21 fell behind. In America, four countries caught up, while 15 fell behind. In Asia, 17 nations caught up, while three fell behind. In Europe and Oceania, 18 countries caught up, while six fell behind.

Figure 1.13 displays pairs of data showing the gap in capital productivity in 1970 and the compound growth rate of capital productivity (ξ, ga) from 1970 to 2019 for 95 countries, organized by continent. The horizontal lines intersect the vertical line at minus 0.43%, the annual compound growth rate of capital productivity of the United States in the period. In 1970, 78 countries had higher capital productivity than the United States; they are located on the left-hand side of the vertical axis. There were 17 countries with lower capital productivity than the leader; eight were in Africa, and nine were in Europe and Oceania. The countries located below the horizontal line had a growth rate of capital productivity lower than the United States.

Catching up in capital productivity primarily involved a downward movement. The 66 countries positioned in the third quadrant had higher capital productivity in 1970 but experienced a lower growth rate of capital productivity between 1970 and 2019 compared to the United States. Additionally, 10 countries in the first quadrant successfully caught up by increasing their capital productivity. The 12 countries in the second quadrant saw an expansion in the gap in capital productivity relative to the leader, while the seven countries in the fourth quadrant further diminished their capital productivity compared to the United States.

Examining catching up by continent reveals that, in Asia, 16 countries caught up, reducing their capital productivity. In America, 16 countries also caught up experiencing a decrease in capital productivity. Africa witnessed 27 countries catching up, with seven increasing their capital productivity and 20 declining it. In Europe and Oceania, 17 nations caught up, three increased their capital productivity, and 14 reduced it.

While there was a general pattern of catching up in capital productivity, the same phenomenon was not observed in labor productivity. The advantages of lower mechanization in follower countries, implying in smaller labor productivity and higher capital productivity and, therefore a higher profit rate, begin to erode when capital productivity declines more rapidly than labor productivity increases. It indicates that the follower country is gradually losing its backwardness advantage as the disparities in profit rates and incentives for capital accumulation diminish relative to the leading country, potentially jeopardizing the catching-up process.

Stylized facts

Building on the EPWT 7.0 dataset, we have explored recurring patterns in economic growth, technical change, capital accumulation, and distribution for a broad spectrum of countries from 1970 to 2019. Following Kaldor (1965), these observed regularities or stylized facts will serve as the foundation for constructing a

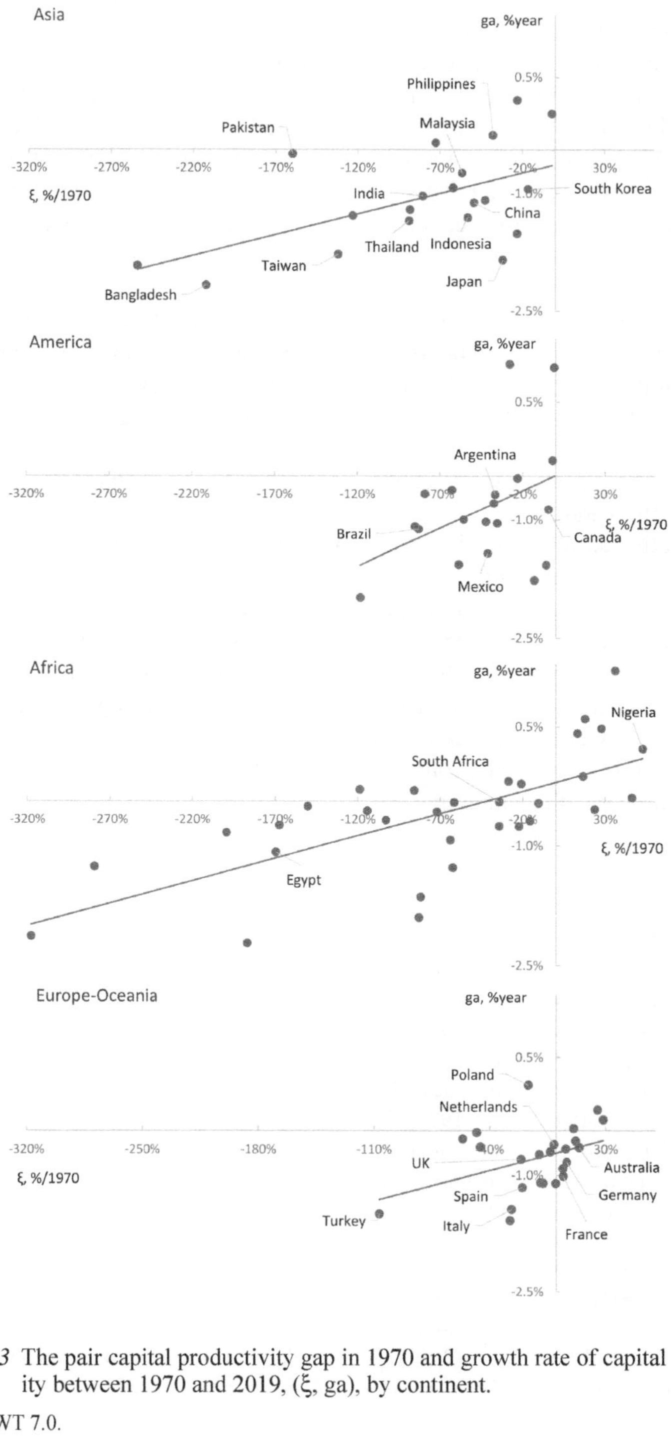

Figure 1.13 The pair capital productivity gap in 1970 and growth rate of capital productivity between 1970 and 2019, (ξ, ga), by continent.

Source: EPWT 7.0.

theoretical model of economic growth encompassing the dynamics of catching up and falling behind, as elucidated in the forthcoming chapter.

The findings revealed a prevailing trend for the technical change to follow a pattern of rising labor productivity, declining capital productivity, and increasing capital-labor ratio. While most countries displayed the Marx-biased technical between 1970 and 2019, other forms of technical change were present. We also observed a positive correlation between the capital-labor ratio and labor productivity and a negative correlation between the capital-labor ratio and capital productivity. The additional stylized facts can be summarized as follows:

1 Differences in the GDP growth rate exist among countries and continents.
2 The follower countries tend to employ techniques with lower labor productivity and capital intensity and higher capital productivity than the leader's technique.
3 The profit rate tends to decline during the process of development and catching up.
4 Real wage increases with economic growth despite declining wage share between 1970 and 2019.
5 A negative correlation exists between profit rate and real wage in the process of economic development.
6 There is a positive correlation between profit rate and capital accumulation.
7 Capital accumulation correlates positively with the growth rate of labor productivity and negatively with the growth rate of capital productivity.
8 Capital accumulation plays a fundamental role in catching up with the leader country. However, high capital accumulation in the follower country can reduce capital productivity and profit rate to a level lower than the leader, posing a risk in the process of catching up.

Bibliography

Feenstra, R., Inklaar, R., and Timmer, M. (2015). The next generation of the Penn World Table. *The American Economic Review*, *105*(10), pp. 3150–3182.

Foley, D., and Marquetti, A. (1997). Economic growth from a classical perspective. In: Teixeira, J. (ed.). *Money, Growth, Distribution and Structural Change: Contemporaneous Analysis*. Brasília: Universidade de Brasília Press

Foley, D., and Marquetti, A. (1999). Productivity, employment and growth in European integration. *Metroeconomica*, 50, pp. 277–300.

Foley, D., Michl, T., and Tavani, D. (2019). *Growth and Distribution.* 2nd edition. Cambridge: Harvard University Press.

Harcourt, G. (1972). *Some Cambridge Controversies in the Theory of Capital*. Cambridge: Cambridge University Press.

Kaldor, N. (1965). Capital accumulation and economic growth. In: Lutz, F., and Hague, D. (eds). *Theory of Capital*. London: Macmillan, pp. 177–222.

Marquetti, A., and Porsse, M. (2017). Padrões de mudança técnica nas economias latino americanas: 1963–2008. *Economia e Sociedade*, 26, pp. 459–482.

Pichardo, G. (2007). Economic growth models and growth tendencies in major Latin American countries and the United States. 1963–2003. *Investigación Económica*, 66(262), pp. 59–88.

Villanueva, L., and Jiang, X. (2018). Patterns of technical change and deindustrialization. *PSL Quarterly Review*, 71(285), pp. 161–182.

2 A growth model in the classical-Marxian tradition

One of the central questions that growth theory faces is how to explain the unequal development observed among nations, a prominent feature of capitalism. As discussed in the preceding chapter, follower countries display lower labor productivity and higher capital productivity in comparison with developed nations. Typically, during the process of development, the increase in labor productivity is accompanied by a decrease in capital productivity. The catch up in labor productivity starts from lower levels, while in capital productivity, it begins from higher levels. Moreover, the profit rate is generally higher in developing countries.

This chapter introduces a classical-Marxian model of catching that incorporates these stylized facts. In the model, the follower country employs a technique characterized by lower labor productivity and higher capital productivity than the leader's. It allows the follower to have a higher profit rate, which enables faster capital accumulation than the leader. In the model, the relationship between profit rate and capital accumulation plays a fundamental role in explaining the dynamics of catching up and falling behind.

We first outline the classical-Marxian canonical growth model, then we extend it to investigate catching up and falling behind trajectories. The growth model encompasses a specific labor market theory, a theory of consumption and saving, and a production model. The present chapter draws on the contributions of Marglin (1986), Foley and Michl (1999), Foley, Michl and Tavani (2018), Blecker and Setterfield (2019), and Marquetti, Ourique, and Morrone (2020).

The chapter is organized into three sections as follows. The first section introduces the classical-Marxian growth model. Section two displays the model for catching up and falling behind. Section three explores extensions for the model and provides avenues for future research.

The standard classical-Marxian model

Initially, we present a simple economic growth model with a classical-Marxian closure. In economic terminology, a closure serves as technical jargon used to define which variables are considered endogenous and exogenous within mathematical models. The closures are defined by economic theory. The only mathematical

DOI: 10.4324/9781003223382-3

constraint is that the number of equations must be equal to the number of endogenous variables, a requirement essential for resolving the model.

The model outlined in the section is straightforward. It throws light on the causal relationship between macroeconomic variables and describes the behavior of a closed economy without a government, with one sector, one commodity, and two social classes: the capitalists and workers. A Leontief production function represents the model of production. The economy produces an output, X, employing capital, K, and labor, N. The constant return to scale Leontief production function is expressed as:

$$X = \min\left(aK, xN\right), \tag{2.1}$$

where a represents the capital productivity and x denotes the labor productivity. The technique of production is defined by labor productivity, capital productivity or capital-labor ratio, and depreciation rate. The capital-labor ratio is computed as the ratio between labor productivity and capital productivity.

Production is distributed in the form of income. Capitalists receive profits and workers receive wages. There is free competition and firms have access to the same technique, which leads to equalization of profit rates and the economy fully utilizes its productive capacity. Competition in the labor market also ensures wage equalization. The real wage-profit rate schedule illuminates the trade-off between wages and profits:

$$w = x - \left(r + d\right)k, \tag{2.2}$$

where w represents the real wage, r is the net profit rate, k is the capital-labor ratio, and d is the depreciation rate. The maximum rate of profit, which occurs when wages are set at zero, is equal to capital productivity, $r + d = a$. The maximum real wage, corresponding to profits equal to zero, is equal to labor productivity, $w = x$.

Output can be invested or consumed. Output growth depends on capital accumulation. The social consumption-growth rate schedule illustrates the trade-off between capital accumulation and consumption:

$$c = x - \left(g_K + d\right)k, \tag{2.3}$$

where c denotes social consumption per worker and $g_K + d$ is the capital accumulation. The maximum rate of capital accumulation is equal to capital productivity, $g_K + d = a$, occurring when social consumption equal to zero. The maximum consumption per worker, corresponding to zero investment, equals labor productivity, $c = x$.

The hypotheses about saving and investment decisions connect the distribution and growth spheres. For simplicity, it is assumed that workers consume all their wages, while capitalists save a proportion s of their profits, where $1 \geq s > 0$. The saving function can be written as:

$$S = sZ = s\left(R + D\right), \tag{2.4}$$

where S is total savings, R is net profits, and D stands for depreciation. Employing the assumption that investment is equal to saving, we obtain:

$$I = S = sZ = s(R + D) \tag{2.5}$$

where I denotes the investment. Dividing the two sides by the capital stock, the Cambridge equation emerges:

$$g_K + d = s(r + d). \tag{2.6}$$

The capital accumulation is a function of the saving rate and profit rate.

Equations (2.2, 2.3), and (2.6) give the framework for different economic traditions. Economic theory provides additional information to close the model (Dutt, 1990; Marglin, 1986). In the classical-Marxian tradition, the distribution is exogenously determined, and the labor supply is elastic at the subsistence wage. Ricardo employed the Malthusian population theory to explain this shape, while Marx postulated the existence of an industrial reserve army of labor. According to Marx, historical and institutional factors determine the real wage, with labor supply adjusting to capital accumulation.

Following this tradition and for simplicity, we assume a constant wage share. The real wage is determined by:

$$w = (1 - \pi)x, \tag{2.7}$$

where $(1 - \pi)$ is the exogenous wage share. Under the assumption that workers consume all their wages, the workers' consumption, c^w, is equal to the real wage, $c^w = w$. Thus, it is possible to compute the capitalist consumption, c^c, by:

$$c^c = c - c^w = c - w. \tag{2.8}$$

The exogenous parameters in the model are the labor productivity, x, capital-labor ratio, k, depreciation rate, d, wage share, $(1\text{-}\pi)$, and savings rate, s. Figure 2.1 pictures the classical-Marxian model. The first and second quadrants present the real wage-profit and the consumption-growth frontier. The fourth quadrant shows the Cambridge equation, revealing the relationship between profit, saving, and accumulation rates. The third quadrant works for analytical exposition. It shows a 45-degree line that connects the Cambridge equation with the consumption-growth frontier.

The endogenous variables are calculated in sequential steps. First, the real wage is determined by equation (2.7), then the profit rate is calculated by equation (2.2), the real wage-profit rate schedule is shown in the first quadrant. The next step is the computation of capital accumulation by equation (2.6), the Cambridge equation, which is depicted in the fourth quadrant. Finally, the consumption-growth rate schedule calculates the social consumption per worker, as seen in the second quadrant. Income distribution and technology determine the profit rate. The profit rate and the saving rate drive the capital accumulation. Thus, distribution is exogenous, and the growth is endogenous in the classical-Marxian tradition.

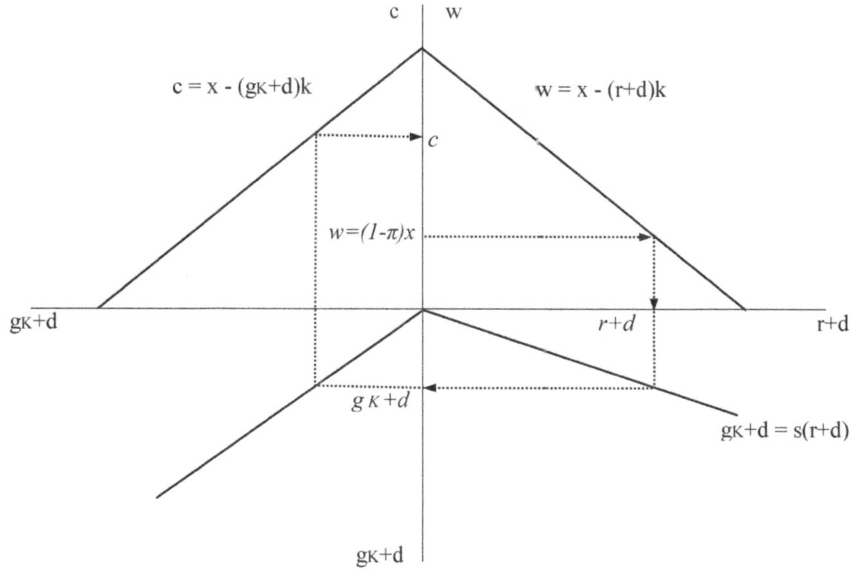

Figure 2.1 The representation of the classical-Marxian growth model. The endogenous variables are determined in a sequence. First, the real wage, w, is computed; then the profit rate, r + d; The next step is determining capital accumulation, g_K + d; and finally, the social consumption per worker, c, is calculated.

Comparative dynamics: The effects of changes in saving rate and income distribution

Comparative dynamics offer a valuable framework for investigating the effects of changes in exogenous parameters on the endogenous variables within a model. In this context, we focus on two-parameter shifts: first, a reduction in the saving rate, followed by a decrease in the wage share. However, in the real world, these parameters frequently change continuously and simultaneously, which makes the analysis markedly more challenging.

First, we investigate the case of a decline in the propensity of the capitalist class to save, denoted as s. This reduction, following a Keynesian perspective, may reflect changes in the expectations of capitalists regarding the future economic landscape. Figure 2.2 illustrates the shifts in the endogenous variables and the new equilibrium of the model, assuming that other exogenous parameters remain constant. A fall in saving rates leads to a decline in capital accumulation and an increase in social consumption per worker. This adjustment occurs through the Cambridge equation channel, which is presented in the third quadrant. The capitalist class reduces its savings and increases its consumption, c^c, while the workers' consumption, c^w, remains constant. Importantly, the real wage and the profit rate remain unaffected by changes in the capitalist saving rate. Consequently, there is a decrease in the GDP growth rate, which equals the capital accumulation rate under the assumption of constant capital productivity.

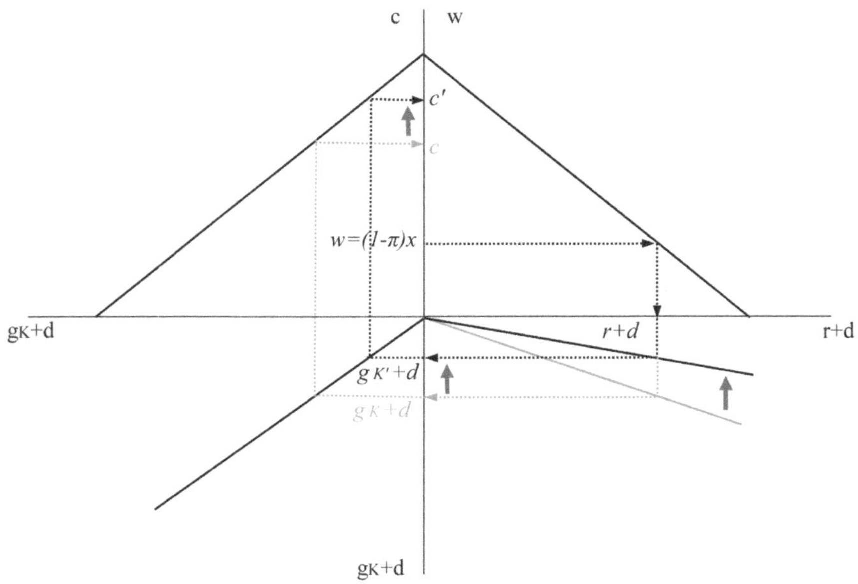

Figure 2.2 The effects of a decline in the savings rate, s, on the classical-Marxian model. the wage, w, and the profit rate, r + d, remain constant, the capital accumulation, g_K + d, declines, and the social consumption per worker, c, due to higher capitalist consumption, c^c.

The impact of a decrease in the wage share on the endogenous variables is illustrated in Figure 2.3. The real wage-profit rate frontier in the first quadrant expresses the trade-off between wages and profits. Ceteris paribus, a redistribution in favor of capital leads to a reduction in real wage, w, and an increase in the profit rate, r + d, which drives an expansion in capital accumulation, g_K + d. There is a decline in social consumption per worker, c, due to the fall in workers' consumption, c^w, which by assumption is equal to the real wage. The increase in capitalist consumption per worker, c^c, is lower than the decline in workers' consumption. In the model, a redistribution from labor to capital drives a higher capital accumulation.

The classical-Marxian model of catching up and falling behind

The classical-Marxian model offers insights into the dynamics of nations in the processes of catching up or lagging behind. In this context, we expand upon the model introduced in the previous section, providing key insights to understand the phenomenon of unequal development in capitalism.

This approach assumes that technical change stems from a historical process in which a country can either develop new production methods or adopt a technique from other countries. The techniques are not a public good and therefore have a

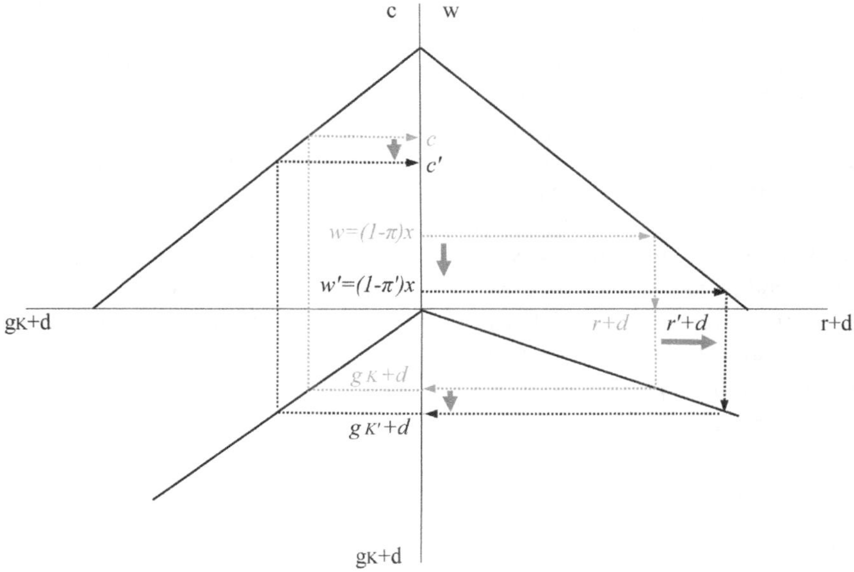

Figure 2.3 The effects of a decline in the wage share, 1 – π, in the classical-Marxian model. The wage, w, falls and the profit rate, r + d, increases, which leads to a rise in capital accumulation, g_K + d. The social consumption per worker, c, declines. The increase in capitalist consumption is lower than the decline in worker's consumption.

diffusion cost. Workers in the follower country require time to learn how to use them effectively. Moreover, the successful adoption of new techniques by a follower country necessitates access to machinery and equipment, education for the labor force, and a learning period for both firms and workers. However, it is generally easier and quicker for a backward country to adapt techniques developed in a leading country rather than attempting to discover new ones.

Follower countries have a technical gap compared to the leader. The gap implies in lower labor productivity ($x^F < x^L$) and in higher capital productivity ($a^F > a^L$) in the follower country in comparison to the leader. Gerschenkron (1962) suggested that a greater technological gap can often translate into larger growth opportunities for the follower countries. In the model, the advantages of backwardness manifest as higher profitability in the follower compared to the leader, which results in higher capital accumulation and in catch up.

Although our model resembles Foley and Michl's (1999), the assumptions we made in the equations for the growth rates of labor productivity and capital productivity growth rates relied on stylized facts. There are two essential differences in our model. Firstly, we consider labor and capital productivities, while Foley and Michl (1999) only employ the equation for labor productivity. Despite raising this possibility, they did not display an equation for catching up in capital productivity.

Secondly, catching up emerges only if accumulation in the follower country is greater than in the leader.

Different economic traditions emphasize the central role of capital accumulation in driving economic growth. Capital accumulation functions as a proxy for a country's efforts to catch up, while considering other crucial factors such as the institutional organization of society. Importantly, investments in new capital goods usually embody the latest technological advancements.

Formally, the growth rate of labor productivity in the follower country depends on the labor productivity growth in the leader, g_x^L, the technical gap in labor productivity, $\mu = (x^L - x^F)/x^L = 1 - x^F/x^L$, and the term of catching up, ψ. The term of catching up in labor productivity, ψ, is either positive when capital accumulation in the follower is higher than in the leader, or equal to zero, or negative in the opposite case. The labor productivity growth rate in the follower country is expressed by:

$$g_x^F = g_x^L + \psi\mu \tag{2.9}$$

where

$$\psi = f\left(g_K^F\right) > 0 \text{ if } g_K^F > g_K^L\text{, and}$$

$$\psi = f\left(g_K^F\right) \leq 0 \text{ if } g_K^F \leq g_K^L.$$

In the process of catching up, the growth rates of labor productivity in the follower are positive and higher than in the leader country.

Similarly, the growth rate of capital productivity in the follower country depends on the growth rate of capital productivity in the leader, g_a^L, the technical gap in capital productivity, $\xi = (a^L - a^F)/a^L = 1 - a^F/a^L$, and the catching up term, θ. The term of catching up in capital productivity, θ, is negative when the capital accumulation in the follower country is greater than in the leader, equal to zero, or otherwise positive. In the follower country, the growth rate of capital productivity is expressed by:

$$g_a^F = g_a^L + \theta\xi, \tag{2.10}$$

where

$$\theta = f\left(g_K^F\right) > 0 \text{ if } g_K^F > g_K^L\text{, and}$$

$$\theta = f\left(g_K^F\right) \leq 0 \text{ if } g_K^F \leq g_K^L.$$

In the catching-up, the growth rate of capital productivity is negative and lower than in the leader. Marquetti, Ourique, and Morrone (2020) prove that under the assumptions of equations (2.9) and (2.10), the follower country will catch up with the leader.

For simplicity, the model assumes exogenous growth rates of labor and capital productivities for the leader country. Foley and Michl (1999) developed a model with exogenous technical change with positive labor productivity growth and negative growth rate of capital productivity. They dubbed Marx-biased this type of technical change. It is possible to endogenize these growth rates following Kennedy (1964) and Duménil and Lévy (1995). For a survey on endogenous labor productivity growth models, see Tavani and Zamparelli (2017).

We consider three additional hypotheses. Firstly, we suppose equal capitalist saving rates in both follower and leader countries, $s^L = s^F = s$. Secondly, we consider equal profit share in both economies, $\pi^L = \pi^F = \pi$. Thirdly, we assume equal depreciation rate in the economies, $d^L = d^F = d$. We postulate that these exogenous variables are equal for easy understanding of the model.

Economic growth in the leader economy is expressed as follows:

$$x^L = x_0^L \left(1 + g_x^L\right)^t$$

$$a^L = a_0^L \left(1 + g_a^L\right)^t$$

$$w^L = \left(1 - \pi\right) x^L$$

$$w^L = x^L - \left(r^L + d\right) k^L$$

$$\left(g_K^L + d\right) = s\left(r^L + d\right)$$

$$c^L = x^L - \left(g_K^L + d\right) k^L$$

where g_x^L is the exogenous labor productivity growth rate, and g_a^L stands for the exogenous capital productivity growth rate. As mentioned earlier, the Marx-biased technical change assumes that $g_x^L > 0$ and $g_a^L < 0$.

Economic growth in the follower country is represented by:

$$x^F = x_0^F \left(1 + g_x^F\right)^t$$

$$a^F = a_0^F \left(1 + g_a^F\right)^t$$

$$g_x^F = g_x^L + \psi\mu$$

where

$$\psi = f\left(g_K^F\right) > 0 \text{ if } g_K^F > g_K^L, \text{ and}$$

$$\psi = f\left(g_K^F\right) \leq 0 \text{ if } g_K^F \leq g_K^L$$

$$g_a^F = g_a^L + \theta\xi,$$

where

$$\theta = f\left(g_K^F\right) > 0 \text{ if } g_K^F > g_K^L, \text{ and}$$

$$\theta = f\left(g_K^F\right) \leq 0 \text{ if } g_K^F \leq g_K^L.$$

$$w^F = \left(1 - \pi\right)x^F$$

$$w^F = x^F - \left(r^F + d\right)k^F$$

$$\left(g_K^F + d\right) = s\left(r^F + d\right)$$

$$c^F = x^F - \left(g_k{}^F + d\right)k^F$$

The exogenous variables of the model are the initial techniques in the leader, x_0^L, a_0^L, and in the follower countries, x_0^F, a_0^F, the depreciation rate, *d*, the profit share, $\pi^L = \pi^F = \pi$, capitalist saving rate, $s^L = s^F = s$, and the growth rates of capital productivity, g_a^L, and labor productivity, g_x^L, in the leader country.

The endogenous variables are the techniques in the leader, x^L, a^L, and in the follower country, x^F, a^F, the net profit rates in the leader, r^L, and in the follower, r^F, the capital accumulation in the leader, $g_K{}^L$, and in the follower country, $g_K{}^F$, the social consumption per worker in the leader, c^L, and in the follower country, c^F, the terms of catching up for labor productivity, ψ, and capital productivity, θ, and the growth rates of capital productivity, $g_a{}^F$ and labor productivity, $g_x{}^F$, in the follower country.

The technical gap in labor productivity, represented by $\mu = (x^L - x^F)/x^L = 1 - x^F/x^L$, is a positive number that decreases as the follower countries catch up with the leader. For example, a gap in labor productivity of one means that the leader has twice the labor productivity of the follower country. Conversely, the technical gap in capital productivity, denoted by $\xi = (a^L - a^F)/a^L = 1 - a^F/a^L$, is a negative number that increases during the process of catching up. For instance, a gap in capital productivity of minus one means that the follower has double the capital productivity of the leader country.

In the initial period, the leader country exhibits higher labor productivity but lower capital productivity compared to the follower country. For an equal profit share, the leader country has higher real wage and lower profit rate. The greater capital productivity in the follower country accounts for its higher profit rate compared to the leader. Assuming equal savings rates, the follower country has higher capital accumulation due to its greater profit rate. In contrast, social consumption is higher in the leader. Figure 2.4 displays a visual representation of the model in the initial period.

Catching-up occurs when capital accumulation in the follower country surpasses that of the leader, in this case we have $g_x^F > g_x^L$ and $g_a^F < g_a^L$. Additionally, the technical change in the follower country follows the Marx-biased pattern. This process leads to a reduction in the differences in the productivities of labor and capital, the

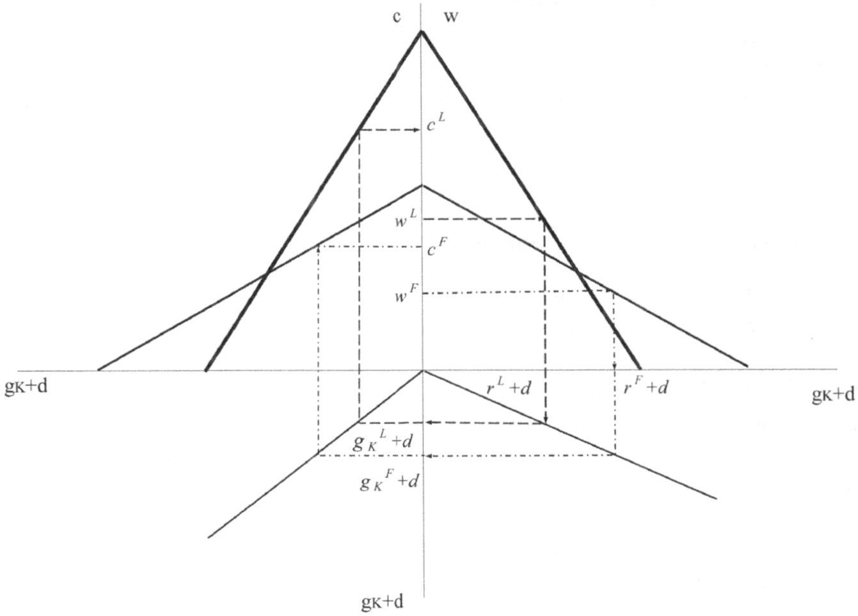

Figure 2.4 The classical-Marxian model of catching up in the initial period. The follower country, represented by the thin line, exhibits lower labor productivity and higher capital productivity than the leader, represented by the thicker line. For the same wage share and saving rate, the follower has lower real wage, $w^F < w^L$, higher profit rate, $r^F + d > r^L + d$, and capital accumulation, $g_K^F + d > g_K^L + d$, and lower social consumption per worker, $c^F < c^L$, than the leader.

capital-labor ratio, the average real wage, the profit rate, capital accumulation, and social consumption per worker between the follower and the leader.

The trajectory of the profit rate depends on technical change and functional income distribution. The presence of Marx-biased technical change, combined with a constant wage share, results in a declining profit rate. The process of catching up hinges on the rate of capital accumulation, a factor explained by both profit and saving rates. The decrease in capital productivity in the follower country reduces the profit rate and capital accumulation.

The increasing capital-labor ratio in the follower country resulting from mechanization and industrialization may not always be enough to eliminate the differences in labor productivity with the leader. There is the possibility for catching up in capital productivity to advance at a faster pace than in labor productivity. If capital productivity in the follower country declines too rapidly, the process of catching up in labor productivity may stop due to a decrease in the profit rate and capital accumulation.

In the cases where the leader experiences higher capital accumulation than the follower country, a process of falling behind process emerges. This can occur in two scenarios. First, when the saving rate of the leader is superior to the follower country. Second, when the leader exhibits a higher profit rate. Moreover, the velocity of catching up may decline when the leader has positive capital productivity growth. In this context, *ceteris paribus*, the profit rate and capital accumulation will expand in the leader. Historically, these periods are associated with the emergence of radical technologies.

Summary and extensions of the model

We have developed a classical-Marxian model that provides insights into the intricate dynamics of catching up and falling behind among nations. Catching up occurs when accumulation rates are higher in the follower country, leading to a reduction in disparities in labor and capital productivities, the capital-labor ratio, the average real wage, the profit rate, capital accumulation, and social consumption between countries. Nevertheless, a rapid decline in the profit rate within the follower country can jeopardize the process. Historical evidence demonstrates that catching up is indeed a challenging endeavor.

The model can be extended to incorporate public investment and external variables. Expanding the analysis to include the role of the state, opening the model to account for foreign trade and investment, and addressing environmental and demographic considerations are vital research questions to consider in the future. Moreover, we may consider integrating aspects such as terms of trade, concerns related to the Dutch disease phenomenon, and questions pertaining to finance. Two main links connect the finance sector with capital accumulation. First, in an open economy, the decisions to finance the investments or the current account deficit with external debt may give rise to financial fragility. Second, the expansion of financial instruments may divert funds from productive investment, reducing capital accumulation.

These additions would enhance the model's capability to explain the dynamics of catching up and falling behind. Economic models simplify reality by emphasizing specific economic aspects to elucidate complex phenomena. The simplifications can be circumvented when economic history is incorporated into the investigation.

The analysis should incorporate the international relations among countries. The international politics often plays an important role in many examples of rapid economic growth. For instance, Japan, South Korea, and Taiwan provide examples of political influence on catching up (Wallerstein, 1979). The development of their economies, facilitated through diplomatic invitation from the United States, served a political purpose, preventing the spread of the Soviet model in Asia.

In the second part of this book, we examine the processes of catching up and falling behind in countries located in Asia, America, Central and Eastern Europe, and Africa. We utilize insights from the model, the statistical information, and the historical perspective on capitalism over the last five decades. We begin our exploration by investigating the leader country, the United States.

Bibliography

Blecker, R., and Setterfield, M. (2019). *Heterodox Macroeconomics: Models of Demand, Distribution and Growth*. Cheltenham: Edward Elgar publishing.

Duménil, G., and Lévy, D. 1995. A stochastic model of technical change, application to the US. Economy (1869–1989). *Metroeconomica* 46(3), pp. 213–245.

Dutt, A. (1990). *Growth, Distribution and Uneven Development*. Cambridge: Cambridge University Press.

Foley, D., and Michl, T. (1999). *Growth and Distribution*, 1st Edition. Cambridge: Harvard University Press.

Foley, D., Michl, T., and Tavani, D. (2018). *Growth and Distribution*, 2nd Edition. Cambridge: Harvard University Press.

Gerschenkron, A. (1962). *Economic Backwardness in Historical Perspective*. Cambridge: Harvard University Press.

Kaldor, N. (1970). The case for regional policies. *Scottish Journal of Political Economy*, 17(3), pp. 337–348.

Kennedy, C. (1964). Induced bias in innovation and the theory of distribution. *Economic Journal*, 74, pp. 541–547.

Marglin, S. (1986). *Growth, Distribution, and Prices*. Cambridge: Harvard University Press.

Marquetti, A., Ourique, L., and Morrone, H. (2020). Measuring the profit rate in an inflationary context: The case of Brazil, 1955–2008. *Review of Radical Political Economics*, 51, pp. 52–74.

Tavani, D., and Zamparelli, L. (2017). Endogenous technical change in alternative theories of growth and income distribution. *Journal of Economic Surveys*, 31, pp. 1272–1303.

Wallerstein, I. (1979). *The Capitalist World-Economy*. Cambridge: Cambridge University Press.

3 The US economy from the demise of the Golden Age to the crisis of neoliberalism

Throughout history, capitalism has undergone distinct phases marked by the combination of institutions and technology. In each phase, a specific institutional organization articulates the roles of both the state and the market in shaping the production process; the power relations and income distribution among and within social classes; the power relations between nations, and the mechanisms by which the income is transferred to the leading country. The institutional organization may postpone the declining trend in the profit rate by activating some of the countertendencies of falling profitability. Structural crises occur when the institutional organization and current techniques are unable to sustain capital profitability. Then, a new set of institutional and technical innovations must emerge to increase the profit rate.

The Great Depression of the 1930s marked the decline of liberalism as the dominant guiding principle for modern societies with the rise of managed capitalism taking center stage. Following World War II, Keynesian economic policies were employed to manage macroeconomics and maintain a low unemployment rate. The objective of enterprises was the expansion of their size through productive investment. The result was high capital accumulation and economic growth, which in turn bolstered the bargaining power of workers. Consequently, the working classes enjoyed an improvement in their living standards.

However, by the late 1960s, there were signs of exhaustion in the Golden Age as capital productivity declined and wages increased, leading to a falling profit rate. It was necessary to restore the power of capitalists through neoliberal reforms. Neoliberalism was imposed in advanced countries in the late 1970s and early 1980s, strengthening the role of the financial markets. After the restoration of capitalist power, the profit rate increased (Duménil and Lévy, 2013). However, the accumulation rate did not rise at the same pace due to the expansion of finance.

As a hegemonic country, the United States has played a leading role in the capitalist transformations, particularly after World War II. The country functions as a source of technical and institutional innovations, which often diffuse to other nations with varying degrees of time lag. The chapter investigates the economic dynamics of the United States by analyzing macroeconomic variables primarily from 1970 to 2019, with some information dating back to 1950. Additionally, it explores the comparison between growth rates during the Golden Age and neoliberalism.

DOI: 10.4324/9781003223382-4

The economic dynamics and major trends of the global economy are shaped by the performance of the leading nation. There are four compelling reasons for selecting the United States as the reference country in the analysis. First, during the period under study, the United States stood as the leading nation, displaying the highest labor productivity. Second, the trajectories of labor and capital productivities of other developed countries mirrored those of the US economy. Third, the dollar and the presence of US financial institutions establish the United States as the epicenter of global finance. Fourth, many international institutions and global policymakers, including the International Monetary Fund and the World Bank, consider the institutional framework of the United States as the ideal model for development.

The United States remained the world economic leader, setting the basic parameters under which developing countries operate and establish their development strategies. It is a demanding task to replicate the growth path of the United States, given its vast reserve of natural resources, large physical and human capital, alongside a remarkable ability to generate technical and institutional innovations. However, particularly after the 2007 financial crisis, US hegemony is in jeopardy, primarily due to its neoliberal contradictions and, secondarily, by the ascendency of China.

The chapter is organized in four sections. The first reviews the US economic performance from the Golden Age to neoliberalism. The second outlines technical change and distribution issues in the US economy. The third presents our conception about the decline growth rates, while critically examining two theories of secular stagnation. The last section concludes by further analyzing the dynamics of capital accumulation during neoliberalism, considering some issues about the global hegemony.

From the Golden Age to the crisis of neoliberalism

From the Golden Age to neoliberalism, the United States underwent substantial changes in its economic and social structures. These changes, driven by a complex interplay between continuities and transformations in its institutional framework and technical change, played a central role in shaping the trajectory of economic growth. A fundamental aspect of the US economy was the decline in growth rates over the last decades.

During the Golden Age from 1950 to 1973, the United States experienced an average annual GDP growth rate of 4.03 percent. However, the trajectory of economic expansion took a different course during neoliberalism, with growth rates showing a marked decrease. Specifically, the average annual GDP growth rate dipped to 3.15 percent between 1980 and 2007 and further diminished to 2.27 percent in the years 2010s.

Capital accumulation and GDP growth exhibit a strong interconnection, as illustrated in Figure 3.1. Capital accumulation appears to function as a gravitational center around which the GDP growth rates tend to fluctuate. The Golden Age featured robust accumulation, which moved to a lower level during neoliberalism, followed by a further decline after the 2007 financial crisis. The 1970s marked the end of the Golden Age and high capital accumulation and economic growth.

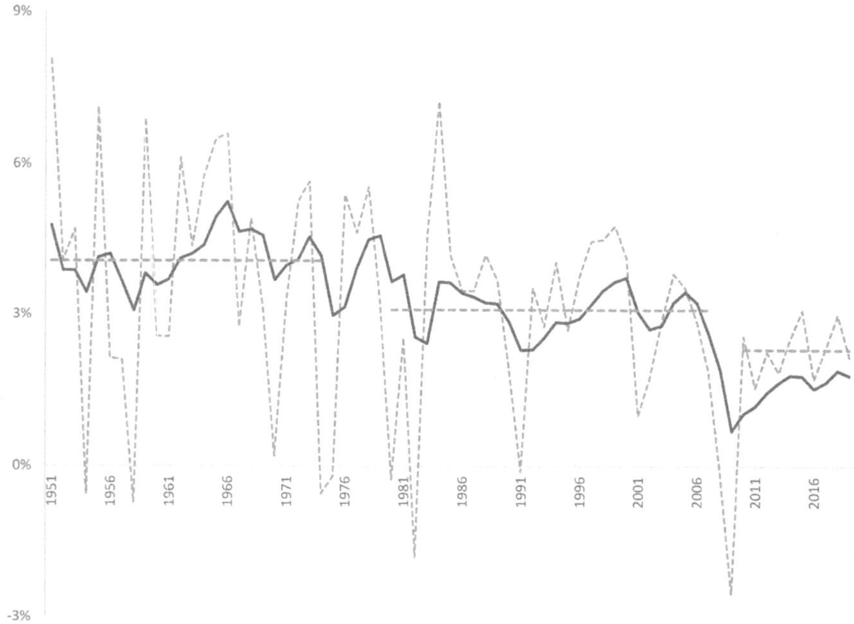

Figure 3.1 The capital accumulation, solid line, and the GDP growth rate and its declining average, dotted line, in the US economy, 1951–2019.

Source: EPWT 7.0

According to the Marxian perspective, the understanding of the trajectory of capital accumulation and economic growth hinges on two key factors: the profit rate and its fluctuations, and the prevailing institutional arrangement, which plays a key role in the conversion rate from profits into investments. Figure 3.2 plots the data on profit rate and capital accumulation from 1951 to 2019.

The profit rate expanded from 1951 to 1966, followed by a gradual decline, reaching its lowest point in 1982. It subsequently experienced an upswing until the late 1990s, declining again until 2001, maintaining, with oscillations, this lower level since then. As the profit rate declined, so did the capital accumulation and GDP growth rates. However, capital accumulation followed the profitability much closer during the Golden Age than in neoliberalism.

The declining path of profits and capital accumulation, coupled with a series of political and economic crises, characterizes the 1970s as a transitional period between two distinct capitalist institutional frameworks. The end of the Golden Age was marked by important events, including the collapse of the Bretton Woods System, surging oil prices, political tensions amid rising inflation, lower economic growth, higher unemployment, and increased international rivalry, all contributing to the 1970s crisis. Additionally, a slowdown in labor productivity was a further sign of the limits of the Golden Age.

The answer to the 1970 crisis materialized through the advent of neoliberalism. It can be broadly characterized as a distinct phase of capitalism marked by

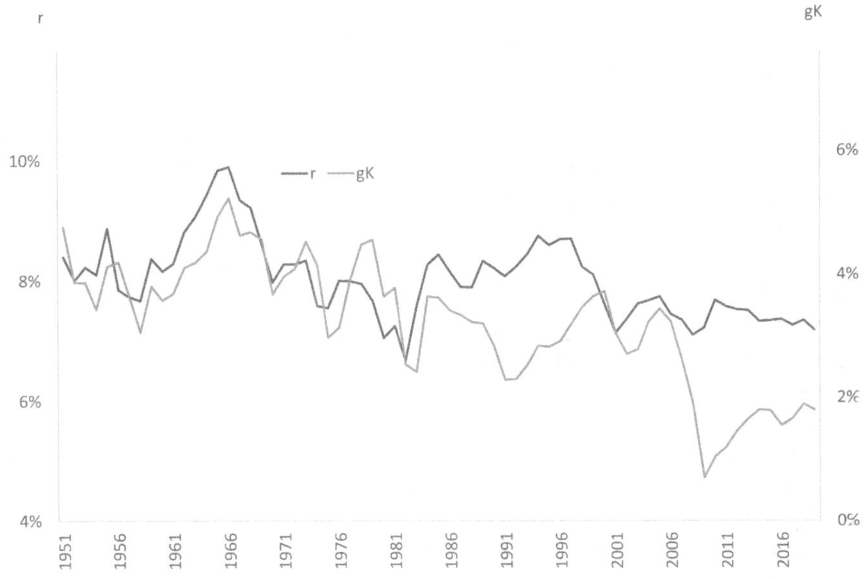

Figure 3.2 Profit rate, r, and capital accumulation, g_K, in the United States, 1951–2019.

Source: EPWT 7.0.

the capitalists' efforts to increase profitability, often at the expense of the working class. As the 1980s progressed, there emerged a pervasive skepticism regarding the role of state in the economy, coupled with a growing emphasis on market and individualist solutions to societal problems. For example, the macroeconomic policy shifted from promoting growth and reducing unemployment to curbing inflation and measures to expand profitability through various mechanisms, in particular, labor cost reduction and tax cuts benefiting both corporations and the wealthy.

Neoliberalism thrived and gained prominence in the United States during the period spanning from the Federal Reserve's decision to raise interest rates in 1979 and 1980, all the way up to the financial crisis of 2007. In the Reagan administration, institutional changes and legislative reforms were adopted based on the belief that "free markets" would allocate resources efficiently, fostering capital accumulation and economic growth. As these changes consolidated, the social sectors that benefited from them became hegemonic, consolidating the basic elements of neoliberalism that greatly favored capital, in particular financial capital.

The events surrounding the fall of the Berlin Wall in 1989 and the subsequent collapse of the Soviet Union in 1991 further solidified the belief that neoliberalism was the only way forward. The slogan "there is no alternative", often referred to by the acronym TINA, served as the rationale behind the adoption of neoliberal policies in many developed and developing countries throughout the 1980s and 1990s.

At the microeconomic level, neoliberalism promoted a transformation in the functioning of large corporations by adopting a corporate governance model focused on maximizing shareholder value. This shift opened the door to the financialization of enterprises, where the primary objective evolved from long-term growth to driving up stock prices. Profits began to be redirected to shareholders rather than being reinvested in the company. Additionally, managers increasingly received compensation in the form of stocks, aimed at aligning their interests with capitalist ownership, as highlighted by Duménil and Lévy (2013).

Moreover, neoliberalism played a pivotal role in the globalization of financial and commercial markets. It led the corporations to expand their operations internationally, driven by the pursuit of lower labor costs and access to larger consumer markets. Industrial production was often relocated to developing countries, especially in Asia. The deepening integration of financial markets further facilitates the rapid movement of financial capital across borders, amplifying the potential for adverse shocks to reverberate globally and impact the broader economy.

Propelled by the information technology boom, the 1990s represented the zenith of neoliberalism in the United States. The increase in the profit rate finally led to higher capital accumulation and growth, despite remaining lower than the levels seen in the Golden Age. By the end of the 20th Century, the United States had established itself as the undisputed global economic leader.

The institutional changes promoted by neoliberalism had far-reaching repercussions on both American society and its economy. These effects included

- i Income inequality: neoliberalism led to a significant expansion of personal income inequality, resulting in a substantial increase in the wealth of the richest individuals. This wealth gap was highlighted by the "We Are the 99%" movement.
- ii Labor relations: neoliberal policies also brought about a transformation in labor relations, resulting in a decline in the wage share. The diminished political power of workers and unions played a significant role in this shift.
- iii Trade deficit: the trade balance in goods witnessed a substantial and rapidly growing deficit, notably with China, primarily stemming from underinvestment in the US economy. The trade imbalance had far-reaching economic consequences, including the dependence on external financing and the weakening of the dollar.
- iv Structural changes: neoliberalism led to a structural transformation in the American economy. On one hand, there was a notable deindustrialization, particularly affecting traditional manufacturing sectors. On the other, there was a surge in financialization, characterized by the increased influence and importance of the financial sector.

Neoliberalism succeeded in partially restoring profitability, but it also gave rise to its own inherent contradictions. The financial sector's profitability demanded new spheres of unrestrained valorization to convert one type of capital asset into another. This process necessitated financial innovations and, if left unchecked, had the potential to trigger speculative bubbles with recessionary consequences after their bursting. As wages stagnated, households sustained their consumption patterns through rising debt, providing demand for the economy.

The families experiencing the wealth effect during the boom further expanded their debts to finance their consumption.

The crash in technology stock prices triggered the 2001 recession. The FED answered the crisis through an expansionary monetary policy, pushing interest rates to unprecedented lows. As interest rates declined, a housing boom emerged. Financial institutions aggressively expanded mortgage lending, including subprime mortgages targeting low-income families. The financial deregulation allowed these institutions to operate under more lenient terms than traditional mortgages, despite the higher interest rates. After securitization, these mortgages were sold to pension funds and other institutional investors worldwide.

The devaluation of the riskiest segments of securities functioned as the catalyst for the financial crisis. Initially confined to the United States, the crisis rapidly propagated to other nations after the collapse of Lehman Brothers in 2008, leading to a significant economic downturn. It represented the structural crisis of neoliberal capitalism which resolution requires major institutional changes, as evidenced by the experience of the 1930s and 1970s.

The US government's response involved expanding the public deficit and implementing an unparalleled expansionary monetary policy. The Federal Reserve promoted a reduction in interest rates and injected a substantial amount of dollars into the economy, providing liquidity and purchasing large quantities of government securities and financial assets through quantitative easing. The Federal Reserve directly financed both the government and the private sector, significantly expanding its balance sheet, with assets increasing from 5.1 percent in 2007 to 14.1 percent of GDP in 2014.

However, the United States maintained some of the central tenets of neoliberalism after the crisis. Economic growth since 2007 financial crisis has been lower than that observed from 1980 to 2006. These developments are related to the reduced profit rate and the country's inability to implement a new set of institutional innovations, abandoning neoliberalism. After an upward movement in 2009 and 2010, the US profit rate declined in the 2010s. Among the effects of quantitative easing was the expansion of corporate indebtedness and financial speculation, which boosted the stock market. Monetary policies preserved firms with negative or reduced profitability that otherwise would have gone bankrupt, limiting the restoration of the profit rate as their fixed capital stock was unliquidated (Roberts, 2016).

The crisis contributed to political polarization and distrust in institutions, fueling a debate about the reduced capacity of democratic institutions to address the interests and needs of large segments of the population, in particular, the sectors most negatively impacted by neoliberalism. The result was an increased mistrust of governmental policies with the expansion of the ultra-right movement worldwide.

In the United States, a consequence of the crisis was the rise of nation-state populism, epitomized by slogans like 'Make America Great Again' (MAGA). However, a fundamental question is whether the United States will be able to reaffirm its capitalist hegemony without abandoning neoliberalism. There appear to be imminent contradictions between the maintenance of US capitalist hegemony and neoliberalism.

Technical change and distribution

There is a long tradition in the economic literature suggesting that the technical change in the leading capitalist country takes a biased form to economize on relatively expensive inputs. Ricardo (2001) considered that machinery competes with labor and can often be introduced when the real wage has reached a certain level. According to Marx (1979), the introduction of machinery and the increase of scale of production aims to reduce the demand for labor by expanding its productive power and lowering cost. The higher labor share compared to the profit share would explain the predominance of Marx-biased technical change.

Following this tradition, Hicks (1932) considers that the changes in the relative share of factors of production induce innovation and inventions to economize in the factor which became more expensive. In the literature on induced technical change, functional income distribution plays a fundamental role in the growth rates of labor and capital productivities.

For example, Duménil and Lévy (1995) developed an economic model in which a new technique is defined by the growth rates of labor and capital productivities. New techniques are generated by a random process with firms searching for new techniques in the vicinity of the technique currently employed. The selection of new technologies is based on the profitability criterion, with only techniques yielding a profit rate higher than the currently employed being adopted. The selection criterion defines a profitability frontier, whose slope is the negative ratio between capital share and labor share. The profitability frontier confers a bias to technical change whenever the ratio between the factor shares is different from one. If the labor share is larger than the capital share, then the savings in labor will tend to be higher than in capital. A decline in wage share reduces the probability of the selected new technique being labor-saving and capital-using.

Figure 3.3 illustrates the wage share in the United States from 1950 to 2019. In the Golden Age, the wage share exhibited stability around a neutral trend, indicating that wages expanded at a rate similar to that of labor productivity. In contrast, during the neoliberal era, the wage share displayed a negative trend, signifying that the gains from labor productivity were predominantly directed toward profits.

The declining wage share reflected the reduced bargaining power of workers in neoliberalism. The decline is attributed to various factors, including reduced labor demand resulting from lower capital accumulation and globalization, as well as diminished labor organization and union density. The falling wage share reduces incentives for the adoption of Marx-biased technical change, while increasing incentives for the adoption of technical change aimed at raising capital productivity. A key factor to expand capital productivity is the decline in the price of capital goods.

Table 3.1 presents the growth rates of capital productivity, ga, and labor productivity, gx, for the United States between 1950 and 2019. For the entire period, the pattern of technical change was consistent with the capital-using, labor-saving Marx-bias. This pattern occurred from 1950 to 1980, in the periods of the Golden Age and its crisis, as well as from 1980 to 2019, during neoliberalism and its crisis.

Figure 3.3 The wage share in the United States and its declining trend, 1950–2019.

Source: EPWT 7.0.

Notably, in the 1980–2019 period, when compared to the 1950–1980 years, there is a difference in the growth rates of capital and labor productivities. Capital productivity declined at a slower pace, while labor productivity expanded at a lower growth rate. This result is consistent with the conception that the fall in the labor share would reduce the incentives for mechanization in the US economy.

However, the Marx-biased pattern is not uniformly present throughout the entire period, there were phases of technical change. First, from 1950 to the late 1960s,

Table 3.1 Growth rates of labor and capital productivities in the US economy, 1950–2019

Periods	*ga, %*	*gx, %*
1950–2019	−0.20	1.75
1950–1980	−0.30	1.98
1950–1967	0.67	2.62
1967–1980	−1.56	1.14
1980–2019	−0.13	1.57
1980–1999	0.62	1.95
1999–2019	−0.83	1.22

Source: EPWT 7.0.

the technical change exhibited rising capital and labor productivities. Second, from the late 1960s to the early 1980s, there was a shift in technical change characterized by a decline in capital productivity and a lower growth in labor productivity. The decline in the capacity of the second industrial revolution to sustain the trajectory of technical change partially explains the productivity slowdown. The large-scale factories demanded big capital investments and yielded modest improvements in labor productivity.

From the early 1980s to the late 1990s, technical change followed a labor-saving, capital-saving technical change. This new pattern of technical change was linked to the so-called third industrial revolution, a set of technical innovations associated with the communications and information sector that allowed product, process, and organization innovations. The increase in capital productivity played a pivotal role in the expansion of the profit rate. Starting in the late 1990s, a Marx-bias technical change, similar to the pattern observed from the late 1960s and 1980, became evident in the US economy. Despite the increase in the profit share, the profit rate declined.

Solow (1987) highlighted the limitations of the third industrial revolution in significantly enhancing the growth rate of labor productivity. The decline in labor share, as expected by the theory of induced technical change, affected the paths of labor and capital productivities. Moreover, the fall in capital accumulation in the US economy also contributed to the diminished growth rate in labor productivity as capital goods incorporate new techniques.

Capital accumulation, profits, neoliberalism, and growth

Currently, there is a resurgence of interest in the secular stagnation thesis, initially suggested by Hansen (1939). He proposed that the US economy could experience prolonged stagnation due to a decline in investment caused by reduced technological innovation and slower population growth. For Hansen (1939), one solution to address the problem involved the government running large investment programs.

The primary evidence supporting the secular stagnation thesis is the decline in both GDP and labor productivity growth rates. As indicated in Figure 3.1 and Table 3.1, both the GDP and labor productivity growth rates have been decreasing since the end of the Golden Age. The thesis attempts to provide an explanation for the low economic growth witnessed in the last two decades and the modest recovery of the US economy following the 2007 financial crisis.

The contemporary argument regarding the secular stagnation thesis can be outlined from two broad perspectives. The first, as proposed by Gordon (2012), emphasizes that the decline in the potential GDP growth rate is a consequence of the limited capacity of scientific discoveries and technological advancements, particularly the digital technologies, to significantly enhance labor productivity. Additionally, the lower population growth and an aging population contribute to this phenomenon.

Summers (2014) presents a second approach rooted in the loanable fund theory, emphasizing its demand-driven nature. He argues that an excess of savings, particularly in the presence of positive interest rates, relative to investment, constrain economic growth in the United States. The increase in savings can be attributed to several factors, including the rising income inequality which expanded the average propensity to save, and the accumulation of large reserves by developing economies. Additionally, sluggish population growth contributes to diminished reduced investment levels. Summers suggests that the solution to the imbalance between savings and investments lies in implementing negative interest rates, which would stimulate economic growth.

However, both arguments give relatively little consideration to the role of the profit rate and the institutional changes associated with neoliberalism. Interestingly, except for the boom of the 1990s, the increase in the profit rate during neoliberalism did not consistently lead to higher levels of capital accumulation. As shown in Figure 3.4, the conversion ratio of profits into investment experienced a notable decline after 1980, with a particularly sharp drop in the 2000s. This decline reduced the link between the profit rate and capital accumulation.

The fall in the conversion rate can be partially attributed to the consequences of policies adopted by the US government, following the embrace of neoliberalism. While the economic policies were designed to rise profitability and increase income for the upper social strata, their outcome resulted in redistribution of profits towards other forms of rent, a reduction in public investment, and the offshoring of productive plants.

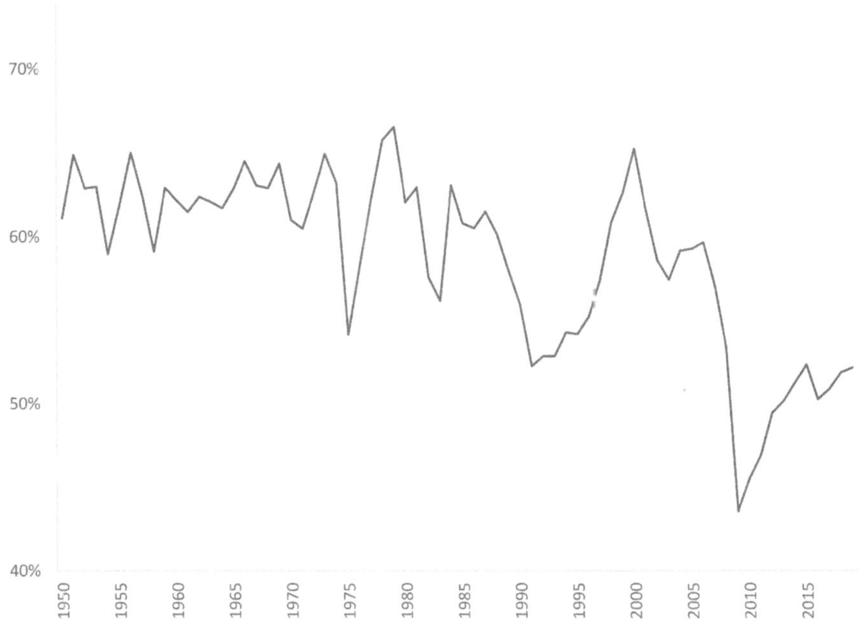

Figure 3.4 The conversion rate of profits into investment in the United States, 1950–2019.

Source: EPWT 7.0

The decline in the conversion rate was also caused by the increased transfer of surplus to capital owners and high-level management, driven by the goal of maximizing shareholder value.

These factors played a central role in exacerbating personal income inequality in the United States. The direct consequence of rising profits and income for the wealthy was a declining in wage share, as the real wages increased at a slower rate than labor productivity. However, the strategy of reducing wage share to boost profitability has, in turn, diminished the incentives for the adoption of technical changes aimed at expanding labor productivity.

From a Marxian perspective, the decline in the GDP growth rate of the United States following the Golden Age is primarily attributed to reduced capital accumulation, driven by the falling profit rate and the institutional changes associated with neoliberalism. Figure 3.5 exhibits the capital-labor ratio in the US economy from 1950 to 2019. Long-term labor productivity growth is associated with the expansion of the capital-labor ratio. However, there was a decline in the growth rate of capital-labor ratio after 1980, and following the crisis of neoliberalism, the capital-labor ratio stagnated in the 2010s.

Neoliberalism influenced the pace of technical change through other channels, negatively affecting the labor productivity growth in the US economy. First, it demanded a short payback period for investments, influencing research and innovation

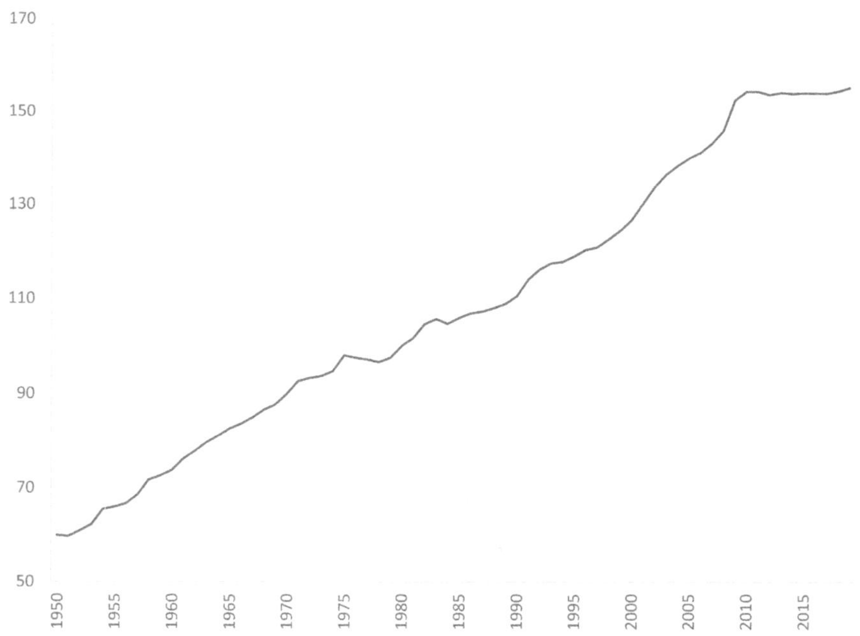

Figure 3.5 The capital-labor ratio in the United States, 1950–2019, 1980 = 100.

Source: EPWT 7.0

that translates into adopted production techniques. Second, the deindustrialization and outsourcing led to the substitution of blue-collar manufacturing workers with lower-paid service sector employees. While U.S. corporations expanded offshore productivity activities, there was a simultaneous increase in non-productive service sectors (Ikeler, 2023). Third, heavy reliance on market allocation resulted in neglecting public investments in infrastructure, including transportation, water distribution, and energy. Fourth, the escalating costs of higher education and healthcare undermine workers' capacity to enhance their labor potential.

Therefore, while the arguments suggesting the limited impacts of technological discoveries on labor productivity growth and the presence of a saving glut may hold true, they play a negligible role in explaining the lower economic growth. A comprehensive investigation of a capitalist country requires to consider the pivotal role of profitability in the economy. As the profit rate falls, it reduces the incentives for capital accumulation and the GDP growth rates declines which is translated in lower expansion of labor productivity. During neoliberalism, the United States witnessed a notable slowdown in capital accumulation. It appears that the decline in profit rates and the partial delink between investment and profits explain the lower economic growth of the US economy.

The analysis of secular stagnation emerged in the aftermath of the neoliberalism crisis. However, the response to this crisis merely reinforced the trends that had prevailed in the final decades of the XX Century. The implementation of quantitative easing and the maintenance of low-interest rates had the consequence of driving up the prices of financial assets. These strategies effectively benefited the financial sector and the wealth tied to it. The safeguarding of wealth also meant that the previous capital accumulation remained relatively unscathed from the typical processes of destruction observed in major capitalist crises.

There is reduced incentives to foster rapid productive investments and technical change within this context. The attempts to reverse globalization trends and encourage the resurgence of industrial activities within the United States may face challenges if the basic principles of neoliberalism remain intact. To ensure the success of such policies, the US government may need to adopt a strategy similar to that originally proposed by Hansen (1939).

Hegemony, neoliberalism, and capital accumulation

It is worthwhile to further explore the effects of neoliberalism on capital accumulation and macroeconomic variables. One of the central features of neoliberalism is the role of finance as a locus for surplus appropriation. This change began with the concept of shareholder value, a euphemism indicating the empowerment of the capitalist class, especially its financial strata. The management of large enterprises also reaped substantial benefits from this shift, resulting in large increase in their remuneration.

The link between capital accumulation and the profit rate began to weaken after 1980, resulting in a reduced conversion rate from profits to investment. A rising portion of profits started flowing into the acquisition of financial assets and distribution among shareholders. This transformation, which solidified in the 1990s, was closely associated with financial deregulation, the growing prominence of investment banks, pension funds, and mutual funds in managing financial assets, alongside a decline in taxation for the wealthy. These processes favored the upper classes in the United States, expanding their share of income, despite declining growth rates.

On the other hand, neoliberalism led to a decrease in the bargaining power of the working class. This reduction was accomplished through various means, including reduced labor demand driven by globalization and deindustrialization, lower economic growth, and the decline of unionization. The result of the diminished labor power was the redistribution of income from labor to capital and rising inequality.

Neoliberalism spread globally under the leadership of the United States. In the 1990s, the US hegemony, grounded on the neoliberal paradigm, was uncontested, particularly after the collapse of the Soviet Union. However, the institutional changes promoted by neoliberalism also gave rise to contradictions. First, there was a concerning reduction in economic growth, which could potentially impact the long-term relevance of the leading nation, particularly, as other countries surge ahead with higher growth rates. Second, globalization and outsourcing led to substantial deficits in the balance of trade in goods and the current account, necessitating the accumulation of external debt and issuance of dollars to cover the deficit, exposing the leading nation to financial fragility. Third, particularly among middle- and low-income families, the expansion in the consumption of goods and services was financed by debt. Fourth, a recurring issue was the financial bubbles and their adverse impact on the economy. The crisis of neoliberalism encompasses elements of the third and fourth contradictions.

A contradiction between neoliberalism and the hegemony of the United States became evident after the financial crisis. The response to this crisis, primarily through quantitative easing, failed to address the underlying contradictions of neoliberalism. As a result, the United States faced the challenge of sustaining long-term economic growth and increasing labor productivity. The nation now confronts obstacles in its quest to maintain leadership in the XXI Century.

The United States, as a nation, perceives the economic emergence of China and the military capacity of Russia as potential competitors to its global leadership. Nevertheless, both countries lag behind the United States in economic and military capacities. However, these developments raise pertinent questions regarding the sustainability of neoliberalism as the prevailing paradigm in the United States. In particular, the Chinese ability to rapidly adopt technical change and the US dependency on imports from China have promoted a reevaluation of the free trade perspectives that have long dominated the US trade policy.

The US. government has made active efforts to revive some of the industrial structures lost during the neoliberal era. However, achieving this goal is not straightforward. Many government initiatives face challenges due to the outlook of reduced profitability. Corporations are more likely to respond favorably to these incentives if their profitability increases. Additionally, there is resistance to the idea of the state playing a role in driving economic growth and industrial development, occupying areas of the private sector.

The trajectory of the US economy will depend on its ability to adapt and move away from the core of neoliberal institutional framework. This transition would necessitate a redefined role for the state in resource allocation and the promotion of productive investments. It may also entail the establishment of a new regulatory framework aimed at reducing the influence of the financial sector, along with increased taxes on the wealthy to address inequality and fund public investments that could yield positive externalities for economic growth. While the private sector will continue to be the primary driver, it would follow government policies designed to induce to "inshore" productive activities and eliminate the deficit in trade balance of goods.

The possibility of rising profit rate partially hinges on the destruction of capital, while the reconnection between profits and investments necessitates a comprehensive reconfiguration of financial activities. While it is politically feasible to discontinue certain sectors, especially those with significant negative environmental consequences, restructuring financial activities with the reduction in the gains of the powerful financial sector poses a more significant challenge. The prospect of adopting a new institutional framework capable of surpassing neoliberalism relies on the construction of a political consensus regarding the necessity of these changes. Therefore, it remains to be seen whether the United States can successfully address these challenges and maintain its leadership in the 21st Century.

Bibliography

Duménil, G., and Lévy, D. (1995). A stochastic model of technical change: An application to the u.S. Economy, *Metroeconomica*, 46, pp. 213–245.

Duménil, G., and Lévy, D. (2013). *The Crisis of Neoliberalism*. Cambridge: Harvard University Press.

Gordon, R. (2012). Is US Economic Growth Over? Faltering Innovation Confronts the Six Headwinds, *National Bureau of Economic Research*, https://www.nber.org/papers/w18315. Working paper.

Hansen, A. (1939). Economic progress and declining population growth. *American Economic Review*, 29, pp. 1–15.

Hicks, J. (1932). *The Theory of Wages*. London: Macmillan.

Ikeler, P. (2023). Are Services post-capitalist? A marxian interrogation. *Critical Sociology*, 50 (1), pp. 11–29.

Marx, K. (1979). *Value, Price and Profit*. Chicago: Charles H. Kerr & Company.

Ricardo, D. (2001). *On the Principles of Political Economy and Taxation*. Batoche: Ontario.

Roberts, M. (2016). *The Long Depression: Marxism and the Global Crisis of Capitalism*. Chicago: Haymarket Books.

Solow, R. (1987). We'd better watch out. *New York Times* (July 12), Book Review, 36.

Summers, L. (2014). U.S. Economic prospects: Secular stagnation, hysteresis, and the zero lower bound. *Business Economics*. 49, pp. 65–73.

4 Running fast

Catching up in Asia

Asia, the world's largest continent in terms of land area, population, and workforce, had undergone a spectacular transformation over the past half-century. In 1999, Asia emerged as the continent holding the highest share of the world's gross domestic product, GDP, contributing with 32.4 percent to the global economy. By 2011, Asia had solidified its position as an economic powerhouse, amassing the largest capital stock, accounting for 36.8 percent of the world's total. This compelling trend persisted throughout the 2010s. In 2019, Asia commanded 45 percent of the world's capital stock, contributing to 46 percent of global GDP, and employing 61.1 percent of the worldwide workforce. This remarkable contemporary context is in stark contrast to the early XX Century when, as noted by Panikkar (2000, p. 63), "only the Japanese empire remained outside the sphere of European authority" in Asia.

Following the Second World War, the continent was characterized by a fierce political dispute, which intertwined the decolonization process and the complex dynamics of the Cold War. At the core of the dispute was the question of which development strategies to pursue, whether capitalism or the Soviet model. This dispute led the state to occupy a leading role in shaping the course of development in Asia. Partially, because of this dispute, the crisis of the Golden Age and the rise of neoliberalism did not impede the catching up in many nations in the continent, as the countries maintained their productive investment. Some benefited from globalization as industrial production shifted from developed region to countries with lower labor costs. Moreover, the debt crisis in the 1980s affected a few Asian countries.

In the last five decades, Asia emerged as the continent showcasing one of the most remarkable catching-up in economic history. It began with Japan, followed by the ascent of the Asian Tigers, Taiwan, South Korea, Singapore, and Hong Kong. Several countries in the region are currently catching up, driven by industrialization, notably China and India, the two most populous nations globally. In 2016, China secured its position as the largest world economy when measured by purchasing power parity, while India ascended to the third-largest global economy in 2009 using the same measure. Nevertheless, a large gap in labor productivity remains in relation to the United States.

DOI: 10.4324/9781003223382-5

However, the Asian regions display a multitude of differences, from levels of economic development to historical formations, cultural diversity, and distinct economic performance. For example, consider the case of the former Asian Soviet republics, which gained independence in 1991 and faced the transition from a centrally planned to a market economy. Meanwhile, some Western Asia countries became involved in wars and civil conflicts, blocking their development. The oil-rich nations were dependent on petroleum and its volatile prices. In response, these countries attempted to diversify their economies with rapid capital accumulation and workforce expansion.

Asia stands as a complex continent, shaped by diverse economic and institutional histories. An analysis of Asian historical development is undoubtedly a difficult endeavor, but one that is essential for a deeper understanding of the dynamics of catching up and falling behind.

When approaching Asia for analysis, we consider five geographical regions: Eastern Asia (China, Hong Kong, Japan, South Korea, Taiwan, and Mongolia); South-eastern Asia (Singapore, Indonesia, Cambodia, Laos, Myanmar, Malaysia, Philippines, Thailand, and Vietnam); Southern Asia (Bangladesh, India, Sri Lanka, Nepal, and Pakistan); Western Asia (United Arab Emirates, Bahrain, Iran, Iraq, Jordan, Kuwait, Lebanon, Oman, Qatar, Saudi Arabia, Syria, Turkey, Yemen, Armenia, and Azerbaijan); and Central Asia (Kazakhstan, Kyrgyzstan, Tajikistan, Turkmenistan, and Uzbekistan).

The complexity of Asia transcends the geographical organization of countries. For instance, Armenia and Azerbaijan, although geographically situated in Western Asia, share significant similarities with Central Asia, primarily due to their shared history as former Soviet republics. Similarly, Mongolia, despite being located in Eastern Asia, shares some characteristics with these countries, particularly as it emerged from a centrally planned economy.

The chapter is structured into five sections. The first section overviews the historical emergence of modern political division in Asia. The second investigates the economic growth within Asian regions, examining the catching up and falling behind during the 1970–2019 period. The third section investigates the interplay between technical change and profit rates in Asian countries. The fourth explores the links between profitability, investment rate, and capital accumulation. The concluding section discusses the dilemmas of economic growth in Asia and the possibilities for the region to sustain its successful trajectory.

A brief historical perspective of modern Asia

After the Industrial Revolution, with the concentration of capital in large enterprises and the expansion of financial capital, occurred a fundamental transformation in the nature of domination during the second half of the 19th century. The period saw major European powers and to a lesser extent, the United States, embark on a quest to expand and acquire colonies and territories in Africa, Asia, and the Pacific. Their goals were to establish control over valuable resources, gaining access to markets, and strategic locations.

The imperialist expansion during this period was propelled by a confluence of factors, including the economic interests of large financial capital, nationalism, and the intense dispute for global dominance between established and emerging capitalist powers. The surplus capital and excess production were exported to colonies and underdeveloped countries in search of greater profitability. Lenin, in his seminal book, "Imperialism, the Highest Stage of Capitalism" published in 1917, provides a compelling analysis of the imperialism during that period.

In the late 19th and early 20th Centuries, imperialism in Asia was a prominent and pervasive phenomenon. The British Empire had a significant presence, exerting influence or direct control in various regions, including India, present-day India, Pakistan, and Bangladesh; Burma, now Myanmar; Ceylon, now Sri Lanka, and other territories, such as Hong Kong and Singapore. France controlled Indochina, modern-day Vietnam, Laos, and Cambodia; the Dutch ruled over the Dutch East Indies, present-day Indonesia. Spain established a presence in the Philippines, which remained under Spanish rule until the Spanish-American War in 1898, resulting in the loss of the Philippines to the United States. Portugal controlled Macau in China, Goa in India, and Timor-Leste.

Japan emerged as an imperial power in Eastern Asia in the early 20th Century. After the Meiji Restoration in 1868, rapid modernization and industrialization formed the basis of its military power. Japan annexed Taiwan, Korea, and parts of China through military victories, establishing its own empire. The Russo-Japanese War of 1904–1905, the first military victory for an Asian country against a major European power, played a role in the events leading up to the Russian Revolution of 1917 and the strengthening of the anticolonialism movements in Asia. In 1914, with the beginning of the First World War, Japan captured German colonial possessions in Asia and Oceania.

Anticolonialism movements expanded during the Great Wars. The Russian Revolution inspired many countries before and during the Cold War, while the Soviet model offered a non-capitalist alternative to development. After the Second World War, there was a wave of independence movements and the decolonization of many Asian countries. The war weakened the colonial powers, shifted global dynamics, and sparked a desire for self-determination among the colonized nations. This, combined with international pressure for decolonization, led to the independence of many Asian countries.

The end of the Second World War also marked the decline of Japanese imperialism. Japan's defeat led to the dismantling of its colonial empire, resulting in the independence of Korea. However, Korea was divided into two zones: the North, occupied by the Soviet Union, and the South, occupied by the United States. Each region became a separate country with different political systems, with the establishment of independent governments in 1948. The Democratic People's Republic of Korea, North Korea, was established in the northern part of the Korean Peninsula, while the Republic of Korea, or South Korea, took root in the southern region. The Korean War, from 1950 to 1953, inflicted extensive damage upon industrial plants and infrastructure in both nations.

China also played a central role during the early days of the Cold War in Asia. The People's Republic of China was established in 1949 after the civil war between the Chinese Communist Party, supported by the Soviet Union, and the Nationalist Party, backed by the United States. The Chinese Communist Party, CCP, was founded in 1921 with the goal of instituting a socialist state in China. The CCP mobilized the peasantry, who constituted the majority of the population, as a revolutionary force against imperialism. The Communist Party was victorious, leading to a retreat of the nationalist government to Taiwan. Until the present day, there is no formal conclusion of the civil war. Macau and Hong Kong, under the control of Portugal and the United Kingdom, were returned to China in 1999 and 1997.

Mongolia became independent from China in 1921, leading to the establishment of the Mongolia People's Republic in 1924 under the influence of Soviet Union. In 1990, Mongolia started its transition to a market economy, a move aligned with the economic shifts seen in many Eastern European and Asian countries in that period.

In Southern Asia, the Indian Independence Act of 1947 created two separate countries: India, with a Hindu majority, and Pakistan, with a Muslim majority. Pakistan was initially divided into two regions, West Pakistan and East Pakistan, which were geographically separated by India. In 1971, East Pakistan declared independence, leading to conflicts and the formation of Bangladesh. Under Mahatma Gandhi's and Jawaharlal Nehru's leadership, the Indian independence movement inspired other countries in South and South-eastern Asia. Sri Lanka gained independence from British rule in 1948.

The Cold War also profoundly influenced the struggle for independence in South-eastern Asia. Indochina, Laos, and Cambodia gained independence from France in 1953. Vietnam, led by Ho Chi Minh, fought against French colonial rule. Vietnam achieved independence in 1954, albeit divided into North Vietnam, with the support of the USSR and China, and South Vietnam, with the support of the United States. In 1975, after the Vietnam War, the North and the South were unified under the leadership of the Vietnamese Communist Party.

Laos and Cambodia were also affected by the war, as the conflict spilled over their borders with repercussions on their internal affairs. The struggle continued after independence in Laos, leading to the Laotian Civil War. The conflict involved various groups, including the communist Pathet Lao and the Royal Lao Government, which the United States supported. The civil war concluded in 1975, when the Pathet Lao emerged victorious, leading to Laos coming under socialist rule. The civil war in Cambodia ended under the control of the Khmer Rouge, which installed a brutal regime. After the Vietnamese intervention in 1979, Cambodia remained in civil war throughout the 1980s. In the early 1990s, negotiations resulted in an agreement to bring about a ceasefire and facilitate a political transition; Cambodia held elections in 1993. Burma, present day Myanmar, became independent in 1948 and faced a prolonged military rule.

In the wake of the decolonization wave, the Philippines gained sovereignty from the United States in 1946. Likewise, Indonesia, after an armed conflict, achieved autonomy from Dutch colonial rule in 1949. Through the 1960s, political conflicts and violence emerged in the country and gave rise to the Suharto dictatorial regime from 1967 until 1998. Federation of Malaya achieved independence from British rule in 1957. In 1963, the Federation of Malaya joined forces with North Borneo, renamed to Sabah after independence, Sarawak, and Singapore to form Malaysia. However, Singapore separated from Malaysia in 1965 to become a sovereign state.

The Western Asian countries underwent a gradual process of independence during the 20th Century. In the XIX Century, the region was under the control of different forces, including the Ottoman Empire, France, and the United Kingdom. Following the First World War, the Ottoman Empire was dismantled, leading to a reconfiguration of control over different parts of the region. The League of Nations placed most of the Western Asian territories, which were part of Ottoman Empire, under the mandate of France and the United Kingdom.

Turkey emerged in 1923 after the war of independence of what remained of the Ottoman Empire. Geographically, it sits on two continents, predominantly in Western Asia, while encompassing a smaller section in Southeast Europe.

Iran, formerly known as Persia until 1935, has a long history of maintaining independence, despite the occupation by Russia of some northern areas until the First World War. Additionally, the British exerted a strong influence on the economy. The Pahlavi Dynasty came to power in 1925, marking an era of centralized rule, and increased Western cultural influence and political interference. In 1979, the Iranian Revolution represented a major turning point in the country's history, with the establishment of an Islamic government, reducing Western influence.

Iraq became independent from the United Kingdom in 1932. Political instability, ethnic tensions, and wars marked its history. Iraq invaded Iran in 1980, initiating a long conflict that inflicted heavy losses on both nations. In 2003, the United States and its allies invaded Iraq, leading to the removal of Saddam Hussein from power and causing destruction within Iraq. The British separated Kuwait from Iraq in the early 1920s, with the country becoming independent in 1961.

The Kingdom of Saudi Arabia was established in 1932 after the unification of various tribal groups into a nation. Oil was discovered in 1938, marking the beginning of a transformation of Saudi Arabia into a leading producer and exporter of petroleum with major impacts on the country's economic growth.

North Yemen achieved sovereignty in 1918, while South Yemen continued under British rule until 1967. After its independence, South Yemen adopted a central planned economy under the influence of the Soviet Union. In 1990, the two regions unified to form Yemen. However, in 2014, Yemen entered into a civil war, partially stemming from unsolved questions after the unification.

Following the Second World War, the increasing relevance of oil production coupled with the dynamics of the Cold War had a profound influence on the region. The United States emerged as the dominant neocolonial power, surpassing the influence of the United Kingdom. The establishment of the State of Israel in 1948 had far-reaching political and military consequences, further solidifying the presence of the United States in the region. Oil production was, at the same time, a blessing and a curse, being a source of political and economic instability in many Western Asian countries.

Lebanon and Syria were parts of the Ottoman Empire that fell under the French mandate after the First World War. They gained independence following anti-colonial movements in 1943 and 1946. However, political instability, sectarian tensions, and conflicts have characterized both countries. After some stability in the 1960s, Lebanon faced a long civil war and external invasions. Siria took part in the six-day war with Israel in 1967 and faced a civil war beginning in 2011. Jordan was under British mandate rule, becoming independent in 1946. In 1971, Bahrain, Qatar, and the United Arab Emirates gained independence from Britain, which marked a significant political shift in the Arabian Gulf region.

Russian colonies in Central and Western Asia were integrated into the Soviet Union after the Bolshevik Revolution. However, in 1991, with the disintegration of the USSR, these former republics emerged as independent states, many of which maintain various connections with the Russian Federation through the Commonwealth of Independent States (CIS). Kazakhstan, Kyrgyzstan, Tajikistan, and Turkmenistan represent the Central Asian countries within the CIS, while Armenia and Azerbaijan are in Western Asia. Uzbekistan, located in Central Asia, has not joined the CIS. These countries maintain economic, diplomatic, and cultural ties with the Russian Federation.

The Asian nations endured a long journey to establish national states, secure independence from external aggression, and ensure internal stability, avoiding intense internal disputes and civil wars. However, certain countries continue facing important challenges related to these necessary conditions for seeking economic growth and development, as in the present cases of Yemen, Afghanistan, Syria, and Myanmar.

Economic growth in modern Asia

Japan was the first Asian country to witness a remarkable surge in economic growth following the Second World War. Interestingly, it stood apart as the sole nation on the continent that had not succumbed to international domination or semi-domination by external powers at the beginning of the 20th century. Furthermore, Japan played a role as an ally for the United States during the Cold War, compellingly demonstrating the capitalist system's capacity to generate substantial economic growth. In the 1980s, the Japanese success led to a misconception that it posed a challenge to the hegemony of the United States.

South Korea, Taiwan, Singapore, and Hong Kong somewhat followed the Japanese model during the Gold Age. Japan and the Asian Tigers experienced similarities: nation-states with a project of national development that promoted high capital accumulation and rapid industrialization; a public bureaucracy capable of organizing the development process; incentives for public and private national enterprises to compete internationally; a relatively egalitarian income distribution, allowing the benefits of economy growth to reach different sectors of society; promoting the expansion of basic education and knowledge within its population; a financial system connected with the industry and a constrained role for the stock and capital markets. The geopolitics of the Cold War allowed these countries to benefit from regional dynamics, trade, and financial networks with the United States and Western Europe.

Through rapid mechanization and industrialization, these nations managed to escape the middle-income trap. As Table 4.1 illustrates, Japan succeeded in catching up until the 1980s, embarking on a trajectory of falling behind the US economy after 1990. The neoliberal reforms and the bubble burst in the early 1990s had long-term consequences for the Japanese economy. Instead of being channeled into capital formation that drives economic growth, the profits were increasingly redirected towards the financial sector.

In contrast, the Asian Tigers continued their catch-up. By 2019, Hong Kong, South Korea, Taiwan, and Singapore had surpassed Japan in both labor and capital productivities. Hong Kong underwent a rapid process of deindustrialization spanning from the 1980s to the middle 1990s, driven by its increasing integration with China, shifting towards specialization in finance and services. South Korea, Taiwan, and Singapore successfully entered the realm of high-tech industrial production. Asian Tigers displayed a pattern of catching up in labor and capital productivities. In 2019, Hong Kong, South Korea, and Japan exhibited lower capital productivity than the United States.

The countries located in Eastern, South-Eastern, and Southern Asia were relatively unaffected by the crises of the Golden Age and the debt crisis in the 1980s, as displayed in Figure 4.1. There were a few exceptions, with the Philippines being one of such cases. Most countries in these regions had the political capacity to implement a national development strategy tailored to suit their own reality. The Asian development strategy of exporting industrialized products was facilitated by the adoption of neoliberalism in developed nations, leading to the offshoring of manufacturing production in these regions.

The result was rapid economic growth led by the industrial sector, contrasting with Latin America, Africa, and some Western Asia nations. Notably, Eastern Asia became a prominent space for capital accumulation. Between 1970 and 2019, this region witnessed the highest average growth rates globally, with Taiwan and South Korea leading the way in the 1970s and China taking the lead thereafter.

China emerged as a focal point of capital accumulation after 1980, adopting a mixed economic model inspired by the New Economic Policy implemented in the USSR in 1921. Following a highly successful mechanization process, the country became the main worldwide manufacturing producer. However, despite having similar capital productivity in 2019, labor productivity in China was approximately one-fifth of that in the United States. Regardless of the rapid catching up, China must demonstrate its ability to avoid the risk of falling into the middle-income trap.

Turning to South-eastern Asia, it is interesting to observe that in 1990, Vietnam, Cambodia, Laos, and Myanmar ranked among the nations with the lowest labor productivity in Asia. However, after 2000, these countries embarked on a rapid trajectory of catching up in labor and capital productivities. Having parallels with other successful Asian experiences, they benefited from industrialization and increased integration with their regional counterparts, particularly China. Malaysia, Thailand, and Indonesia rapidly industrialized, leading to increased labor

Table 4.1 Labor productivity and capital productivity in Asian countries relative to the United States, 1970–2019

Country	*Labor productivity*						*Capital productivity*					
	1970	*1980*	*1990*	*2000*	*2007*	*2019*	*1970*	*1980*	*1990*	*2000*	*2007*	*2019*
China	4.8	5.3	5.8	7.9	12.4	19.8	149	145	127	125	138	107
Hong Kong	30.8	44.4	60.5	61.1	69.8	73.8	123	121	107	85	109	72
Japan	43.2	59.0	72.3	65.3	62.5	56.1	147	94	82	65	69	65
South Korea	14.1	21.4	36.1	49.0	55.9	63.0	117	146	142	106	108	91
Taiwan	17.1	28.6	42.9	59.4	67.8	75.5	232	184	180	143	123	119
Mongolia	n.a.	15.2	17.4	11.9	13.9	20.5	n.a.	79	70	49	71	102
Singapore	49.8	62.8	79.2	92.6	92.2	99.2	162	127	109	110	131	127
Indonesia	9.1	13.1	12.8	12.5	14.4	18.3	153	253	173	129	131	99
Cambodia	6.3	2.7	3.1	3.4	4.5	6.4	123	71	102	166	217	168
Laos	n.a.	4.4	5.3	5.9	7.1	12.0	n.a.	341	321	261	236	151
Myanmar	2.3	2.4	2.0	2.7	5.2	9.7	354	275	239	447	553	169
Malaysia	17.2	27.5	30.1	35.0	38.5	41.8	157	160	120	116	142	135
Philippines	17.6	19.2	14.3	11.8	12.4	16.9	138	146	116	121	143	151
Thailand	9.7	12.4	16.1	18.4	20.5	25.2	189	148	123	81	105	120
Vietnam	4.4	4.0	4.5	5.9	6.9	11.3	173	199	242	149	156	180
Bangladesh	7.5	6.1	5.8	5.7	6.4	9.0	312	202	136	147	155	132
India	5.6	4.9	5.6	6.5	8.2	14.2	181	162	120	111	125	134
Sri Lanka	12.1	14.0	16.1	17.3	19.2	26.8	223	163	167	179	204	146
Nepal	n.a.	4.3	4.6	4.6	4.3	5.1	n.a.	223	150	126	132	117
Pakistan	10.4	10.9	14.0	13.0	12.5	13.2	260	222	209	210	228	253
Kazakhstan	n.a.	n.a.	37.4	26.1	37.1	44.8	n.a.	n.a.	90	37	80	131
Kyrgyzstan	n.a.	n.a.	18.9	9.8	9.7	11.7	n.a.	n.a.	95	64	82	92
Tajikistan	n.a.	n.a.	16.7	5.7	7.5	11.8	n.a.	n.a.	100	11	12	25
Turkmenistan	n.a.	n.a.	37.8	18.1	21.0	36.9	n.a.	n.a.	93	52	83	76
Uzbekistan	n.a.	n.a.	18.1	12.6	14.1	20.8	n.a.	n.a.	169	119	172	158
Armenia	n.a.	n.a.	12.9	9.1	22.6	34.5	n.a.	n.a.	89	58	103	110
Azerbaijan	n.a.	n.a.	17.4	8.3	21.1	22.0	n.a.	n.a.	96	75	197	171
United Arab Emirates	747	466	240	175	114	86	72	133	80	82	141	120
Bahrain	327	254	146	134	90	79	101	116	86	107	127	98
Iran	69.8	54.8	45.1	36.9	37.2	31.3	109	79	55	68	96	92
Iraq	44.8	83.6	54.2	44.0	34.8	40.0	303	330	152	256	236	198
Jordan	59.6	83.4	52.1	37.9	42.3	33.7	188	138	78	78	116	128
Kuwait	767	265	94	135	124	75	448	435	127	165	297	176
Lebanon	163	98	56	54	49	39	120	95	60	71	84	112
Oman	122	148	129	106	78	40	204	157	123	140	172	131
Qatar	566	427	162	194	160	112	260	178	131	179	215	117
Saudi Arabia	411	386	167	151	126	92	230	229	124	129	192	143
Syria	29.8	49.2	34.0	36.3	40.1	19.8	143	158	103	113	154	103
Turkey	36.5	40.3	44.5	45.4	55.6	61.5	207	176	162	135	151	122
Yemen	n.a.	n.a.	17.2	17.0	18.0	5.6	n.a.	n.a.	114	134	194	91

Source: EPWT 7.0.

Note: n.a. Information not available.

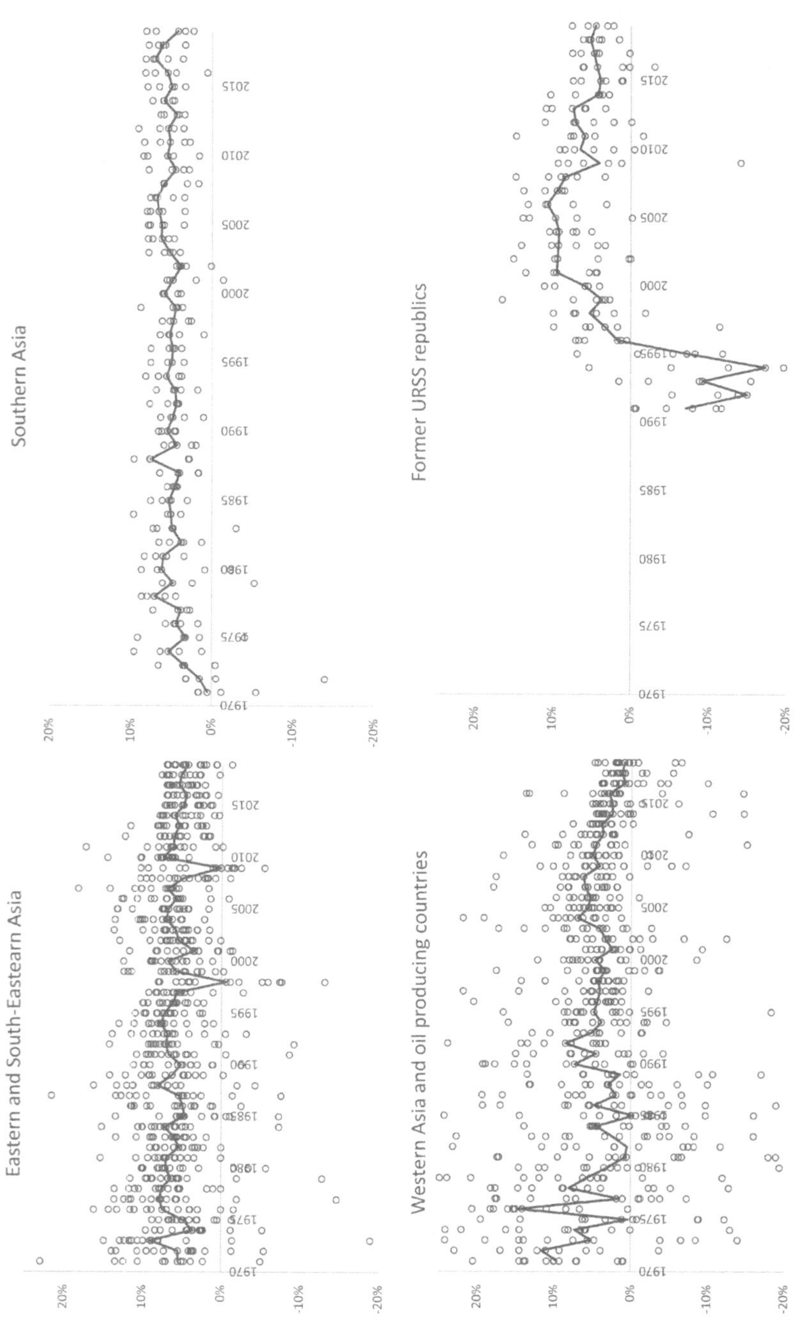

Figure 4.1 GDP growth rates and its median in Asian countries.

Source: EPWT 7.0.

productivity through mechanization. The Philippines, despite experiencing higher growth in the last two decades, stands as the main exception in the region, with its 2019 labor productivity relative to the United States remaining similar to its initial value.

In the early 1990s, many Asian countries implemented neoliberal reforms, reducing tariffs on imports, opening financial accounts, increasing the convertibility of local currencies, privatizing state-owned enterprises, attracting foreign direct investment, and disciplining the labor force. Wade (2017) suggests that, despite the neoliberal turn on Asian countries, the developmental state has adapted and evolved, performing roles much beyond what a typical neoliberal economic policy would consider. With some exceptions, like Japan and Hong Kong, a sizable portion of the profit remained directed toward fixed capital formation.

In the early 1990s, many Asian countries introduced neoliberal reforms, which involved reducing tariffs on imports, opening financial accounts, increasing the convertibility of local currencies, privatizing state-owned enterprises, attracting foreign direct investment, and disciplining the labor force. Wade (2017) suggests that, despite this shift towards neoliberalism, the developmental state in most Asian countries adapted and evolved, taking on roles that go beyond the scope of traditional neoliberal economic policies. With some exceptions, such as Japan and Hong Kong, a sizable portion of profits continued to be directed toward fixed capital formation.

The 1997 Asian financial crisis originated from a combination of industrial, financial, and monetary government policies aimed at stimulating export-led growth and investment. These policies led to high current account deficits, substantial foreign debt, and imbalanced capital flows, often associated with currency pegs to the US dollar. A financial bubble with a heavy inflow of foreign capital and external borrowing expanded the risks of exchange rate devaluation.

When Thailand allowed the baht to devalue, a contagion effect rapidly spread across the South-eastern and Eastern Asian countries, resulting in significant currency devaluations. Subsequently, the crisis propagated to developing countries across the globe, causing widespread economic turmoil. The International Monetary Fund provided financial aid conditioned on implementing further neoliberal economic reforms.

The resolution of the Asian crisis was much faster compared to the experiences of Latin America and Africa in the 1980s. One contributing factor to the recovery was the large foreign exchange reserves accumulated by some countries, which provided a buffer during the turbulent times. These experiences influenced some developing nations to maintain large foreign reserves to safeguard against external crises. Indonesia, Malaysia, and Thailand continued to catch up in labor productivity after 2000. The Philippines, which was less impacted by the 1997 financial crisis than most of its neighbors, finally embarked on a path of catching up in labor productivity.

As Figure 4.1 shows, the crisis of neoliberalism negatively impacted economic growth after 2007, resulting in a declining GDP growth rate throughout the 2010s in most countries of these regions. Interestingly, the Southern Asia nations experienced a relatively minor impact compared to other countries, except for Pakistan, as their GDP growth rates continued to expand steadily over the years. For example, the economic growth in India during the 2010s surpassed that of the previous decades, coming closer to the levels observed in China.

During the 1970s, the Western Asia countries, especially oil-exporting, experienced a phase of high and volatile GDP growth rates due to fluctuating petroleum prices. The first oil shock occurred in 1973 when the prices quadrupled as the Organization of Arab Petroleum Exporting Countries, OAPEC, implemented an oil embargo against the nations supporting Israel in the Yom Kippur War. The event enormously affected oil-importing developing countries, leading to higher import bill and adverse effects on their balance of payments. The second oil shock occurred in 1979 with the Iranian Revolution.

The 1980s witnessed a decline in economic growth, primarily driven by a fall in oil prices, alongside the emergence of political conflicts and regional disputes. The advent of neoliberalism and the strengthening of the US dollar contributed to the decline in commodity prices, including petroleum. The importance of oil prices in the region cannot be overstated, as the oil rent constituted a substantial portion of GDP. For instance, on average, during the study period, Saudi Arabia's oil rent accounted for 39.2 percent of its GDP, while Iran's was 21.3 percent (World Bank, 2023).

In response to the volatility of prices, some countries embarked on economic diversification efforts to reduce dependence on oil and establish a more complex economic base. There were substantial investments in infrastructure and services, as well as an impressive rise in number of workers. For instance, from 1970 to 2019, the number of workers, in Saudi Arabia, was multiplied 11.8 times, in Bahrain by 14.8, in Oman by 25.2, in Qatar by 44.2, and an astonishing 57 times in the United Arab Emirates.

Despite the efforts, the region's economic growth has remained sensitive to fluctuations in global oil prices. Low oil prices have led to economic slowdowns in oil-exporting countries, in contrast, high oil prices have provided a boost to their economies. As a result, the growth in the region expanded during the 1990s and 2000s but declined after the 2007 financial crisis.

The trajectory of labor productivity in relation to the US economy within these countries was influenced by both oil prices and the substantial expansion of the workforce. Capital productivity fell due to oil price fluctuations and efforts aimed at diversifying their economies. Labor productivity also experienced a decrease, attributed to the oil price changes and the expansion in labor force.

The region has faced several political and regional conflicts, adversely affecting economic stability and growth. Wars, civil unrest, and geopolitical tensions, such as the Iran-Iraq War, the Gulf War, the invasion of Iraq, the civil war in Lebanon, the sanctions in Iran, and the conflicts in Syria and Yemen, have disrupted economies and posed challenges for growth and development. The impact of the war, as seen in cases like Iraq, Syria, and Yemen, led to a decline in labor and capital productivities.

In line with the experience of other post-Soviet states, the Asian republics of the former USSR witnessed a collapse in their GDP. Between 1990 and the middle

1990s, these nations had an average GDP decline of 47 percent. The impact varied across countries, with Tajikistan being the hardest hit, experiencing a 68 percent decline, partly due to the civil war. Uzbekistan, the country which suffered the least among the former Soviet Asian republics, had a 19 percent decline in its GDP. This economic turmoil resulted from the rapid transition from a planned economy to a market one. Mongolia underwent a similar transition in the early 1990s, also suffering a decline in GDP.

Considering their labor productivity, these countries displayed lower capital productivity compared to other developing Asian nations. There was an overinvestment in the former USSR economic model. After 2000, most of these countries experienced an increase in labor and capital productivities, benefiting from the commodity boom. However, when the commodity boom ended, their GDP growth rate declined. These countries received a large percentage of their GDP as remittances, except by Kazakhstan. There were differences in the economic growth of these landlocked countries. Uzbekistan, Kyrgyzstan, and Tajikistan had a decline in labor productivity relative to the United States compared to the 1990 levels. However, Armenia, Azerbaijan, and Kazakhstan managed to reduce their gap in labor productivity.

The case of Turkey shared some similarities with most Latin American nations in terms of economic shifts and strategies. Until the late 1970s, Turkey followed an import substitution industrialization strategy, expanding domestic industrial production. The country also accumulated a high external debt after the first oil shock. Turkey shifted toward a neoliberal economic model in 1980 after the military coup, expanding the financialization of the economy during the 1990s.

Nevertheless, Turkey faced a minor decline in economic growth during neoliberalism compared to most Latin American nations. Between 1970 and 2019, the Turkish economy experienced a narrowing in labor productivity gap. Despite the fall in capital productivity, it remained higher than that observed in the US economy. Thus, the trajectory in economic growth and productivity trends in Turkey is different from the patterns observed in the Latin American context.

Technical change and profit rate: Industrialization, institutional change, oil rent, and conflicts

The Asian regions and nations, as discussed previously, display enormous disparities in institutional organization, economic structure, rents from natural resources, and development level. Nonetheless, examining the patterns of technical change, we find some similarities between them, especially in the long term. Additionally, neighboring countries often exhibit parallels in their patterns of technical change driven by shared common characteristics and historical trajectories.

Figure 4.2 illustrates the growth rates of capital productivity and labor productivity, denoted as the pair (ga, gx), during the periods 1970–2019, 1970–1980, 1980–2000, 1990–2000, and 2000–2019. It displays the technical change in the long term, in the crisis of the Golden Age during the 1970s, and in neoliberalism. The subperiods were selected to highlight the distinct experiences of Asian regions

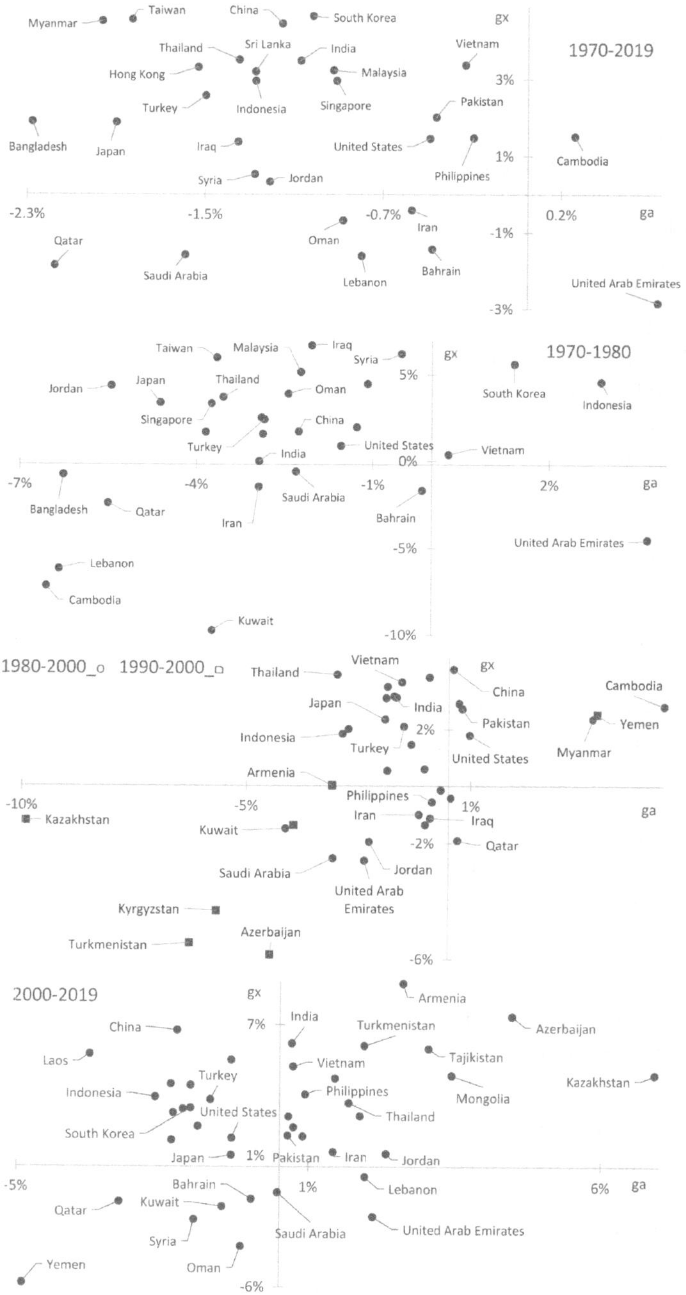

Figure 4.2 The growth rates of capital and labor productivities, (ga, gx), for Asia countries and the United States: 1970–2019, 1970–1980, 1980–2000, 2000–2019.

Source: EPWT 7.0.

and countries. Growth rates falling within the open interval from −0.1 percent to 0.1 percent are treated as zero.

From 1970 to 2019, the technical change exhibited the labor-saving, capital-using Marx bias pattern in the cases of China, Hong Kong, South Korea, Singapore, Indonesia, Myanmar, Malaysia, Philippines, Thailand, Taiwan, and Vietnam. These countries achieved remarkable annual labor productivity growth rates of three percent or more. Japan, Bangladesh, India, Pakistan, Sri Lanka, Turkey, Jordan, Iraq, and Syria also presented the Marx-biased technical change. The last three countries fell behind, while the others narrowed the gap with the United States during the study period.

The pattern of technical change in Cambodia was input saving, reflecting, at least partially, its recovery after the civil war. In contrast, Iran, Kuwait, Oman, Qatar, and Saudi Arabia exhibited a technical regress with a labor-using, capital-using pattern. The United Arab Emirates presented a labor-using, capital-saving technical change. The pattern of technical change in oil-rent countries reflected the fluctuations in petroleum prices, the substantial workforce expansion, and the capital accumulation aimed at diversifying their economies. Countries heavily reliant on primary commodity exports often see their terms of trade playing a pivotal role in shaping their economic dynamics.

From 1990 to 2019, the technical change in the former USSR republics followed distinctive patterns. Armenia, Azerbaijan, and Kazakhstan experienced an input-saving pattern, while Turkmenistan, Uzbekistan, and Tajikistan had a Marx-biased technical change. On the other hand, Kyrgyzstan exhibited a labor-using, capital-using technical change. Mongolia displayed an input-saving pattern from 1990 to 2019, and a Marx-biased from 1980 and 1990.

During the crisis of the Golden Age from 1970 to 1980, the pattern of technical change was predominantly Marx-biased. This pattern was observed in four Eastern Asian countries, five in South-eastern Asia, two in Southern Asia, and five in Western Asia. A labor-saving, capital-saving pattern was identified in one Eastern Asian country, South Korea which displayed an impressive growth rate, and two South-eastern Asian countries involved in conflicts in the previous decade, Vietnam until middle 1970s and Indonesia which had internal disputes in the 1960s. The labor-using, capital-using pattern was predominant in Western Asia with six instances. It was also observed in two countries also involved in conflicts, Bangladesh in Southern Asia and in Cambodia in South-eastern Asia. The only occurrence of a labor-using, capital-saving pattern was presented in the United Arab Emirates in Western Asia.

In the phase spanning from 1980 to 2000, which extended from the implementation of neoliberalism to the Asian financial crisis, distinct patterns of technical change emerged. There were five cases of Marx-biased technical change in Eastern Asia, five in South-eastern Asia, three in Southern Asia, and two in Western Asia, Turkey, and Syria. China displayed a Harrod-neutral change, with rising labor productivity and constant capital productivity. The institutional changes and the high economic growth may have played a role in the Chinese pattern of technical change observed in the period.

Furthermore, there were two instances of labor-saving and capital-saving technical changes in South Asia and two in South-eastern Asia. In Western Asia, there was one instance of Harrod-neutral technical regress, one instance of labor-using, capital-saving technical regress, and seven cases of labor-using, capital-using technical regress. The Philippines which was impacted by the 1980 external debt crisis also displayed a labor-using, capital-using technical regress.

From 1990 to 2000, among the former USSR republics, six displayed a labor-using, capital-using while Armenia presented a Solow-neutral technical regress. On the other hand, Yemen presented a labor saving, capital saving technical change in the period.

The phase from 2000 to 2019 is closely associated with the emergence of China and, to a lesser extent, India, and the challenges faced by the follower countries with the crisis of neoliberalism. The labor-saving and capital-saving was the predominant form of technical change, with one case in Eastern Asia, five in South-eastern Asia, two in Southern Asia, three in Western Asia, and across all seven former Soviet republics. The Marx-biased pattern was observed in five Eastern Asian countries, four South-eastern countries, three Southern Asian experiences, and two Western Asia countries. Additionally, there were seven cases of labor-using, capital-using and two cases of labor-using, capital-saving in Western Asia.

Asian nations that caught up through industrialization and infrastructure building displayed a prevailing Marx-biased pattern of technical change over the long term. Other patterns emerged in countries dependent on commodity rents, those transitioning from the Soviet economic model to mixed economies, and those involved in conflicts. The impact of the financial crisis is also discernible. Nevertheless, it appears to have exerted a short-term effect. Hence, the process of technical change is shaped by many factors, encompassing industrialization and structural change, institutional transformations, the dynamics of natural resources and commodity prices, conflicts such as wars and civil disturbances, and the repercussions of financial crises.

The path of technical change significantly influences the determination of the profit rate. As capital productivity diminishes, a parallel decline in profitability occurs unless countered by a rise in the profit share. Figure 4.3 displays the profit rate for six Eastern, seven South-eastern, and three Southern Asian countries, while Figure 4.4 presents the profit rate for six former Soviet republics and twelve Western Asian countries.

The profit rate exhibited similar movements to those observed in capital productivity. There was a tendency for a declining profit rate in the Eastern Asian countries, except for Mongolia. Similarly, in the South-eastern region, the downward trend is observed across all countries except Cambodia and Myanmar. In the Southern Asian region, the profit rate fell in Sri Lanka, while it expanded in India and Bangladesh due to increased profit share. One of the effects of neoliberalism was the disciplining of the working force, leading to a drop in the wage share across many countries. The decline of the profit rate to a similar level or lower than that of the leading country can potentially result in falling behind, as demonstrated by the case of Japan.

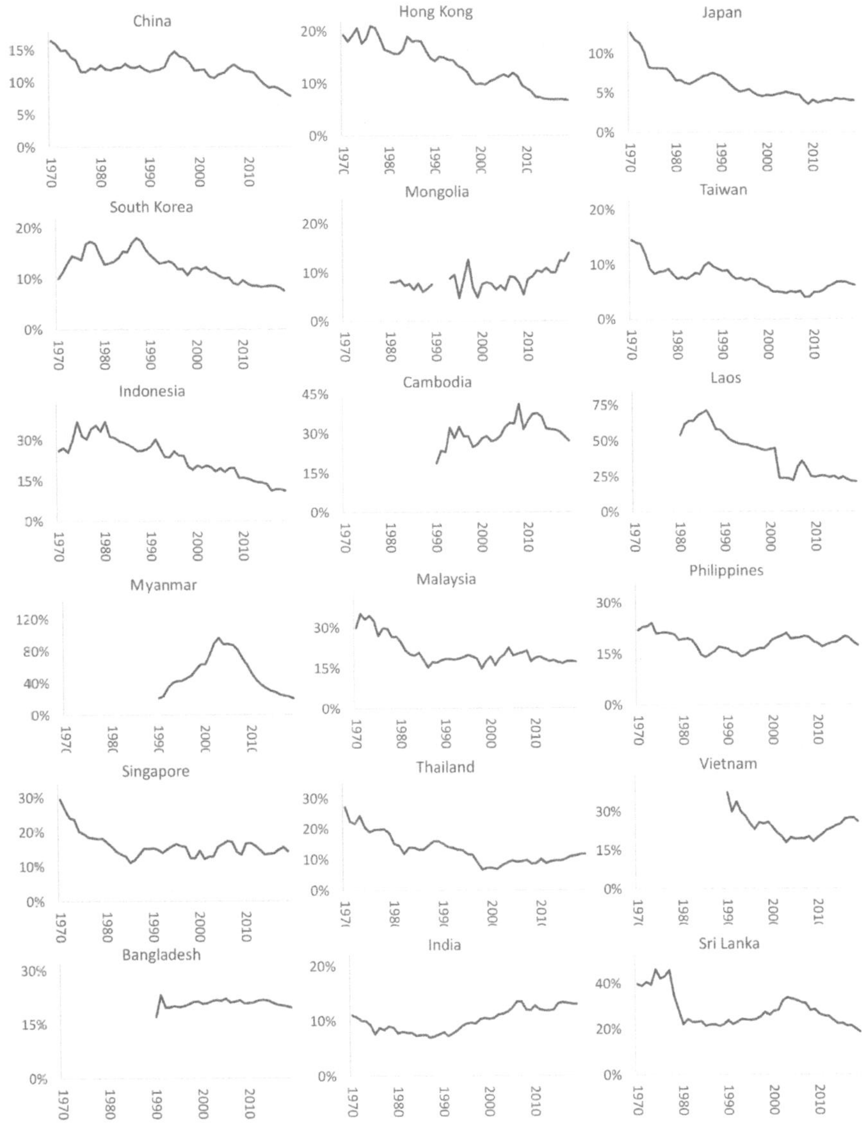

Figure 4.3 The net profit rate for six Eastern, seven South-eastern, and three Southern Asian countries: 1970–2019.

Source: EPWT 7.0.

In the former Soviet republics, except for Uzbekistan, the profit rate expanded from 1990 to 2019, marking a reversal after falling during the 1990s. Mongolia also underwent a similar expansion in its profit rate during this time frame. There was a tendency for overmechanization in these countries before the institutional change, allowing the markets to play a role in capital accumulation. Turning attention to the

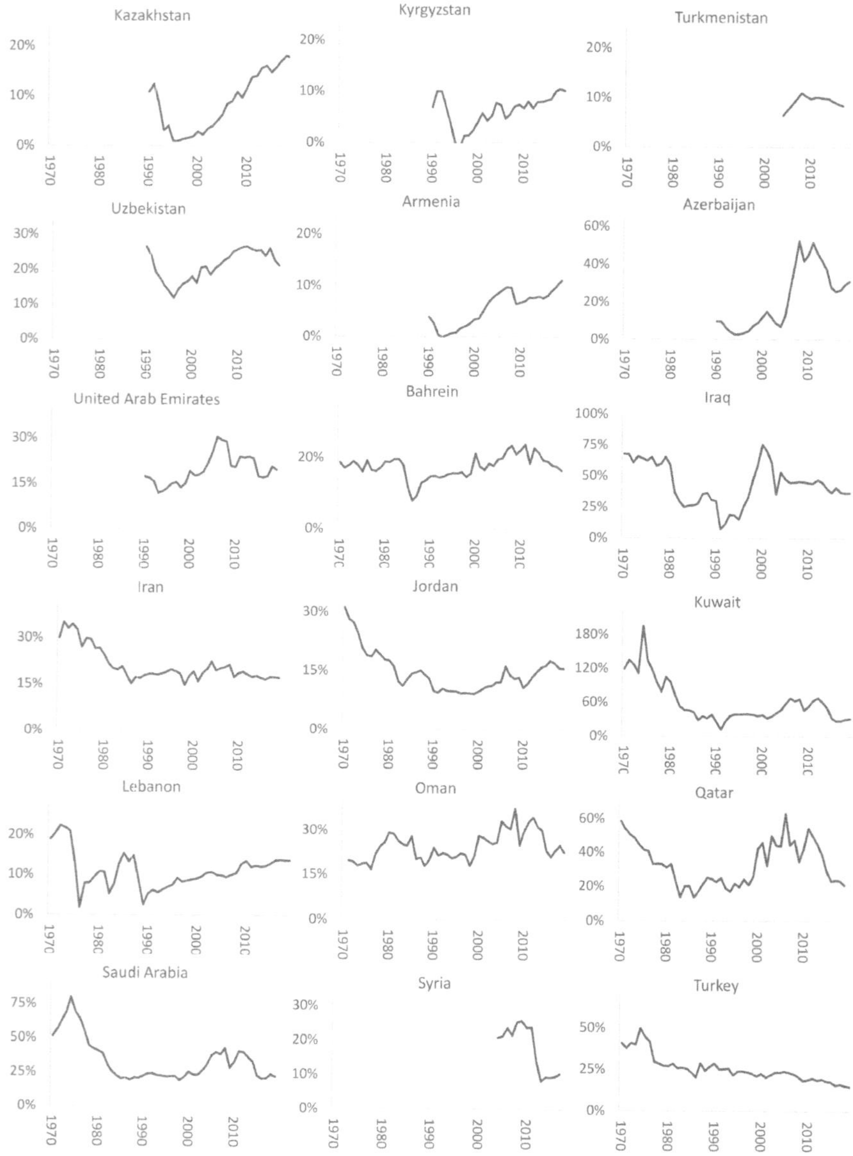

Figure 4.4 The net profit rate for six former Soviet republics, and 12 Western Asian countries: 1970–2019.

Source: EPWT 7.0.

Western Asian countries, the profit rate expanded in the United Arab Emirates and Oman while it was trendless in Bahrain. The other countries exhibited a declining trend, consistent with the fall in capital productivity.

Despite their differences, Asian countries share similarities in their profit rate phases, a decline from 1970 to the late 1990s, followed by either stabilization or expansion across many countries. Several factors may contribute to the increase in the profit rate. The adoption of information technology, coupled with declining prices of capital goods and rising commodity prices, positively influenced capital productivity. Implementing neoliberal economic policies led to a fall in wage share, increasing the profit rates as observed in India.

This general pattern also had significant variations during the periods investigated, particularly evident in Eastern Asia. In China, the profit rate remained relatively stable between 1980 and the mid-1990s, despite the rapid pace of industrialization. However, the profit rate decreased after the middle 1990s. South Korea experienced an expansion until the late 1980s, followed by a decline. In Japan, it fell until the late 2000s, stabilizing at a low level. Meanwhile, Indonesia and Turkey, two countries that caught up during the period, exhibited a downward trend since the middle 1970s. Moreover, the profit rate sharply declined in countries engaged in armed conflict, such as Iraq, Lebanon, and Syria.

The links between profitability, capital accumulation, and catch-up

The leading country employs a more capital-intensive technique with greater labor productivity due to its better-equipped workforce and lower capital productivity compared to the follower nations. Expanding the capital accumulation beyond that of the leading country is fundamental for the followers to bridge the gap. The capital accumulation hinges on the profitability and the interplay between profits, savings, and investment.

Figure 4.5 illustrates the differences in capital accumulation for six Eastern, seven South-eastern, and three Southern Asian countries and the United States, while Figure 4.6 displays the same information for six former Soviet republics and 12 Western Asian countries. The graphical representation shows a dotted line to depict the actual difference and a solid line to portray the three-year moving average.

Interestingly, China, one of the most successful countries in narrowing the labor productivity gap after 1980, maintained the largest and very stable difference in capital accumulation in relation to the United States throughout the examined period. It contrasts with the Japanese case, where the difference in capital accumulation declined and turned negative after 1990, a period during which Japan lagged behind.

Among the Asian Tigers, there was a decline in capital accumulation after the late 1990s. This decline only led to a negative difference in capital accumulation in Hong Kong in relation to the United States. Nevertheless, Hong Kong managed to maintain the catch-up, suggesting that the transition from manufacturing to finance and services might be more achievable for smaller nations. Deindustrialization is a movement from sectors with lower to higher capital productivity, as the capital searches for higher profitability.

The Asian financial crisis in 1997 had a detrimental impact on capital accumulation in the Asian Tigers and other countries located in South-eastern Asia, such as Indonesia, Malaysia, Thailand, and the Philippines, resulting in a slowdown of their catching-up process. Conversely, Vietnam, Cambodia, Laos, and Myanmar remained unaffected by the crisis, experiencing rapid expansion in their capital

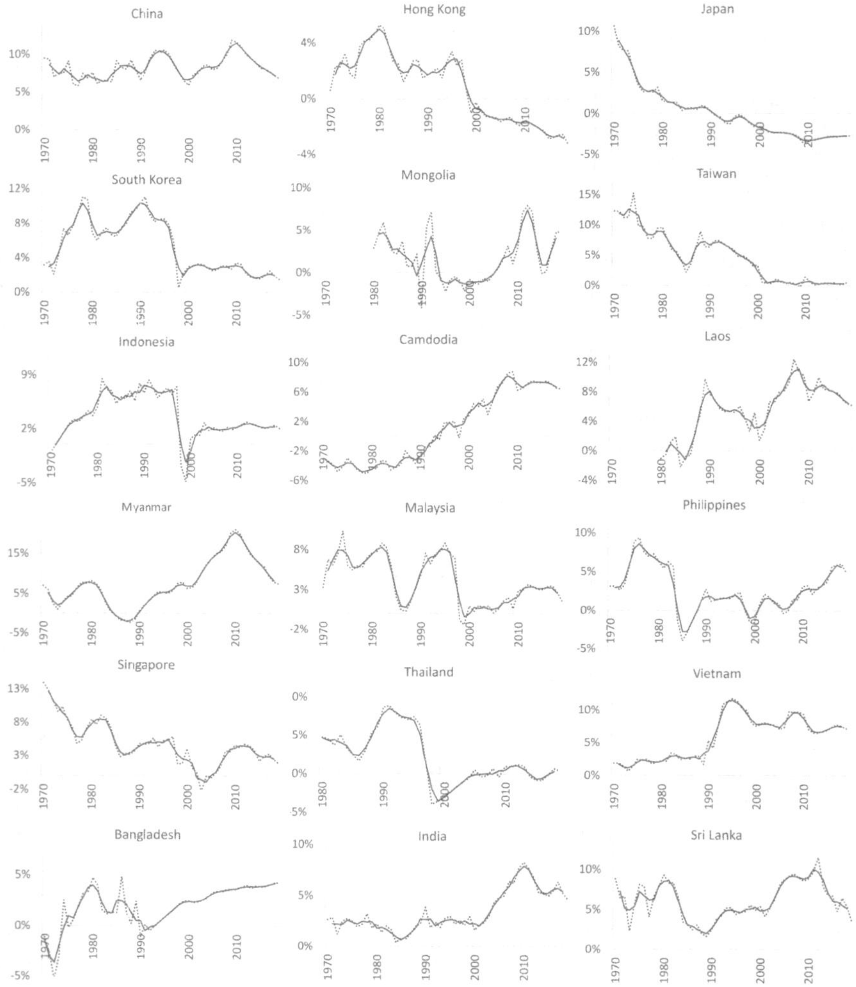

Figure 4.5 The difference in capital accumulation between six Eastern, seven South-eastern, and three Southern Asian countries and the United States: 1970–2019. The dotted line is the actual difference, and the solid line is the three-year moving average.

Source: EPWT 7.0.

accumulation after 1990. This enabled them to successfully narrow the gaps in labor and capital productivities.

In Southern Asia, India exhibited slightly higher capital accumulation than the United States between 1970 and 1990. This difference grew during the 1990s and expanded further after 2000. The catching-up process in India gained momentum in 1990, suggesting that the progress of catching up in larger countries might necessitate the difference reaching a certain positive threshold to initiate. Similarly,

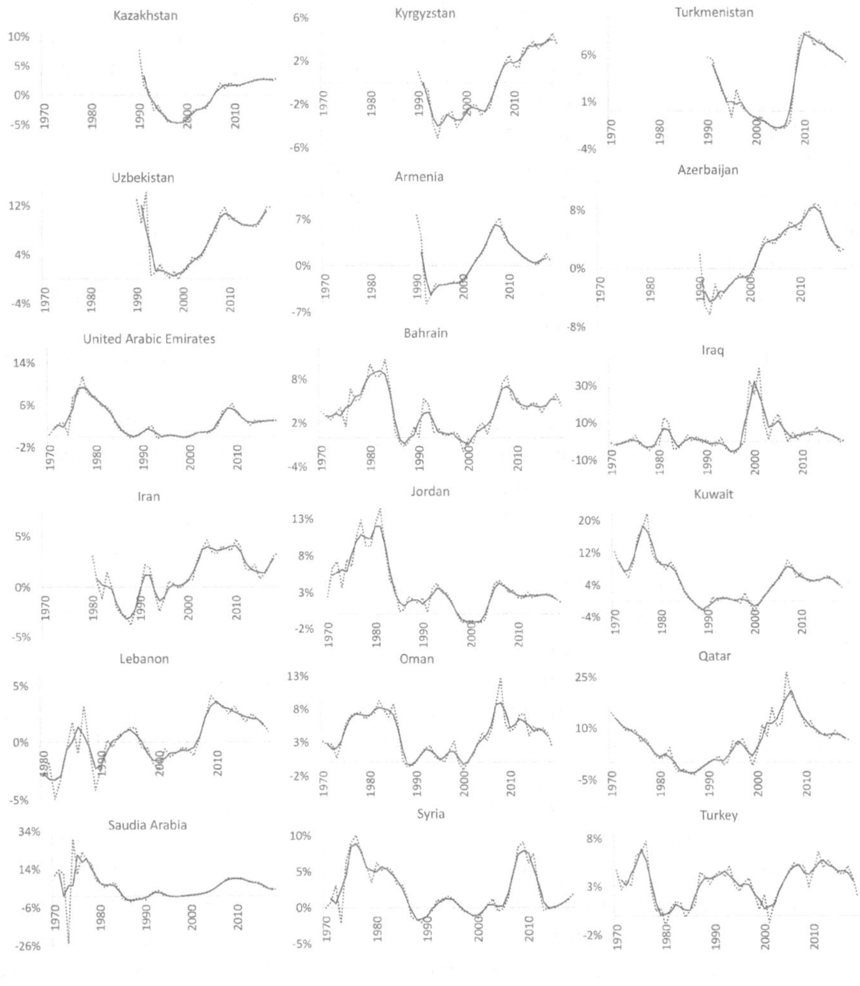

Figure 4.6 The difference in capital accumulation between six former soviet republics and 12 Western Asia and the United States: 1970–2019. The dotted line is the actual difference, and the solid line is the three-year moving average.

Source: EPWT 7.0.

Bangladesh and Sri Lanka observed an expansion in the difference of capital accumulation post-1990, particularly after 2000, leading to a rapid upsurge in labor productivity in both countries in comparison to the United States.

Within the former Soviet republics, the difference in capital accumulation declined quickly in the early 1990s, turning negative, then it expanded rapidly after 2000. A comparable movement occurred in Mongolia. As previously anticipated, these countries experienced falling behind and subsequently catching up. The difference in capital accumulation among oil rent Western Asian nations, in relation to the United States, exhibited significant fluctuations over the years. It expanded during the 1970s, declined in the 1980s and 1990s, and expanded again after the 2000s. Changes in oil prices explained these fluctuations. Capital accumulation decreased in countries involved in conflicts, such as Lebanon, Iran, Iraq, and Syria. As expected, these nations suffered a process of falling behind.

In Turkey, capital accumulation followed a cyclical trajectory. The debt crisis and the advent of neoliberalism triggered a decline in the 1980s. However, as the decade progressed, there was an expansion until the middle 1990s, with a subsequent fall and a robust recovery in the 2000s. Turkey emerged as a standout success in catching up within the Western Asian region. The effects of its unique geographical position and its integration with the European economy might have played a role in Turkey's economic performance.

After the neoliberal crisis of 2007, there was a decline in capital accumulation across several Asian nations, underlining their greater integration into the global economy. This integration has rendered these economies more susceptible to external shocks. Notice that historical instances of economic turmoil, such as the 1980 debt crisis and the 1997 financial crisis, impacted a smaller number of countries.

The profit rate and investment rate explained the differences in capital accumulation in relation to the leader. Figures 4.7 and 4.8 display scatterplots showing the relationship between the difference in the profit rates and capital accumulation, alongside their linear fit for Asian countries. A prevalent positive correlation emerged among most of them: a decrease in the difference in profit rates is associated with a reduction in the difference in capital accumulation. The fall in capital productivity during the catching-up can endanger the process, resulting in a lower profit rate and capital accumulation compared to the leader, as observed in Japan. Consequently, a fundamental question for follower countries involves catching up on labor productivity while maintaining the distance in capital productivity.

There were three exceptions in this general pattern. In China and Vietnam, the decline in the difference in profit rate did not result in a reduction of the difference in capital accumulation. It indicates that no direct links existed between these variables in China and Vietnam. In Laos, a negative correlation was observed between them. These findings suggest that factors beyond profitability influenced investment decisions in these countries. China, Vietnam, and Laos adhered to a market socialist economic model, where the state and the public enterprises play a central role in driving capital accumulation (Hansen, Bekkevold and Nordhaug, 2020). A bureaucratic elite controls the economic surplus, directing it to investment (Roberts, 2022). However, in countries which fully adopted neoliberalism, the profits are redistributed, and the investment rates declined. The extent to which this model aligns with the Keynesian proposition of investment socialization remains an open question.

The difference in the net investment rates between followers and the leader also contributes to disparities in capital accumulation. The net investment rate is the ratio of net social surplus advanced in the production process as fixed capital to the GDP. Figure 4.9 displays the scatterplot and the linear fit for the differences between the net investment rate, λ^{i}-λ^{USA}, and capital accumulation, $g_K{}^{i}$-$g_K{}^{USA}$, between six Eastern, seven South-eastern, and three South Asian countries and the United

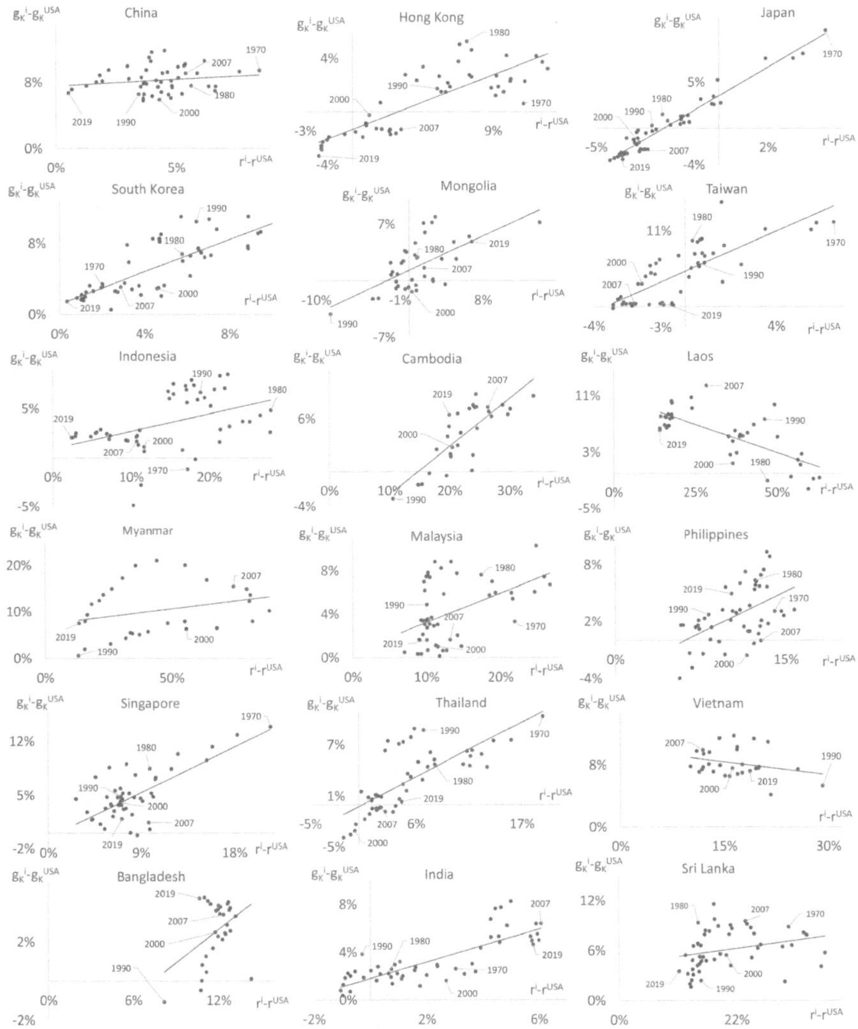

Figure 4.7 The scatterplot and the linear fit for the differences in profit rate, r^i-r^{USA}, and capital accumulation, $g_K{}^i$-$g_K{}^{USA}$, between six Eastern, seven South-eastern, and three Southern Asian countries and the United States: 1970–2019.

Source: EPWT 7.0.

States from 1970 to 2019. Figure 4.10 shows the same information for six former Soviet republics and 12 Western Asian countries.

As expected, a positive correlation emerged between the variables, a greater difference in the net investment rate corresponded to a higher difference in capital accumulation. China stands out with the largest investment rate and capital accumulation difference throughout the period. India amplified these differences after 1990, accelerating the pace of its catching up with the United States. Conversely,

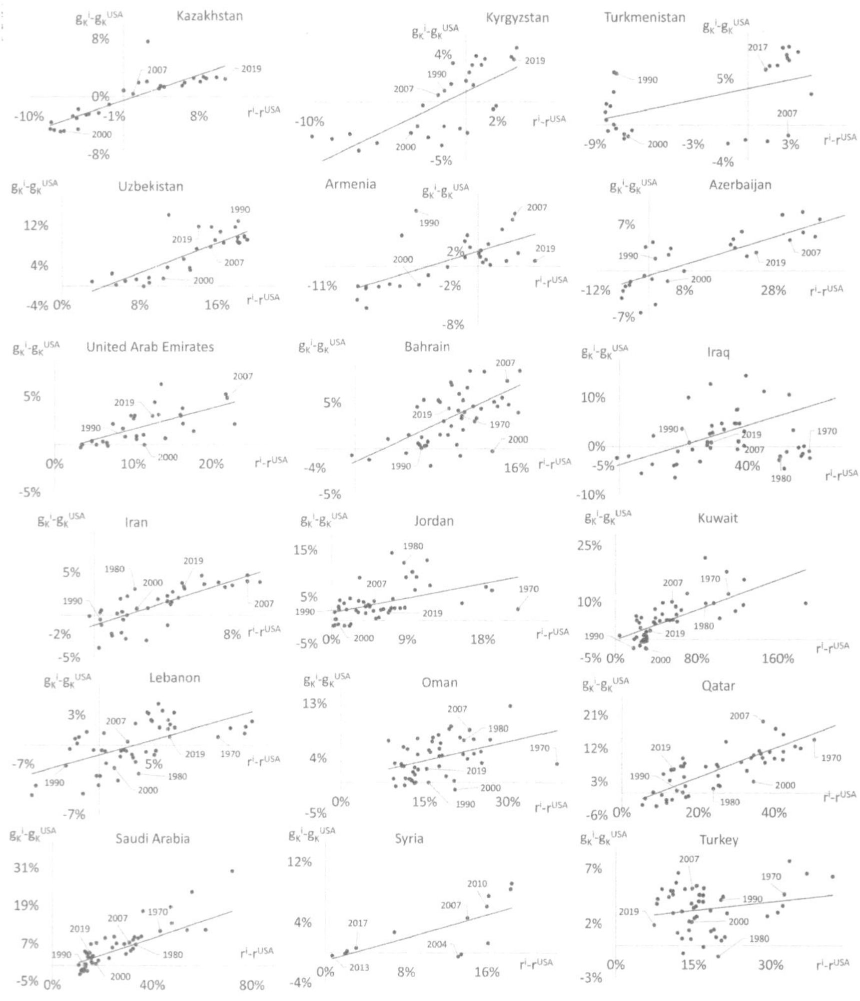

Figure 4.8 The scatterplot and the linear fit for the differences in profit rate, r^i-r^{USA}, and capital accumulation, $g_K{}^i$-$g_K{}^{USA}$, between six former Soviet republics, and 12 Western Asian and the United States: 1970–2019.

Source: EPWT 7.0.

Japan began falling behind after 1990, coinciding with the net investment rate falling below that of the United States.

In terms of the relationship between profitability and investment, neoliberalism had varying impacts on Asian countries, with some remaining relatively unaffected. For example, in Japan, the average profit-to-investment conversion rate decreased from 95.6 percent in the 1970s to 56.7 percent in the 2000s, while in South Korea, it declined from 76.7 to 66.2 percent. Contrarily, in China and India during the same periods, it increased from 85.1 to 96 percent and from 64 to 70 percent, respectively.

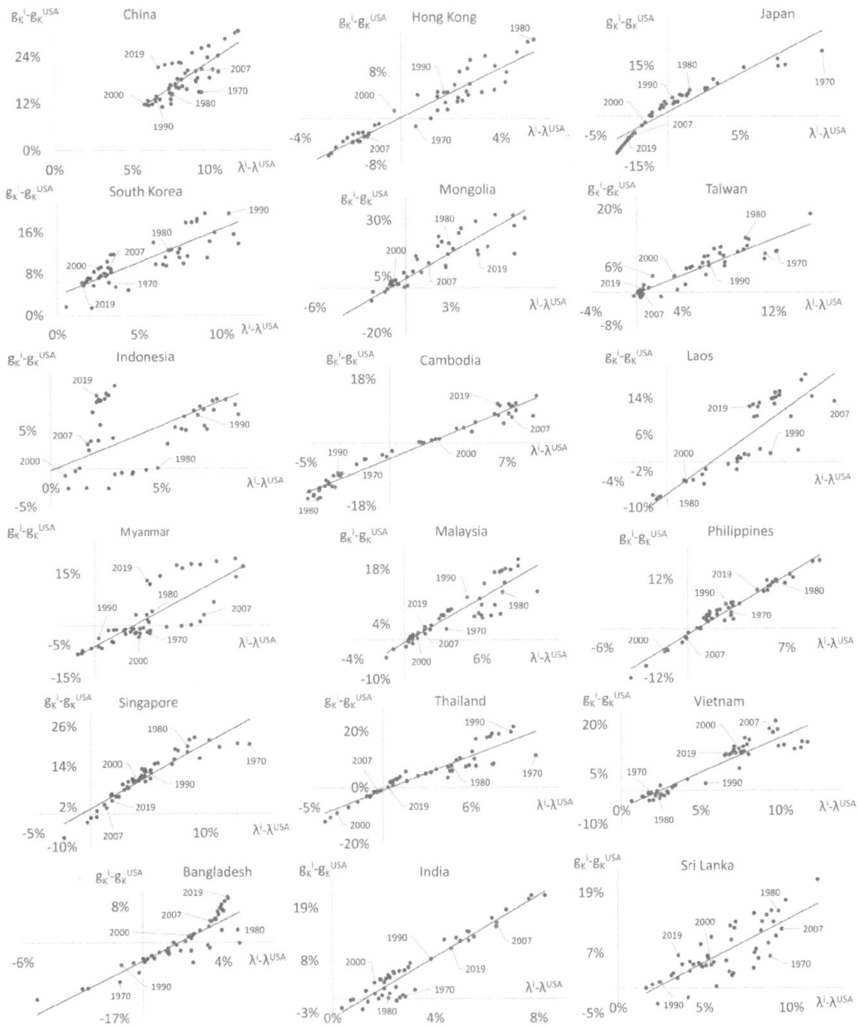

Figure 4.9 The scatter plot and the linear fit for the differences in investment rate, λ^i-λ^{USA}, and capital accumulation, $g_K{}^i$-$g_K{}^{USA}$, between six Eastern, seven South-eastern, and three Southern Asian countries and the United States: 1970–2019.

Source: EPWT 7.0.

If the investment rate in the follower country is determined by profitability in a market economy or by the state bureaucracy, it must be higher than the leader in order to have catching up in labor productivity. The problem is that, in most cases, a high capital accumulation reduces capital productivity and the profit rate for a relatively stable wage share. The decline in profit rate would require further social control over savings and investments to maintain the process.

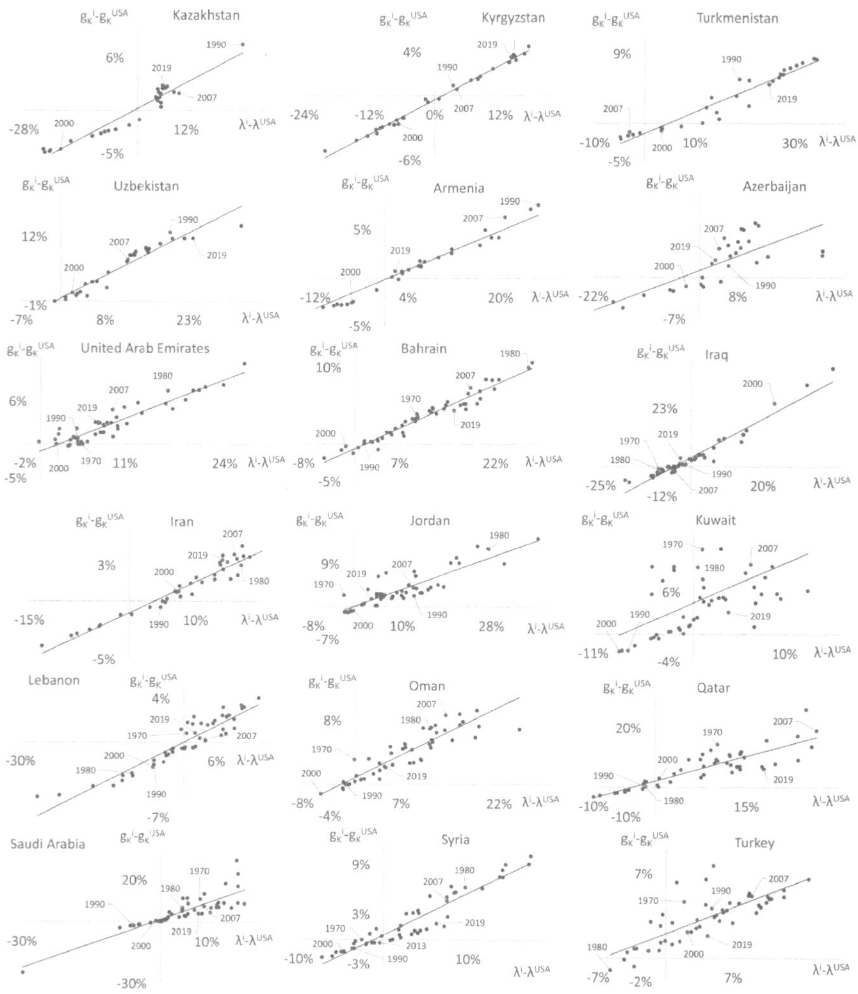

Figure 4.10 The scatter plot and the linear fit for the differences in investment rate, λ^i-λ^{USA}, and capital accumulation, $g_K{}^i$-$g_K{}^{USA}$, between six former soviet republics, and 12 Western Asian countries and the United States: 1970–2019.

Source: EPWT 7.0.

Dilemmas of catching up, profitability, neoliberalism, and environmental sustainability

Many Asian countries have been successful in reducing the gap in labor and capital productivities in the past five decades, experiencing substantial and prolonged economic growth. However, the catching up has been concentrated in Eastern, South-eastern and Southern Asian nations. Even within these regions, there are large variations in the degree of backwardness. While Japan and the Asian Tigers managed to elevate their labor productivity, joining the league of developed nations, other countries had in 2019 a labor productivity around 10 percent of the level observed in the United States.

A common element among many Asian experiences, notably in the regions referred above, was the formation of nation-states that implemented comprehensive development strategies. Establishing robust institutional frameworks to foster rapid economic growth requires prerequisites such as national sovereignty, both domestic and international stability, and a solid financial foundation. It is worthwhile to point out that the success of the export drive strategy of Japan was an inspiration for those nation-states.

The emergence of neoliberalism in Western developed countries in 1980s led to the offshoring of industrial activities and adoption of free trade policies. There was a peculiar and sometimes contradictory combination of national development strategies in Asia alongside neoliberalism in Western developed countries. Some Asian nations adopted state-induced strategies to foster growth and benefited from neoliberalism without adopting its central tenets.

The countries that emerged following the dissolution of the USSR faced the challenging tasks of establishing a national state, forging an identity, and transitioning toward a market-oriented economy. Many of the ongoing challenges faced by these nations were rooted in these complex objectives.

Similarly, nations in Western Asia are also faced with the problem of establishing and consolidating their identities and state structures. Many of these countries have employed the strategy of utilizing revenue from oil resources to invest in infrastructure and diversify their economies, aiming to reduce their reliance on petroleum. Additionally, there is an ongoing effort to foster a unified national identity. Civil conflicts and war have posed major obstacles to development for some countries, as exemplified by cases in Iraq, Afghanistan, Yemen, Lebanon, and Syria

As a hegemonic imperialist country, the United States has played a pivotal role in this process, sometimes nurturing economic growth in certain countries while taking opposing conduct in others. For example, it supported economic growth in Japan and the Asian Tigers while imposing restrictions on Iran. Similarly, China benefited from increased integration into the global production channels and the US economy.

During the process of catching up, the prevalent pattern of technical change observed in Asian countries was Marx-biased, with rising labor productivity and declining capital productivity. There was rapid infrastructural development and industrialization of the productive process through mechanization, and the adoption of capital-intensive technologies from the leading countries. The fall in capital productivity led to a decline in the profit rate in many Asian countries.

In the initial stages, an elevated profit rate holds the potential to propel rapid capital accumulation and economic growth. However, as the benefits of backwardness expressed in the higher profitability began to decline, the incentives for capital accumulation through market mechanisms also diminished.

The Asian countries responded to the decline in the profit rate in various ways. For example, Japan adopted neoliberalism, channeling profits into the financial system and reducing investments and economic growth. China pursued a distinct path, expanding the investment rate as the profit rate declined. The capital accumulation was delinked from profitability. It raises the question of whether a threshold exists beyond which the diminishing profit rate might impede capital accumulation within the Chinese model. India employed a different approach, the adoption of neoliberalism drove a decrease in the wage share, boosting the profit rate and capital accumulation. The question for India pertains to the limits within which the wage share can be reduced to allow higher profit rates and capital accumulation. Despite the decline in capital productivity, China and India managed to maintain their catching up using different strategies.

After the 2007 financial crisis, a structural capitalist crisis, the process of globalization and the integration between China and the United States have experienced a change. In addition to the deficit in commercial balance, the ascendence of China has increasingly positioned it as a potential competitor to the US hegemony. Consequently, the United States has imposed a series of escalating restrictions on China and its enterprises, while expanding its alliances with other countries. The impact of these measures on the Chinese economy and the potential responses remains uncertain. Nevertheless, China has displayed a capability to respond positively to its developmental obstacles.

The rapid capital accumulation in many Asian countries has driven a vigorous expansion in both GDP production and greenhouse gas emissions, positioning the continent as a global leader in both GDP production and emissions. In 2019, China ranked as the largest emitter of carbonic gas, followed by India in the third position, while a large gap in average labor productivity in relation to the US economy persisted.

The continuity of the catching up requires further capital accumulation and the employment of energy, whose main source is fossil fuel. The absolute decoupling between economic growth and greenhouse gas emissions is imperative to mitigate the consequences of global warming. It can be obtained either by a reduction in the pace of capital accumulation in developing and developed countries or by boosting environment-saving technical change.

The first option implies that developing countries might have to accept not reaching the living standards of their developed counterparts, which could result in a lower velocity in the reduction of the productivity gap or even a standstill. There is no indication that this path is under consideration in the Asian countries currently experiencing catching up.

The second alternative appears favored at the present time, particularly in its more dynamic economies. Adopting environment-saving technical change has the potential to stimulate growth, as it implies investment in new technologies and capital accumulation. Moreover, these investments are likely to be readily promoted in countries where the links between investment and profit are weaker, as in the case some Asian countries. Promoting the expansion of green manufacturing to balance economic growth with reduced environmental impact could be a promising direction for many developing countries worldwide.

Asia is characterized by heterogeneity and complexity. The economies of numerous Asian nations heavily rely on oil resources, making imperative to ponder their response to the global movement toward decarbonized energy sources. Moreover, a more comprehensive examination is needed to assess whether the new avenues for capital accumulation in Asian countries which could accompany the potential departure from neoliberalism and deglobalization. The intricate interplay of these distinct forces will be crucial in shaping the future trajectories of the continent.

Bibliography

Hansen, A., Bekkevold, J., and Nordhaug, K. (2020). *The Socialist Market Economy in Asia: Development in China, Vietnam and Laos*. Singapore: Palgrave Macmillan.

Lenin, V. (2010). *Imperialism: The Highest Stage of Capitalism*. London: Penguin Classics.

Panikkar, K. (2000). The twentieth century in Asian and world history. *India Quarterly*, 56 (1–2), pp. 63–96.

Roberts, M. (2022). China As a transitional economy to socialism? *Journal of Global Faultlines*, 9 (2), pp. 180–197.

Wade, R. (2017). The developmental state: Dead or alive? *Development and Change*, 49(2), pp. 518–546.

World Bank. (2023). *World bank open data*. Available at: https://data.worldbank.org/. Accessed on:18June 2023.

5 From hope to frustration

Falling behind in Latin America

Latin America encompasses the countries located south of the United States, where Romance languages predominate. The origin of the term remains subject to debate, blending elements of geography, language, and reactions to imperialism (Gobat, 2013). The region has natural resources, fertile lands, and a suitable climate for agricultural production. Yet, many countries have failed to achieve high living standards and stable political institutions, grappling with high-income inequality. While a few nations have made progress in industrialization and productive diversification, most continue to depend on primary commodity exports, rendering them vulnerable and susceptible to recurrent boom and bust cycles.

Scholars in Latin America have played a central role in the debates on economic development, especially concerning the relationship between structural change and economic growth. They argued that industrialization would mitigate the unequal exchange between the central and the peripheral countries associated with falling terms of trade (Prebisch, 1968). Many Latin American nations adopted the strategy of import substitution industrialization (ISI), from the 1930s to the 1970s. Under state leadership, ISI aimed to replace foreign industrial imports with local production, expanding the autonomy of the region's largest economies. During the Cold War, the United States supported developmentalism through ISI to foster capitalist development.

During the crisis of the Golden Age, many Latin American countries massively increased their loans from commercial banks to finance current account deficits, support capital accumulation, and sustain economic growth. However, the profit rate sharply declined in the region during the 1970s. Moreover, the debt service soared after the Federal Reserve skyrocketed the interest rate in 1979, leading to the external crisis in the 1980s. In "lost decade," a period marked by slow growth and high inflation, the premature deindustrialization started along with the expansion of the financial sector.

Neoliberalism was implemented in the 1980s and the early 1990s, further connecting the national and international financial bourgeoisie. Developmentalism and the perspective of a national project of development was abandoned. Neoliberalism led to an increased extraction of financial rents from the periphery, it is a form of financial imperialism. While successful in achieving price stability, neoliberalism fell short in reigniting economic growth. Most countries fell

DOI: 10.4324/9781003223382-6

behind after 1980, including the largest economies in the region, Brazil, Mexico, and Argentina. Despite the increase in profitability after the early 1990s, the accumulation of capital declined.

Reduced growth led to rising unemployment and a growing wave of political resistance against neoliberalism. In the late 1990s and early 2000s, left-wing parties came to power. The surge in commodity prices, driven by Chinese demand, improved terms of trade and profitability. Some Pink Tide governments adopted a pragmatic economic policy that combined elements of both neoliberalism and developmentalism. The outcome was a modest increase in capital accumulation, facilitating catching up in the 2000s, despite the persistent trend of deindustrialization.

However, the terms of trade declined after the 2007 financial crisis, which coupled with the rise in wage share drove a fall in the profit rate. As a result, the Pink Tide governments lost political support and eventually their power. By the late 2010s, most Latin American nations embraced a late version of neoliberalism.

The chapter provides an in-depth analysis of the processes of catching up and falling behind in Latin American countries from 1970 to 2019 in relation to the United States, drawing comparisons between neoliberalism and developmentalist periods. It is structured into four sections. The first offers an overview of the economic history of Latin America over the last five decades. The second investigates the relationship between technical change and the profit rate, providing an analysis of economic performance since the 1980s. The third examines the effects of the profit rate and investment on capital accumulation, particularly during neoliberalism. Finally, the last section explores the conditions under which countries in the region can catch up, answering whether the abandonment of neoliberalism is a prerequisite for expanding capital accumulation.

Neoliberalism in Latin America: A brief account

Most Latin American nations adopted neoliberalism in the early 1990s, roughly a decade after the United States. However, the structural break in the growth rates in the region occurred in 1980, coinciding with the emergence of neoliberalism in the capitalist center. Figure 5.1 displays the GDP growth rates and their median for 20 countries from 1950 to 2019. The median growth rate declined from 5.1 percent between 1950 and 1980 to 3.1 percent from 1981 to 2019. It peaked in 1973 during the Golden Age and in 2007 during neoliberalism, both years marked the onset of structural crises in the US economy.

After World War II, many Latin American countries adopted the ISI regime to drive economic growth. Developmentalism was characterized by extensive state intervention and protectionism, combining large public enterprises with national and multinational private companies. The ISI was an attempt to build an economic model that prioritizes internal markets and aimed to reduce dependence on the external sector. The resulting high capital accumulation proved beneficial to the national industrial bourgeoisie, prompting urbanization and the emergence of an urban working class and a state bureaucracy. However, the industrialization and the urbanization also fueled social inequalities and political unrest.

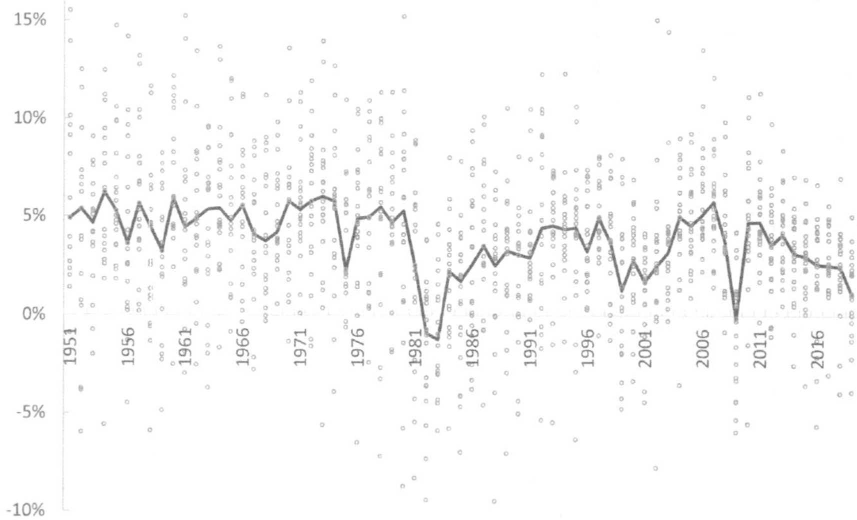

Figure 5.1 Latin American GDP growth rates and its median, 1951–2019.

Source: EPWT 7.0.

Note: There were 19 observations outside the y-axis limits.

The expansion of the working class and its organization played a role in the political conflicts that unfolded in Latin America during the Cold War. Except for Mexico and Costa Rica, the region witnessed successive coups and dictatorships, particularly during periods of reduced economic growth and rising class struggle. The US government supported many of these coups to preserve its economic and political dominance in the region. The case of Chile stands out as a significant example. The violent overthrow of Allende's government in 1973 marked one of the earliest instances of a country adopting neoliberalism.

The United States has historically intervened in Latin American nations when governments clashed with its political and economic interests. The Monroe Doctrine, which emerged during James Monroe's presidency in the 1820s under the motto "America for Americans," was initially aimed at preventing European nations from interfering in the affairs of Americas, safeguarding the newly independent nations from the threat of recolonization. However, this doctrine served as a foundational rationale for US interventions in Latin America, persisting from the XIX Century to the present day. There are many cases of the employment of this doctrine from 1970 to 2019, including economic sanctions in Venezuela and interventions in civil wars, such as the cases of Nicaragua and El Salvador in Central America during the late 1970s and the first half of the 1980s.

Latin American countries implemented the ISI during the Golden Age. The signals of exhaustion of the developmentalist model became apparent in the early 1970s, with the crisis of the Golden Age. Industrialization raised labor productivity and reduced capital productivity, a major determinant of the profit rate. After the first oil shock in 1973, the countries relied on growing external indebtedness to finance the deficit in trade balance and expand capital accumulation. There was a sharp decline in profitability in Latin American countries during the 1970s. Moreover, commercial banks in the capitalist center recycled the petrodollars, rapidly expanding external indebtedness in the peripheral countries. The conjunction of falling profitability and mounting external debt escalated the financial fragility in the region.

The emergence of neoliberalism unleashed the debt crisis with the Federal Reserve's rising interest rate and the second oil shock in 1979. In the early 1980s, the debt crises reached most countries in the region, even those exporting oil. There was a foreign currency shortage, high inflation, and lower investment due to falling profitability and rising fiscal fragility. In the 1980s, the terms of trade declined, further reducing the profit rate. The sharp fall in economic growth, coupled with a substantial expansion in servicing the external debt, resulted in increased poverty, as well as political and economic consequences.

A wave of democratization emerged during the 1980s. Nevertheless, the newly elected governments embraced a neoliberal economic model. The ongoing crises and high inflation opened the possibilities for significant institutional reforms and the adoption of the Washington Consensus agenda, which marked the deepening of neoliberalism in Latin America. The International Monetary Fund and the World Bank played a fundamental role in this process, promoting neoliberalism through conditional lending. Their agenda pursued macroeconomic austerity, currency devaluation, and market-friendly reforms (Babb and Kentikelenis, 2018).

Two phases marked the transition from the Golden Age to neoliberalism. The first was the years from the late 1970s to the onset of the debt crisis of the early 1980s. The second was the adoption of neoliberalism in the middle 1980s and early 1990s. Neoliberalism aims to make the market the central mechanism for resource allocation and capital accumulation, reducing the role of state in these processes. Neoliberal reforms aimed to eliminate protectionism via a commercial and financial opening, dimmish the state's intervention in economic activity, privatize public companies, lower labor market regulations, and place smaller taxes on capital gains. A distinctive outcome of neoliberalism is the increasing share of income directed toward both national and international finance, leading to the decline in the investment rate.

Neoliberalism succeeded in reducing inflation rates. However, with few exceptions, notably in Chile, it failed to spur economic growth despite a partial recovery in the profit rate. Profit was increased channeled to financial sector. As the 1990s unfolded and the neoliberal reforms consolidated, the region experienced growing financial instability. Premature deindustrialization and specialization in commodity production were common features.

Starting with the Mexico peso crisis in the mid-1990s, a series of financial crises struck the Latin American nations later in the decade. There was growing disappointment with the unfulfilled promises of neoliberalism, leading to a loss of support for the political parties espousing neoliberalism. Venezuela, Nicaragua, Brazil, Ecuador, Bolivia, Uruguay, Honduras, Argentina, and Paraguay elected center-left governments around 2000 in a wave called Pink Tide.

In the early XXI Century, the surge in commodity prices in the context of Pink Tide governments triggered economic growth, leading to seemingly contradictory outcomes: improved living standards alongside continued deindustrialization. The decline in poverty was attributed to higher economic growth and the implementation of redistributive programs by the center-left governments. Some countries attempted to blend aspects of neoliberalism with developmentalism. However, the Pink Tide governments were unable to change the productive structure of the economies.

Following the 2007 financial crisis, terms of trade declined with the fall in commodity prices. The structural crisis of neoliberalism hit Latin America in early 2010s. As the GDP growth rate dropped, the political support for the center-left governments waned. The Pink Tide governments that had initially benefited from the new international division of labor also suffered the consequences of commodity price volatility.

Around 2015, most center-left parties were out of government. Some, like Argentina, through elections, and others, like Brazil, Bolivia, and Paraguay, through hard and soft coups. Toward the end of the 2010s, Latin America was under what can be called late neoliberalism, which aimed to reestablish the political power and the economic gains of the financial bourgeoisie.

Figure 5.2 shows the labor productivity of 20 Latin American countries in relation to the United States from 1970 to 2019, and the average for countries with complete observations for the entire period. In this time frame, the labor productivity gap widened for most countries, except for Chile, the Dominican Republic, Panama, Paraguay, and Uruguay. In these nations, the 2019 labor productivity gap was either similar to or lower than in 1970.

The process of catching up and falling behind in the region occurred in three distinct phases. The first phase, consistent with ISI, saw catching up during the 1970s. In the second phase, between 1980 and the early 2000s, there was a substantial rise in the labor productivity gap, leading to falling behind. The third phase, between the early 2000s and 2019, initially witnessed a narrowing of the gap, followed by a falling behind in the middle 2010s. These results align with the capitalist phases observed in Latin America, where countries caught up during developmentalism but fell behind during neoliberalism, with mixed outcomes during the Pink Tide. The following section delves into the relationship between technical change and the falling behind process.

Technical change, profit rate, and premature deindustrialization

There is a tendency for countries to display a pattern of technical change with declining capital productivity and rising labor productivity. Yet, there are substantial variations in the paths that national economies follow during economic development. Figure 5.3 graphs the rates of change in capital productivity and labor productivity, the pair (ga, gx), for the periods 1970–2019, 1970–1980, 1980–2003, and 2003–2019. It reveals the technical change in the long term, in the last years of the ISI, in neoliberalism, and the Pink Tide. For simplicity, we consider the growth rates in the open interval from -0.1 percent to 0.1 percent as equal to zero.

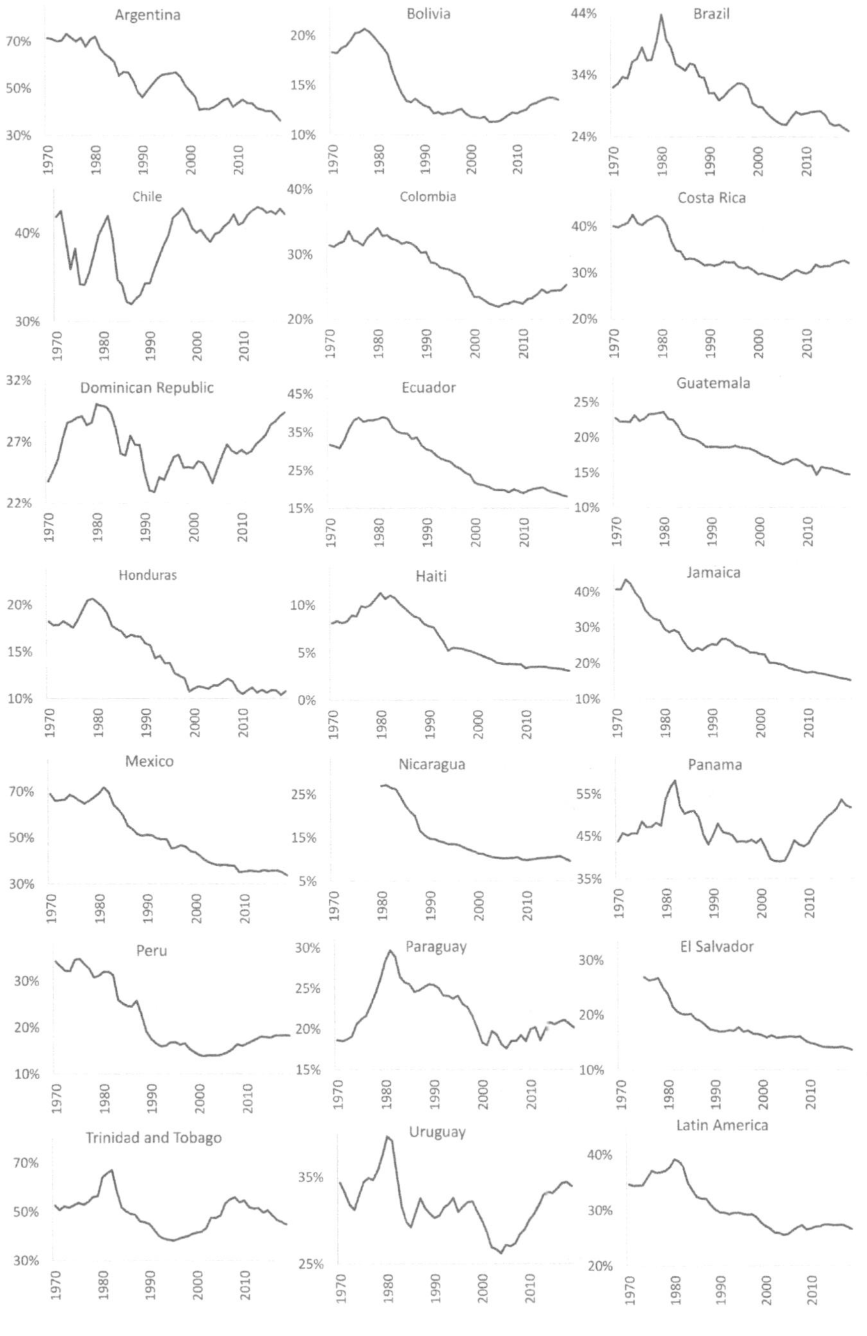

Figure 5.2 Labor productivity in Latin American countries relative to the United States, 1970–2019.

Source: EPWT 7.0.

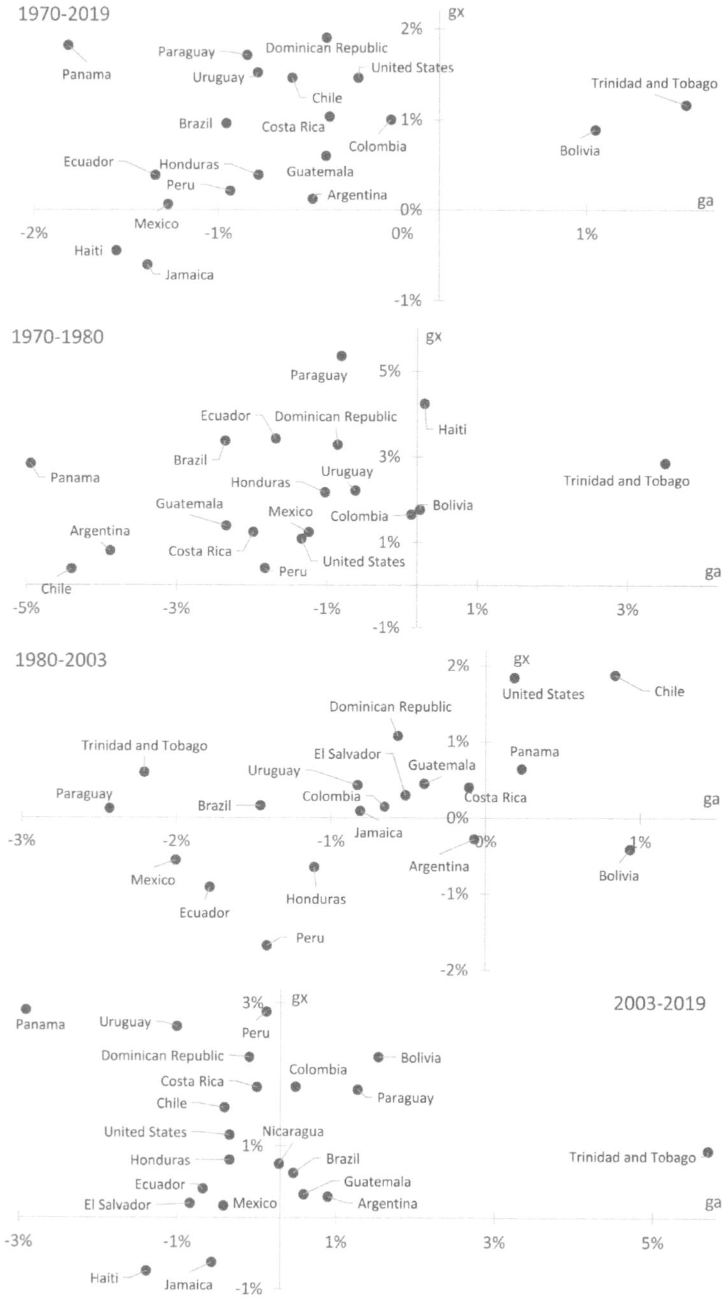

Figure 5.3 The (ga, gx) points for Latin American countries and the United States: 1970–2019, 1970–1980, 1980–2003, 2003–2019.

Source: EPWT 7.0.

The technical change was consistent with the labor-saving, capital-using Marx bias in the long term for Argentina, Brazil, Chile, Colombia, Costa Rica, Ecuador, the Dominican Republic, Ecuador, Guatemala, Honduras, Panama, Peru, Paraguay, and Uruguay. Bolivia and Trinidad and Tobago exhibited an input-saving technical change. Haiti and Jamaica presented a technical regress with declining labor and capital productivities, while Mexico displayed a Solow-neutral technical regress.

From 1970 to 2019, there were three phases of technical change. First, between 1970 and 1980, when 14 out of 18 economies exhibited the Marx-biased pattern. This phase encompassed the last ten years of the ISI regime, a strategy that delivered high growth rates in many Latin American countries, particularly in Brazil and Mexico. Bolivia, Colombia, and Haiti presented the Harrod-neutral technical change, and Trinidad and Tobago displayed a labor-saving, capital-saving technical change.

Industrialization is a form of mechanization with a structural change toward sectors with higher labor productivity and lower capital productivity. Historically, industrialization displays a Marx-biased pattern of technical change. Deindustrialization, whether premature or not, is a countertendency to the falling profit rate, as capital relocates to sector with higher average capital productivity.

Second, from 1980 to 2003, seven countries experienced technical regress, four had a labor-using, capital-using technical change, including Mexico; Bolivia exhibited a labor-using, capital-saving pattern; Jamaica a Solow-neutral technical regress; and Argentina had a Harrod-neutral technical regress. Nine countries displayed the Marx-biased technical change. Chile and Panama presented the input-saving technical change. The annual average growth rate of labor productivity was over 0.5 percent for just three countries.

This phase corresponds to the lost decade and the implementation of neoliberal reforms in Latin America. There was a structural change, the manufacturing share in value-added declined while the mining and services shares increased. The region's economic autonomy decreased while the dependence on the terms of trade expanded. The reduced GDP growth rates and two additional factors may explain the fall in capital productivity. First, there was a sharp fall in terms of trade in the 1980s. Second, deindustrialization implied physical capital destruction, which is unaccounted by the perpetual inventory method, which measures fixed capital.

In the third phase, between 2003 and 2019, nine economies exhibited the Marx-biased technical change; Nicaragua revealed a Harrod-neutral technical change; and Haiti and Jamaica the labor-using, capital-using technical change. There were seven cases of labor-saving and capital-saving technical change. The input-saving technical change may result from four possibilities: the employment of innovations that reduce the price of capital goods, the rise in terms of trade, the structural change in direction to higher capital productivity sectors, and the increase in the degree of capacity utilization. In the early 2000s, the boom in commodity prices boosted the terms of trade with the rising demand from China and the financialization of commodity markets. Some countries in the region also witnesses a higher degree of capacity utilization as a result of the distributive policies adopted by the Pink Tide governments.

The trajectory of the profit rate is determined by capital productivity and profit share. It rises in tandem with an increase in profit share and capital productivity. The profit share, in turn, grows when labor productivity outpaces the average wage. Figure 5.4 displays the net profit rate for 18 Latin American countries between 1970 and 2019. There was a declining trend for 14 countries, including Brazil,

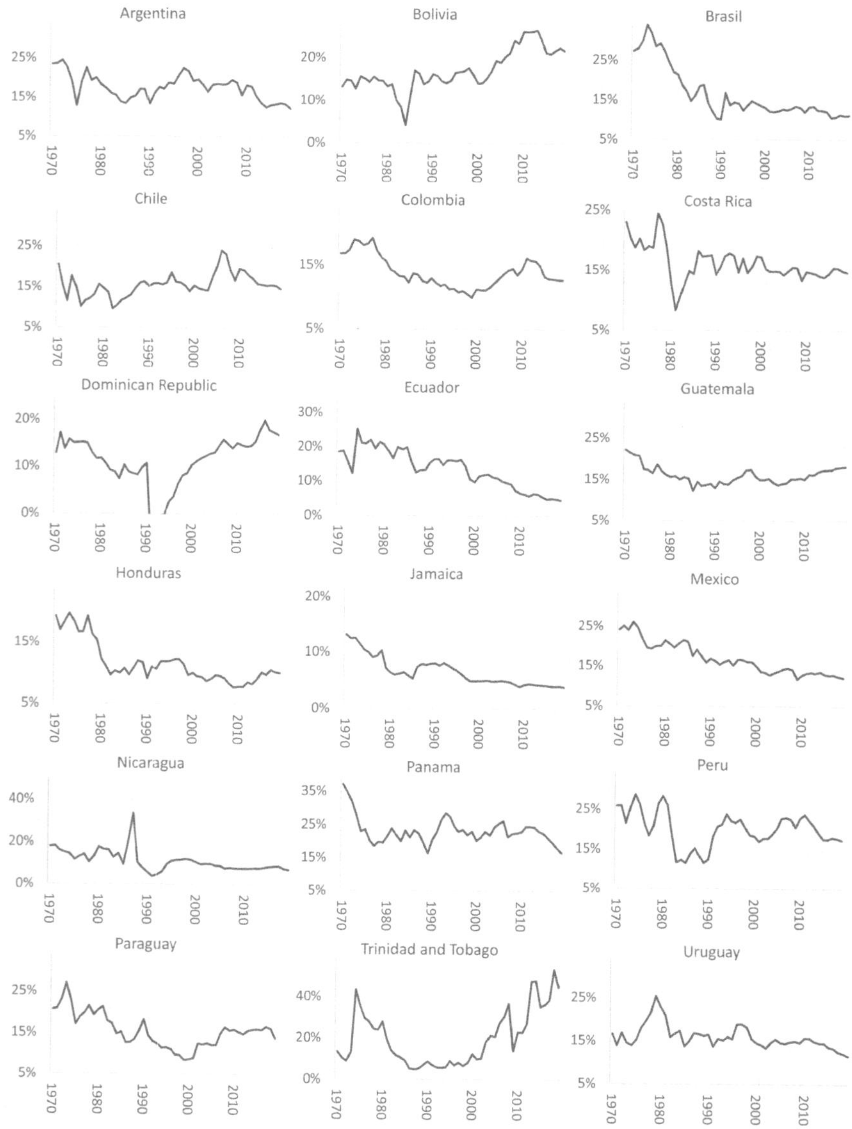

Figure 5.4 The net profit rate for 18 Latin American countries: 1970–2019.
Source: EPWT 7.0

Argentina, and Mexico, the largest economies in the region, a positive trend for Bolivia, Dominican Republic, Trinidad, and Tobago, and it was trendless for Chile. The trend in the profit rate reflected the movements of capital productivity except for the Dominican Republic, where the increase in the profit share offset the falling capital productivity.

The profit rate displayed similar phases to the ones observed in capital productivity. For most countries, the profitability was stable or increased at the beginning of the 1970s. Then, it started to decline after 1973, the year which symbolizes the end of the Golden Age, falling until the late 1980s. During the 1990s, the profit rate increased due to rising capital productivity. The deindustrialization and the employment of information and communication and technology may explain the higher capital productivity. With the neoliberal reforms, the wage share remained stable or declined in most countries during the 1990s. There was a re-primarization of exports, even in the countries that were able to diversify their exports during the ISI. Mexico, on the other hand, expanded its *maquila* exports to the United States.

In the 2000s, despite the rise in wage share promoted by center-left governments, most countries experienced rising profit rates due to higher terms of trade. Initially, the 2007 neoliberal crisis had a limited impact on commodity prices, by 2010, they had reached or surpassed their previous peak due to booming demand and limited supply. However, prices started to decline in the early 2010 as demand faded with the slowdown in economic growth.

During the Pink Tide, there was limited political leeway to reduce the wage share, even as the terms of trade deteriorated. Consequently, a rapid decline in the profit rate occurred in many countries, driven by the simultaneous decrease in terms of trade, falling capital productivity, and rising wage share. In the long term, an inherent contradiction exists between the wage share and the profit rate.

Profit rate, capital accumulation, and neoliberalism

A necessary condition for catching up is that capital accumulation in the follower country is greater than in the leader. Capital accumulation is a function of profit rate, as well as saving and investment rates. Figure 5.5 highlights the difference in capital accumulation between Latin American countries and the United States in the 1970–2019 periods. The dotted line is the actual difference, and the solid line is the three-year moving average.

For most countries, the difference in capital accumulation declined relative to the United States between the early 1970s and late 2010s. It is consistent with the observed falling behind in labor productivity. The three phases are clearly illustrated in the graphs. In the 1970s, except for Chile and Bolivia, the Latin American countries had higher capital accumulation than the United States. During neoliberalism, the difference in capital accumulation turned negative in the 1980s and slightly positive in the 1990s. With the lower capital accumulation, there was an increase in the labor productivity gap in Latin America. Chile was an exception, as the country increased its capital accumulation in the mid-1980s, reducing the

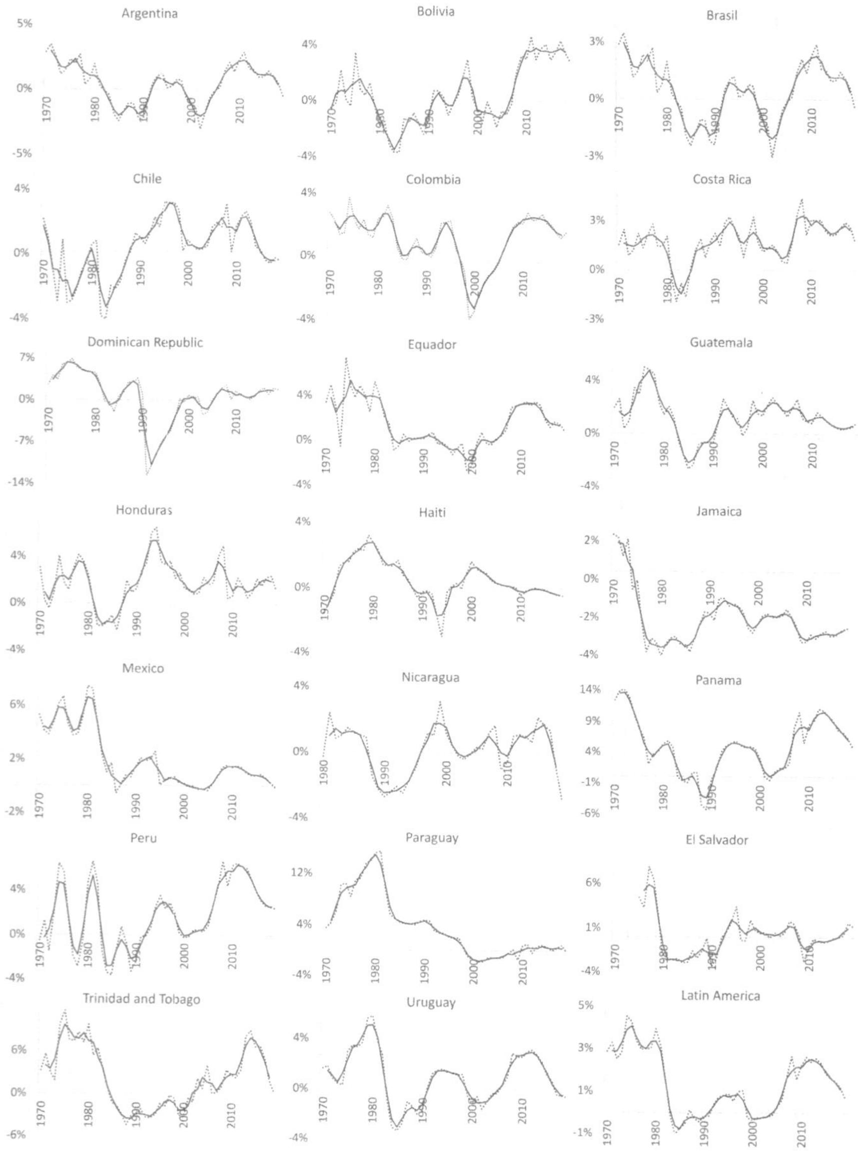

Figure 5.5 The difference in capital accumulation between Latin American countries and the United States: 1970–2019. The dotted line is the actual difference, and the solid line is the three-year moving average.

Source: EPWT 7.0.

labor productivity gap. During the Pink Tide, the difference in capital accumulation increased in the 2000s, declining in the 2010s.

The result is consistent with our model in chapter two. A higher capital accumulation in the follower country is required to catch up. Two factors drove the decline in capital accumulation in Latin America in relation to the United States. The first was the fall in the differences in the profit rate between the countries in the region and the United States. Figure 5.6 displays the scatterplot between the differences in the profit rate, r^{i}-r^{USA}, and in capital accumulation, $g_K^{\ i}$-$g_K^{\ USA}$, and their linear fit for 18 Latin American countries and the United States. There was a positive correlation between the variables; the distance in capital accumulation diminished as the difference in profit rate declined. The profit rate in Latin American nations was higher than in the United States between 1973 and 2019, except for some years during the neoliberalism in Bolivia (1984), Ecuador (2010–2019), Jamaica (1979–2019), Nicaragua (1989–1993, 2006–2013, and 2018–2019), Paraguay (1999–2001), and Trinidad and Tobago (1986–1999).

The second factor was the decline in the net investment rate, which represents the ratio between net profits advanced in production as fixed capital and GDP. Figure 5.7 displays the scatterplot and the linear fit for the differences between the net investment rate, λ^{i}-λ^{USA}, and capital accumulation, $g_K^{\ i}$-$g_K^{\ USA}$, for 18 Latin American countries and the United States from 1970 to 2019. A positive correlation is observed between the variables. The drop in the net investment can be attributed to four main causes: the fall in the profit rate, the increase in factor income paid abroad, the decrease of public investment, and the increase in financial rents in neoliberalism.

The conversion rate from profits to investment generally declined from developmentalism to neoliberalism in the region, with few exceptions. For instance, in Brazil, the average conversion rate decreased from 43.8 percent in the 1970s to 39.5 percent in the 1990s. Similar trends were observed in Mexico, 46.1 to 38 percent, and Argentina, 38.4 to 27.5 percent. However, Chile stood out, with its ratio increasing from 31.9 to 47.8 percent during these periods.

Whither Latin America: Leaving neoliberalism?

Latin American countries experienced falling behind in labor productivity during neoliberalism. The drop in profit rate in the 1970s followed by the fall in the investment rate in the 1980s drove a sizable decline in capital accumulation and output growth after 1980. The institutional changes associated with the crisis of the Golden Age sharply contrast with the Keynesian reforms adopted to address the crisis of liberalism in the 1930s. Most Latin American countries embraced the developmentalist model during that period, combining state intervention with protectionism.

Some nations, particularly those endowed with large populations and expansive geographical areas, industrialized in the ISI years, thereby reducing their reliance on commodity exports. This phase saw the expansion of a national bourgeoisie class and the emergence of an organized urban working class. Between World War II and the late 1970s, several countries in the region experienced robust capital accumulation and managed to make significant strides toward catching up with the United States.

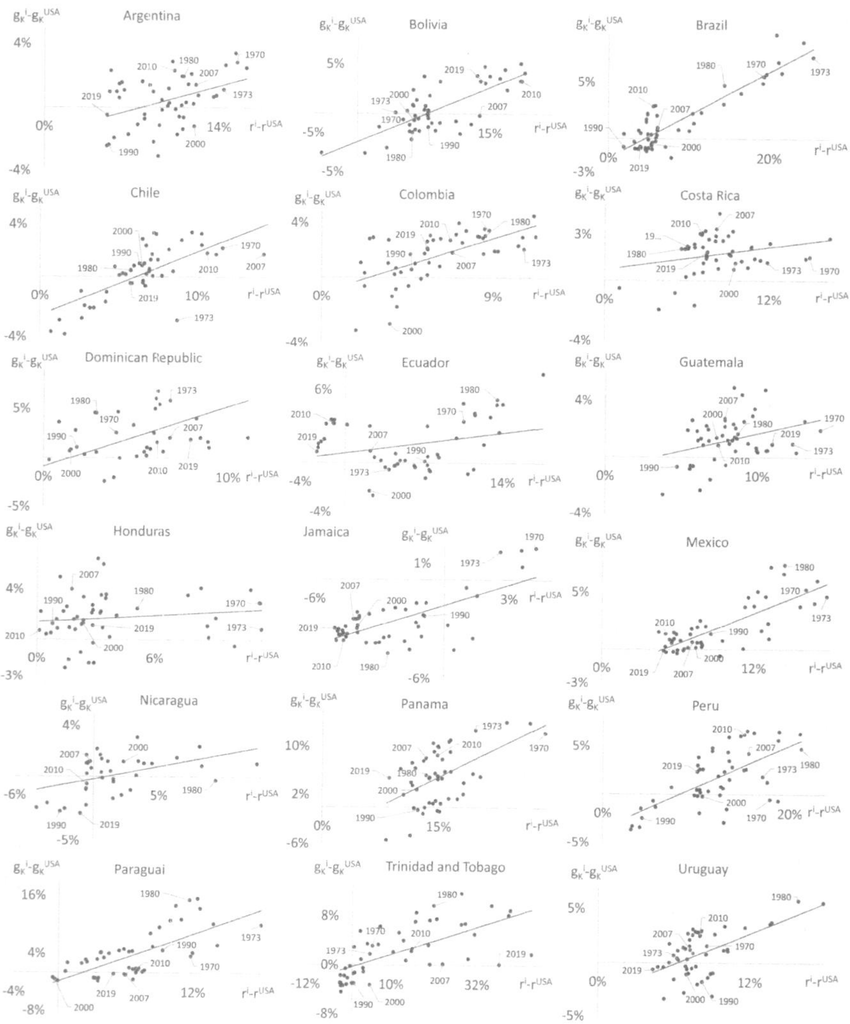

Figure 5.6 The scatterplot between the differences in profit rate, r^i-r^{USA}, and capital accumulation, g_K^i-g_K^{USA}, for 18 Latin American countries and the United States: 1970–2019.

Source: EPWT 7.0.

The crisis of developmentalism in Latin America coincided with the parallel crisis of the Golden Age in developed nations. Many countries in the region rapidly expanded the external debt, while the profit rate declined, rising their financial fragility. The increase in the interest rate by the Federal Reserve as the United States adopted neoliberalism was a determinant factor for the external debt crisis in the 1980s.

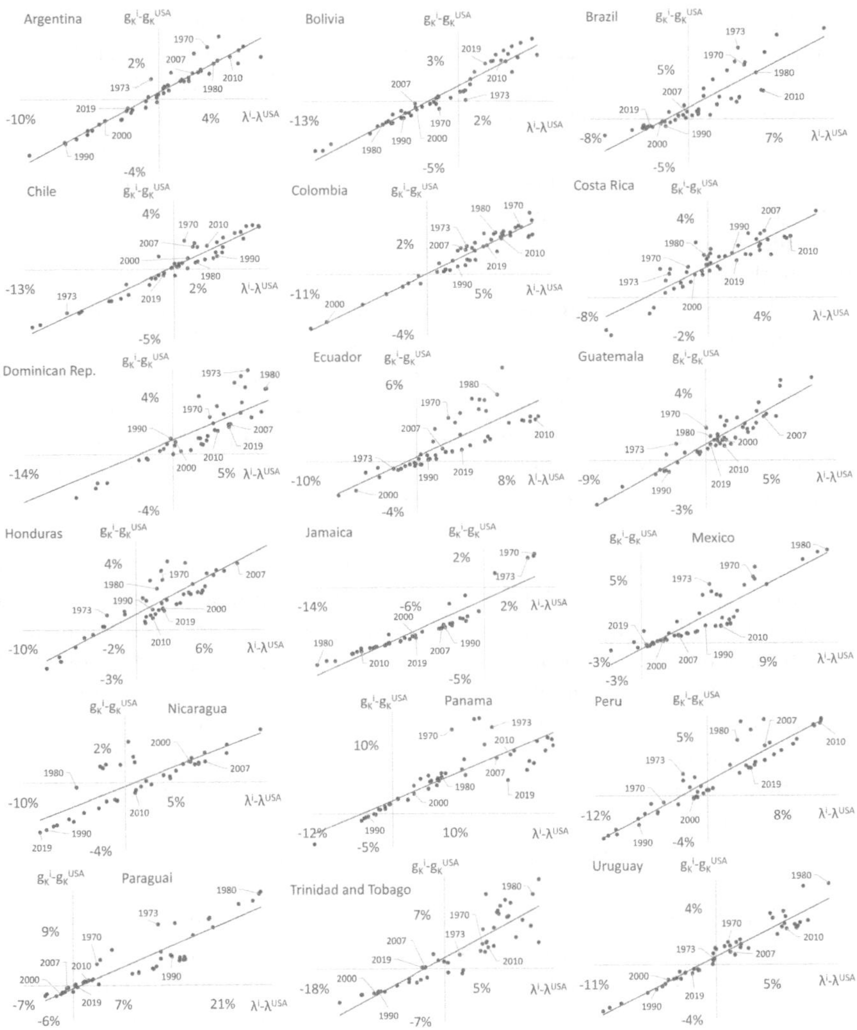

Figure 5.7 The scatterplot between the differences in the net investment rate, λ^{i}-λ^{USA}, and in capital accumulation, $g_K{}^{i}$-$g_K{}^{USA}$, for 18 Latin American countries and the United States: 1970–2019.

Source: EPWT 7.0.

The influence of international financial institutions, notably the International Monetary Fund and World Bank, expanded significantly in the region. Their support became contingent upon the adoption of neoliberal reforms. As the profit rate declined, the local bourgeoisie began advocating for neoliberal reforms, attributing the economic crisis to the developmentalist model. During the 1980s, a transition to neoliberalism occurred with the gradual dismantlement of the developmentalist state.

Following the reintegration of Latin American countries into the international financial markets, they accumulate significant reserves, enabling them to peg their currencies to the dollar and control inflation. This opened political space to a comprehensive adoption of the neoliberal agenda in the 1990s. These institutional changes propelled the financialization of the economy and solidified the role of Latin American nations as commodity producers. The premature deindustrialization emerged as a consequence of neoliberalism and declining profitability in the manufacturing sector. Most Latin American countries fell behind from 1980 to the early 2000s.

The 1997 Asian financial crisis rapidly spread to Latin America. The impact was felt through a decline in commodity prices and disruptions in foreign exchange flows, which affected the region, triggering an economic crisis, fueling a growing political resistance against neoliberalism. Around the turn of the century, left-wing governments came to power across many countries, with the notable exceptions of Mexico and Colombia. The Pink Tide period marked the first attempt of center-left governments in Latin America to depart from neoliberalism.

The surge in demand and the financialization of raw materials fueled a boom in commodity prices in the early 2000s. As China continued its industrialization, it ascended as the principal trading partner for Latin America. The governments benefited from the expanded role of Latin America as a commodity producer in the international division of labor. The period witnessed heightened profitability and expanded capital accumulation in the region, leading to a rise in real wages at a pace exceeding labor productivity growth. As a result, income inequality and poverty declined, particularly in South America. However, the Pink Tide was accompanied by further deindustrialization, contributing to the region's expanded re-primarization.

The 2007–08 financial crisis marked a structural crisis of neoliberalism with profound consequences for the Latin American region. As the Pink Tide governments implemented expansionary fiscal policies to stimulate economic growth, a decline in terms of trade and an increase in labor share caused the collapse of profit rates. By the middle 2010s, the reduction in the profit rate drove a fall in capital accumulation and economic growth. The economic crisis led to the political defeat of the Pink Tide governments. However, many Latin American economies caught up with the United States during the Pink Tide.

After elections or soft coups, numerous countries embraced a late neoliberalism agenda. The reinforced neoliberal economic policies, although successful in stabilizing the profit rate through a declining wage share, proved insufficient to counter the decline in capital accumulation. Neoliberalism failed again in delivering higher capital accumulation, resulting in reduced economic growth and higher income inequality in the region.

The economic history of Latin America has highlighted the importance of a "big push" in capital accumulation for successful catching up. In the region, the experiences of catching up have coincided with periods marked by high accumulation rates, often driven by robust profit rates and developmental policies.

In this context, the state assumes a critical role in coordinating investments to mitigate declines in capital productivity and counteract profit squeezes. Moreover, the social control of investment, often achieved through public enterprises, becomes indispensable to foster sustained capital accumulation, particularly during periods of diminishing profit rates.

The state must play a crucial role in coordinating investment to prevent the decline in capital productivity and profit squeeze. The social control of investment through public enterprises is also necessary to foster capital accumulation, particularly during periods of declining profit rates. To achieve catch-up and sustain it, Latin America must transcend the constraints of late neoliberalism. This entails the construction of new political and social institutions prioritizing sustainable and inclusive economic growth as a paramount objective.

Bibliography

Babb, S., and Kentikelenis, A. (2018). International financial institutions as agents of neoliberalism. In Cooper, D., Cooper, M., Konings, M., and Primorose, D. (eds). *The Sage Handbook of Neoliberalism*. Thousand Oaks: Sage.

Gobat, M. (2013). The invention of Latin America: A transnational history of anti-imperialism, democracy, and race. *American Historical Review*, 118, pp. 1345–1375.

Prebisch, R. (1968). *Dinâmica Do Desenvolvimento Latino-Americano*. Rio de Janeiro: Fundo de Cultura.

6 Restarting capitalism in Central and Eastern Europe

From 1917 to 1991, the developing countries had a model of development alternative to capitalism, represented by the centrally planned economy and the Soviet Union, the first nation to identify itself as socialist. Fierce opposition confronted the Soviet Union from its rise until the end of the Second World War. The aftermath of the war implied the broadening of the socialist realm with the incorporation of several Central and Eastern European countries into the Soviet sphere of influence. At the same time, the Cold War was unleashed and implied in a continuous political, economic, diplomatic, and military competition between the Soviet Union and the United States for influence zones around the world.

The three decades after the end of the Second World War, which corresponded to the capitalist Golden Age, were also a period of robust growth for socialist economies. Until the seventies, capitalist economies perceived socialist economies as their competitors. However, in the late 1970s, their dynamism began to fade. At the end of the 1980s, Central and Eastern European countries started their transition from socialist planned economies to capitalism. The region had high-income equality and a well-educated population. Neoliberal market reforms were quickly implemented, commonly called "Shock Therapy," leading to the dismantling of established institutions and their substitution with market-driven mechanisms (Amsden, Kochanowicz and Taylor, 1998).

Central and Eastern European scholars have significantly contributed to the extensive literature on planned economies and development economics. They have played a crucial role in economic debates on the conditions required for countries to achieve development. For instance, their contributions to development economics include Chayanov in the relationship between agriculture and industry, Leontief in input–output economics, Rosenstein-Rodan's theory of the Big Push, and Kalecki in the theory of effective demand. The discussions about imperialism and Marxism include names like Lenin, Trotsky, and Lange.

Despite these critical contributions, their theories were largely ignored in favor of market fundamentalism. The dominant view was that the market mechanism would promote economic growth. Like in Latin America and Africa, the World Bank and International Monetary Fund promoted liberalization through conditional loans. The shock therapy approach led to economic instability, high unemployment, inflation, a decline in output, and a collapse of health indicators.

DOI: 10.4324/9781003223382-7

The region possesses natural resources, mainly gas and fertile lands, high educational level and income equality which have the potential to contribute to economic growth. After 1990, many countries diminished their manufacturing share in the overall economy, relying instead on primary commodities to stimulate their economies, and expanding services.

By the end of 1991, the Soviet Union had disintegrated, leading to its division into multiple countries. Subsequently, Central and Eastern European countries underwent a massive transition to capitalism through comprehensive market reforms. The toolkit comprised bankruptcy policies, tight monetary policy, trade and capital account liberalization, and rapid privatization (Scheiring and Lawrence, 2023). Many believed the vast privatization of state-owned enterprises would boost labor productivity and spur growth. It was taken for granted that the capital previously allocated to the military-industrial complex would spontaneously migrate to other private sectors, positively impacting the economy.

The reforms placed a strong emphasis on property rights and the significance of the price mechanism, while assigning a relatively minor role in institutional development. The expectation was that capital inflows would bring modern management and technology. Workers who lost their jobs in state-owned enterprises were expected to find employment in manufacturing and service firms. Low real wages were seen as critical for fostering international competition, with "stick and carrot" incentives used to revive the region's economies. However, despite low real wages and incentives, neoliberal reforms failed to reignite output growth, leading to deindustrialization and high-income inequality. The output collapsed, and inflation soared after implementing market reforms.

Many Central and Eastern European countries began negotiations for their accession to the European Union (EU) in the mid-1990s. These countries included the Czech Republic, Hungary, Poland, Estonia, Lithuania, Latvia, Slovakia, and Slovenia, all of which joined the EU in 2004. These last five countries also adopted the Euro between 2007 and 2014. The accession of Bulgaria and Romania occurred in 2007, and Croatia became a member in 2013. This marked the integration of these economies into the EU, leading to the adoption of new technical and institutional practices within these countries (Foley and Marquetti, 1999). It also involved their integration into the heart of capitalist economies through investments and participation in more complex value chains, often serving as suppliers of labor-intensive activities.

Access to the EU has been selective. In some cases, countries had an easier process, while others had to wait or are still waiting for the accession. Serbia, Bosnia-Herzegovina, Albania, among others, remain in the negotiation phase of their accession to the EU. Notably, countries under the influence of the Russian Federation did not apply for EU membership. In 1992, the Russian Federation was accepted by the Council of Europe. However, as the country recovered from the effects of the transition, there was a gradual departure from the Council of Europe. In 2022, the country was expelled from the Council of Europe. After the Ukraine war, Georgia, the Republic of Moldova, and Ukraine applied for EU membership.

In the late 1990s and early 2000s, these now capitalist countries recovered as they integrate into the world economy, particularly with Western Europe. In the 2000s, the countries in the region benefited from establishing more robust and functional state structures. This period was marked by the consolidation of their capitalist economic systems. The rise in commodity prices proved especially advantageous for nations rich in natural resources, notably the Russian Federation and Ukraine.

During the 2000s, the drive of developed economies like Germany, France, Italy, and the Netherlands to lower labor costs and higher profitability led to a surge in productive investments within the newly admitted EU member states. Notably, countries in Central and Eastern Europe with larger populations became prime destinations for European investments and vital markets for European products. The countries outside the EU specialized in supplying commodities to the EU. The economies of both groups of countries intensified their ties with the economic dynamics of the EU. The economic growth in the region picked up during the late 1990s and early 2000s.

However, the 2007 financial crisis had a significant impact on the region, leading to lower growth rates in many countries during the 2010s. Central and Eastern European economies, in particular, were severely affected as they adopted measures that involved reductions in wages, pensions, and government expenditures. Countries outside the EU also felt the crisis, primarily due to lower growth rates and a decrease in commodity demand. As Europe gradually overcame the effects of the crisis, the economic trajectories of Central and Eastern European countries began to diverge. EU member states intensified their economic performance, deepening their integration with Western Europe and the United States. Meanwhile, countries outside the EU, particularly the Russian Federation, increased their ties with other developing nations, particularly in East Asia. The question of which group will be more successful in catching up in the following decades remains open, especially as international competition between the United States and China intensifies.

This chapter investigates the economic performance of Central and Eastern European countries before and after the transition in the early 1990s. Our analysis covers the period from 1970 to 2019. As in previous chapters, we employ the Extended Penn World Tables, version 7.0, to track changes in the region's labor productivity, capital productivity, and profit rates. These variables serve as essential indicators to assess whether the region is making progress in catching up with or falling behind the U.S. economy.

The data availability for the period before the 1990s is limited, and there is information for five countries, Albania, Bulgaria, Hungary, Poland, and Romania, from 1970 to 2019. For the period 1990 to 2019, there are data for thirteen nations: Belarus, Bosnia and Herzegovina, the Czech Republic, Croatia, Georgia, Lithuania, Latvia, the Republic of Moldova, the Russian Federation, Serbia, Slovakia, Slovenia, and Ukraine.

The chapter is organized into four sections. The first section briefly introduces Central Eastern Europe's economic performance before and after the transition to capitalism, including the breakdown of the centrally planning system and the emergence of peripheral capitalism. The second section explores the relationship between technical change and profit rate in Central and Eastern European nations. The third section investigates capital accumulation in the region. The fourth presents two possible economic pathways, one aligned with Western European countries, and another led by Russia with strong ties with Asian nations.

From breakdown to peripheral capitalism

At the end of the 1960s, in the Golden Age apex, socialist countries were perceived as an effective threat to capitalism. However, there were sights that the economic growth dynamic associated with the reconstruction after the Second World War was starting to fade. In the Soviet Union, the government of Nikita Khrushchev, between 1953 and 1964, promoted some mild reforms. However, they were overturned after his fall and the rise of Leonid Brezhnev to the leadership.

In the then Czechoslovak Socialist Republic (or Czechoslovakia, later divided into the Czech Republic and Slovakia), the episode known as the Prague Spring in 1968 represented a tentative reform blocked by a foreign invasion of the Warsaw Pact forces, the military alliance between the socialist nations. In 1970, there were strikes and protests in Poland, contributing to the resignation of the then-Polish leader Gomulka. Hungary, after the 1956 Soviet invasion, was able to promote some reforms.

The 1970s were described by the last Soviet leader, Mikhail Gorbachev, as the Era of Stagnation in the Soviet Union. Improvements in the production of consumer goods did not follow the successful development of the heavy and defense industries. The debate about the causes of economic stagnation in the Soviet Union remains to this day. Failures of planning and control, the lack of reforms, and the high level of military expenditures generated by the Cold War are some reasons usually pointed out for the stagnation. Nonetheless, the Soviet Union and, by extension, the Central and Eastern European countries, benefited from rising oil prices in the 1970s. Oil exports prompted economic growth and reduced the impetus for reforms.

At the beginning of the 1980s, tensions arose with the changes in the global environment, and oil prices declined. Terms of trade declined sharply following the advent of neoliberalism and the increase in interest rates by the Federal Reserve. Moreover, the region's economic systems lacked technological dynamism with growing difficulty in incorporating technical advances outside the military sector (Amsden, Kochanowicz and Taylor, 1998).

In the Soviet Union, economic problems and the turbulent succession process of Leonid Brezhnev with the ephemerous governments of Andropov and Chernenko led to the rise of Gorbachev. There were subtle criticisms and demands for reforms in some countries like Czechoslovakia, Hungary, and the German Democratic Republic, also known as East Germany. Bulgaria and Romania were subject to more authoritarian governments, and the dissatisfaction with their government was not visible due to the repressive nature of these regimes. In Poland, criticism was more explicit. The strike at the Gdansk shipyard and the formation of the Trade Union

Solidarity under the leadership of Lech Walesa marked the 1980s. Mass demonstrations were against the government until 1982, and repression followed suit with minor concessions.

In the 1980s, the planned economies of Central and Eastern Europe faced significant challenges. These economies operated without institutions capable of delivering a democratic decision-making process, meaning that workers did not participate in decisions to organize production. The regimes were inefficient, relying excessively on central economic planning to guarantee resource allocation. Resource allocation was centralized within the political party, with bureaucracy playing a significant role in determining the production levels in the economies.

As a result, there was low labor and capital productivity (Foley and Marquetti, 1999), an insufficient supply of goods, and long queues were common in the region's countries. The lack of quality in consumer goods produced was also notable. Low wages engendered reduced incentives to adopt labor-saving techniques. Furthermore, the system failed to reward high-performing workers, providing low incentives for proper job engagement (Cockshott and Cottrell, 1993).

Despite the challenges, centrally planned economies achieved significant progress in education and industrialization through their economic policies. Additionally, compared to capitalist nations, they exhibited high levels of equality. These accomplishments occurred in a context marked by trade embargoes from the United States. In addition, the Soviet planning regime was shaped by the demands of military production during the arms race, starting from a lower level of economic development compared to the US economy (Kotz, 2023).

The stagnation and crises in the 1980s placed political pressure on these countries. Austerity measures were implemented in indebted nations such as Romania, Bulgaria, and Poland, leading to a decline in living standards. The Gorbachev government policies, known as Perestroika (meaning "restructuring") and Glasnost (meaning "transparency"), aimed to promote economic and political reform, were launched in 1985. The policies in the Soviet Union inspired growing demands for reform in Central and Eastern Europe.

Hobsbawm (1996) pointed out that the political reforms created more openness to criticism and political participation in socialist countries. However, economic reforms were unable to overcome the previous patterns of low growth. Glasnost advanced as Perestroika failed. These developments opened the space for the demise of the "real" socialist regimes in Europe. Starting with the fall of the Berlin Wall in 1989, a series of regime changes occurred at the beginning of the 1990s, resulting in the reunification of Germany, the division of Czechoslovakia, and later the fragmentation of the Soviet Union and the formation of the Russian Federation.

In 1990, the Central and Eastern European countries could be considered semi-industrialized economies with a highly skilled labor force. Another prominent feature of the region was income equality, which was shared across these societies. This high-income equality and skilled labor were two positive aspects of the region's economies, which were also key ingredients presented in the successful experiences of East Asian countries.

In the aftermath of the dissolution of the Soviet Union in 1991, it gave rise to 15 independent countries. In Europe, these nations include Belarus, Estonia, Georgia, Latvia, Lithuania, Moldova, Ukraine, and the Russian Federation, which spans both Europe and Asia. Meanwhile, in Asia, we find Armenia, Azerbaijan, Kazakhstan, Kyrgyzstan, Tajikistan, Turkmenistan, and Uzbekistan.

The former Yugoslavia underwent a similar process, resulting in the division into six distinct nations: Croatia, Montenegro, Serbia, Slovenia, Bosnia and Herzegovina, and North Macedonia (formerly known as Macedonia). This fragmentation of Yugoslavia was marked by violent conflicts, particularly during the early 1990s. Kosovo also sought independence from Serbia and declared itself as an independent state, although its sovereignty remains a subject of ongoing international debate. In contrast, Czechoslovakia peacefully separated into two countries, the Czech Republic and Slovakia.

In the early 1990s, the Central and Eastern European countries began to adopt a neoliberal economic model that aimed to deregulate their economies quickly. The goal was to solve economic problems through the market mechanism, which involved disregarding all the previous qualities of the planning system. This approach was commonly referred to as "shock therapy," as it rapidly freed markets and allowed the price system to work.

The local elite embraced the free market ideas. The World Bank and the International Monetary Fund also pushed for free market reforms through conditional lending. In this context, the primary goal of the institution reforms was to ensure private property rights and the enforcement of contracts and laws. Privatizing state-owned enterprises was the primary tool used to modernize the regional economy. However, there needed to be more emphasis on developing institutions that could facilitate long-term economic growth (Amsden, Kochanowicz and Taylor, 1998).

As a result, the region's output collapsed after 1990. The rapid deregulation of prices led to high inflation, which provoked a drop in real wages, negatively impacting demand. The decline in internal demand caused a corresponding drop in output, as firms had to adjust their production to match the lower demand in the short run. Additionally, declining exports of the socialist bloc further exacerbated the fall in demand, resulting in negative consequences on the supply side. Moreover, a mortality crisis emerged, leading to a significant increase in death rates and a sharp decline in life expectancy (Scheiring and Lawrence, 2023). In the case of post-socialist Russia, criminal groups dominated the economy, and a class of opportunistic operators emerged to seize the previous regime's assets (Kotz, 2023).

Figure 6.1 displays Central and Eastern European output's growth rates and median from 1970 to 2019. There was a sharp decline in output growth rates in the early 1990s. Furthermore, the impact of the transition varied across countries, leading to significant variability in growth rates during the 1990s. The adverse effects were less pronounced in nations with stronger economic ties to Western countries and those that did not experience border disintegration.

Between the mid-1990s and the early 2000s, economic growth expanded significantly. The average GDP growth rate for the 18 Central and Eastern European countries in the 2000s was 4.7 percent per year, a marked improvement compared

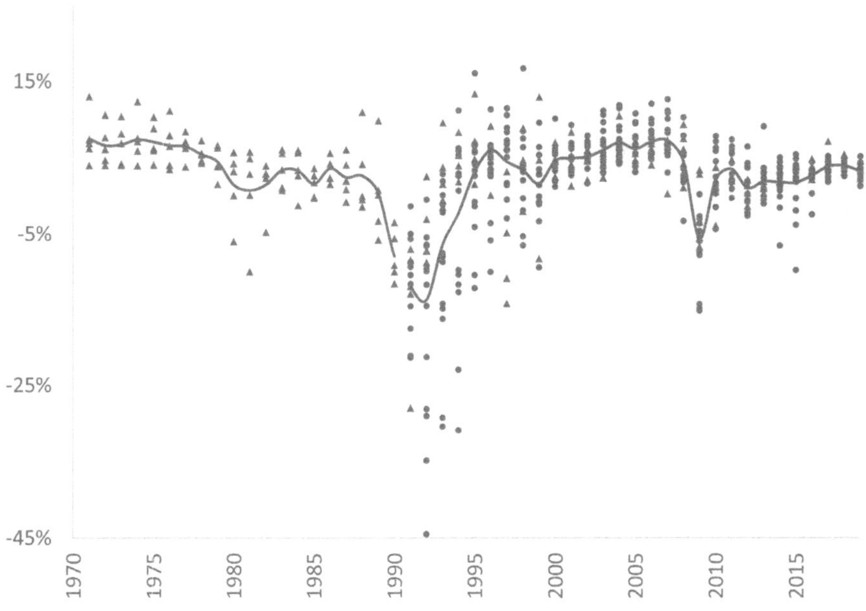

Figure 6.1 Central and Eastern European GDP growth rates and its average, 1970–2019.

Note: The sample includes four countries represented by triangles from 1970 to 2019, and 11 countries represented by circles from 1990 to 2019.

Source: EPWT 7.0.

to the −2.7 percent average growth rate during the 1990s. However, economic growth began to decline after the 2007 financial crisis, with the average growth rate in the 2010s dropping to 2.6 percent annually. Nevertheless, there were important differences in the performance between the countries, for example, the countries that entered the EU performed better than those that did not.

Figure 6.2 presents labor productivity for Central and Eastern European countries compared to the US economy. It covers the period from 1970 to 2019 for five countries and from 1990 to 2019 for 13 countries. Bulgaria, Hungary, Poland, and Romania rapidly caught up in labor productivity in the 1970s, followed by a stabilization in their relative labor productivity compared to the US economy during the 1980s. The labor productivity gap expanded in Albania between 1970 and the early 1990s.

The transition years of the 1990s marked one of the fastest and most widespread declines in labor productivity worldwide. Recovery was unequal with different speeds among countries. Over the decade, the labor productivity gap narrowed in five countries: Albania, Hungary, Poland, Slovenia, and Slovakia, while it increased in the other nations.

In the 2000s, Central and Eastern European countries experienced a catch-up in labor productivity. Some benefited from their integration and assessment of the EU, while others saw gains from raising commodity prices. In the 2010s, with the repercussions of the 2007 financial crisis, the pace of catching up decelerated for

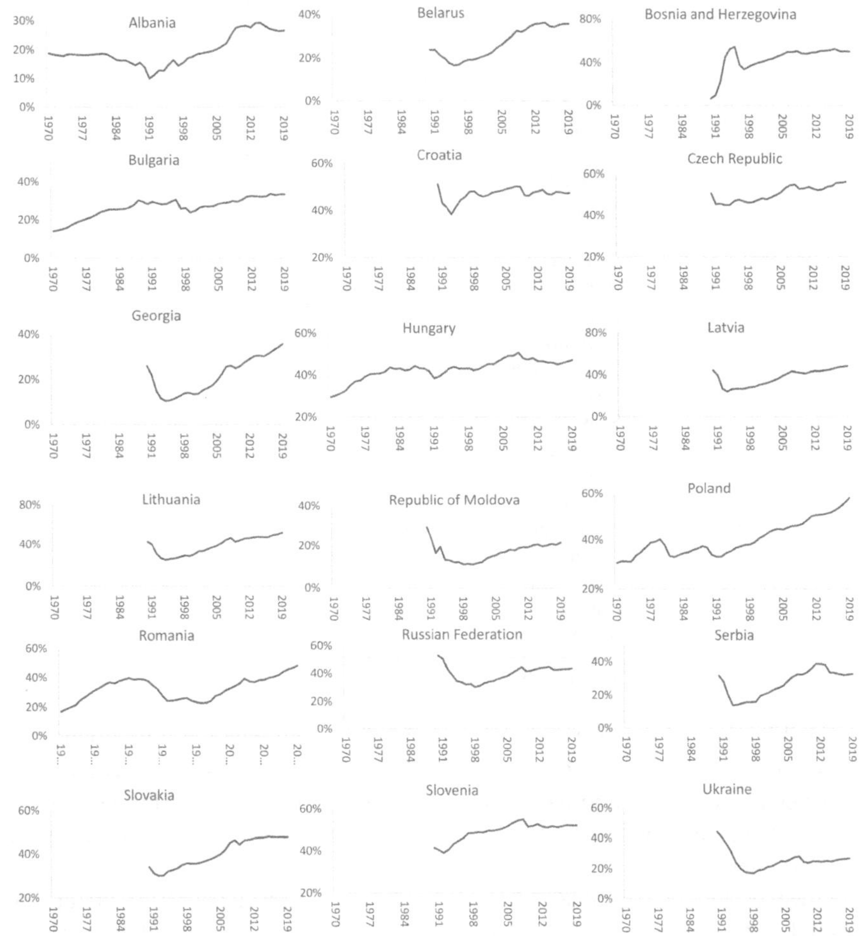

Figure 6.2 Labor productivity in Central and Eastern European countries in relation to the US economy, 1970–2019.

Source: EPWT 7.0.

some and stagnated for others. The adoption of the Euro apparently did not affect the dynamics of catching up.

By 2019, the labor productivity in Central and Eastern European nations in relation to the United States had generally increased compared to 1990. The exceptions were the Russian Federation, Ukraine, and the Republic of Moldova, which in 2019 had a lower labor productivity gap than in 1990. In 1990, the Russian Federation, the largest economy in the region, had a labor productivity rate of 52.9% of that of the United States. However, by 2019, it had declined to 43.5%. Ukraine faced the most dramatic transition to capitalism, experiencing in 2019 lower absolute values of GDP and labor productivity than in 1990.

Table 6.1 Variation in the number of workers in Central and Eastern European countries between 1990 and 2019

Country	*gN*
Bulgaria	−16.5%
Belarus	−16.0%
The Czech Republic	1.2%
Hungary	−8.1%
Republic of Moldova	−30.6%
Poland	7.1%
Romania	−20.4%
Russian Federation	−4.8%
Slovakia	0.8%
Slovenia	−7.3%
Ukraine	−34.2%
Georgia	−52.1%
Albania	−18.7%
Bosnia and Herzegovina	−59.2%
Croatia	−16.6%
Lithuania	−19.1%
Latvia	−28.5%
Serbia	−37.0%

Source: EPWT 7.0.

Notably, the reduction in the labor productivity gap was more pronounced in the countries that participated in the EU enlargement to the East. On average, these countries displayed around half of the labor productivity of the United States in 2019. Poland stood out as the former centrally planned economy with the highest labor productivity.

However, the labor productivity growth in most of these countries can also attributed to the decrease in the number of workers from 1990 to 2019, as shown in Table 6.1. The number of workers increased in just three countries, the Czech Republic, Poland, and Slovakia. Five countries experienced a workforce reduction above 30 percent, namely, the Republic of Moldova, Ukraine, Georgia, Bosnia and Herzegovina, and Servia. Interestingly, these are nations that are not part of EU. This declined can be attributed to falling natality rates and increased immigration. As immigration gains prominence, countries exporting labor rely more on personal remittances, but this, coupled with low birth rates, can strain social security due to a shrinking employment-to-retired ratio.

Technical change and profit rate Before and after the fall

This section investigates the relationship between technical change and profit rates in the economies of Central and Eastern Europe. During economic development, capitalist countries typically experience declining capital productivity and increasing labor productivity. An interesting question is whether the same pattern occurred in the centrally planned economies.

Typically, follower countries tend to exhibit lower labor productivity and higher capital productivity than their leader counterparts. Interestingly, this pattern is not observed in the former centrally planned economies, as depicted in Figure 6.3. In 1990, these nations had lower labor and capital productivities when compared to the United States, except Bulgaria, which demonstrated higher capital productivity. In the case of these economies, catching up would involve an increase in both labor and capital productivities. Institutional innovations and new processes of production could partially drive this growth in capital productivity. Moreover, these countries would have a higher profitability than the United States only if they had a lower wage share.

Figure 6.4 presents the rates of change in capital productivity and labor productivity, denoted as the pair (ga, gx), for the entire period of 1970–2019, as well as for the sub-periods 1970–1980 and 2000–2019. The results reveal a long-term trend of labor-saving, capital-using Marx-biased technical change from 1970 to 2019, except for Poland, which exhibited positive growth rates in both labor and capital productivities.

These findings remain consistent for the 1970–1980 and 1980–2019 subperiods. Except for Albania, the other four countries displayed high growth rates in labor productivity during the 1970s. However, the results should be interpreted with caution due to the limited data available for only a few countries in the 1970s and 1980s. Interestingly, the countries in the region generally displayed a similar

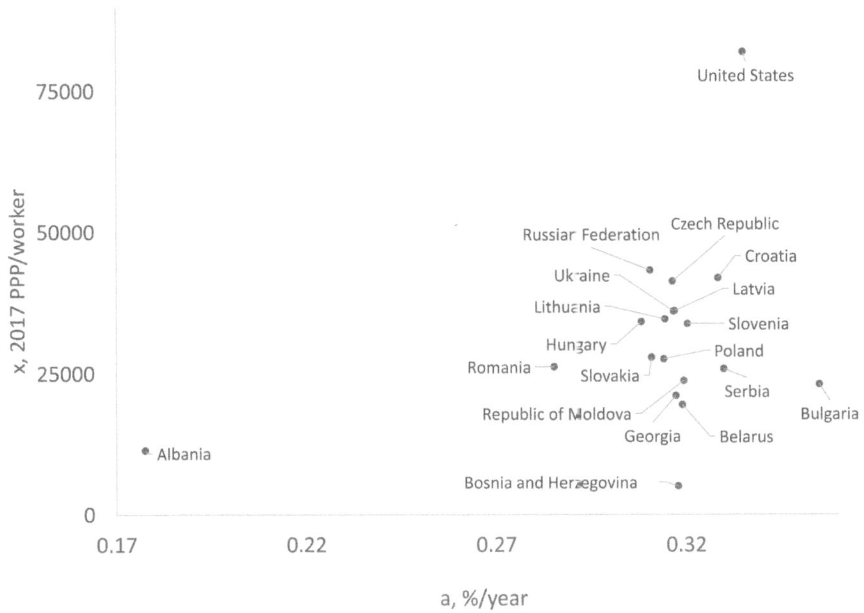

Figure 6.3 The comparison between capital productivity and labor productivity in Central and Eastern European countries and the United States in 1990.

Source: EPWT 7.0.

Figure 6.4 The growth rates of capital and labor productivities, (ga, gx), in Central and Eastern European countries, 1970–2019, 1970–1980, 1980–2019.

Source: EPWT 7.0.

pattern of technical change to that observed in the leading capitalist economy, the United States.

The sample size considerably increases when we turn our analysis from 1990 to 2019. Figure 6.5 illustrates the results for Central and Eastern European countries in this period. In the long term, the labor-saving, capital-using pattern of technical change displayed ten cases, including Belarus, Croatia, the Czech Republic, Georgia, Hungary, Latvia, Russian Federation, Serbia, Slovenia, and the Republic of Moldova. The labor-saving, capital saving occurred in seven countries, Albania, Bosnia and Herzegovina, Bulgaria, Lithuania, Poland, Romania, and Slovakia, the last five countries joined the EU. In contrast, Ukraine experienced labor-using, capital-using technical regression. Notably, ten out of the 18 countries approached their capital productivity in relation to the United States.

From 1990 to 2019, two main phases of technical change emerged. In the first phase (1990–2000), six countries exhibited a Marx-biased pattern: Albania, Belarus, Bosnia and Herzegovina, the Czech Republic, Latvia, Slovakia, and Slovenia. Romania, on the other hand, experienced a reverse Marx-biased pattern, marked by declining labor productivity and rising capital productivity. Bosnia and Herzegovina, Poland, Bulgaria, and Hungary displayed a factor-augmenting technical change pattern during this phase, with both labor and capital productivities expanding. Meanwhile, Georgia, Latvia, Belarus, Serbia, the Republic of Moldova, the Russian Federation, and Ukraine encountered technical regress, with both labor and capital productivity declining. While Serbia suffered from armed conflict, the other countries emerged from the former Soviet Union. To simplify the analysis, growth rates within the open interval of –0.1 percent to 0.1 percent are considered as zero.

This phase marked the rapid transition from a centralized planned economy to capitalism. The Central and Eastern European region faced output decline, rising unemployment, and income inequality. The distinct patterns of technical change were the product of the different impacts of the demise of their economic model.

In countries that experienced a labor-saving, capital-saving technical change or a Marx-biased technical progress with higher increases in labor productivity a more “soft-transition” to capitalism was evident. This shift toward raising capital productivity often coincided with deindustrialization, which became a noticeable trend in many nations. The lack of industrial policies and privatization initiatives contributed to a decline in industrial production across the region. Technical regress was associated with the fragmentation of the Soviet Union, where supply chains were disrupted, leading to a disarticulation of the economic structure.

In the second phase, from 2000 to 2019, 13 out of 18 countries displayed a labor-saving, capital-saving technical change, with both productivities rising over time. The countries with this pattern include Albania, Belarus, Croatia, the Czech Republic, Georgia, Poland, the Russian Federation, the Republic of Moldova, Romania, Serbia, Slovakia, and Ukraine. Bosnia and Herzegovina, Bulgaria, Hungary, Latvia, and Slovenia exhibited the Marx-biased technical change pattern, also observed in the US economy. The productivity of capital in relation to the United States increased in 16 countries.

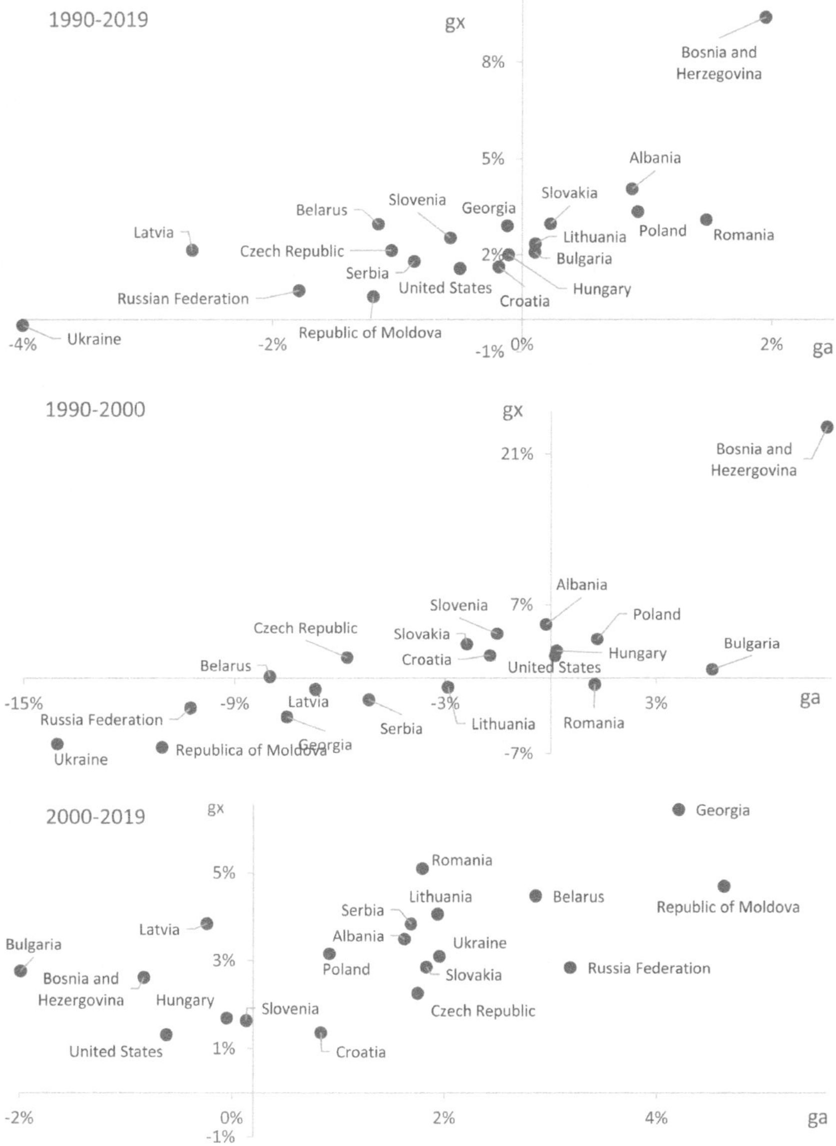

Figure 6.5 The growth rates of capital and labor productivities, (ga, gx), in Central and Eastern European countries, 1990–2019, 1990–2000, 2000–2019.

Source: EPWT 7.0.

The results reflected the higher GDP growth driven by the new roles embraced by these countries in the capitalist economies. The eastward enlargement of the EU allowed many nations to benefit from special conditions associated with the assessment, including investments in infrastructure, subsidies, and the enlarged consumer market. Some countries specialized in industrial activities that complemented the production in main European economies, while others entered into the service sectors with high labor productivity. The economic structure of most Central and Eastern countries moved in the direction of the developed countries.

Other countries primarily entered international markets as providers of commodities and natural resources, relying on the increasing global demand for raw materials and energy (Kotz, 2023). Additionally, worker remittances played a vital role in some of these nations. The Russian Federation emerged as a significant economic and military power. In 2000, it ranked ninth globally with a GDP corresponding to 15.5 percent of the U.S. economy, and by 2019, it had risen to the sixth position with a production equivalent to 19.7 percent of the U.S. production.

Technical change and profit rates are interrelated. The path of the profit rate depends on capital productivity and the functional distribution of income, which is determined by the evolution of the average real wage relative to labor productivity. When labor productivity outpaces average wage growth, the profit share rises, leading to an increase in the profit rate.

Figure 6.6 illustrates the net profit rates for eighteen Central and Eastern European nations spanning the years 1970 to 2019. Before 1990, the profit rates in these countries may be interpreted as a measure of the economic surplus which was used to capital accumulation, maintaining the social consumption, and the state bureaucracy. For the countries with data available from 1970 to 1990, the profit rate remained relatively stable in the 1970s but experienced a sharp decline in the 1980s, mirroring trends seen in many capitalist nations worldwide. During the 1980s, centrally planned economies faced a substantial decrease in their ability to generate economic surpluses.

In the early 1990s, profit rates sharply declined as a consequence of the crisis linked to shock therapy and the transition to a capitalist economy. The nations formed by the former Soviet republics and Serbia experienced rates near zero, suggesting that these nations had the hardest impacts from transitioning as their economic system were disintegrated.

From the middle 1990s to the 2007 financial crises, the profit rate increased as the countries adapted to the market economy. This rise in profitability was driving by expanding capital productivity and declining wage share. The higher capital productivity resulted from a combination of factors, including institutional change, capital destruction from deindustrialization, rise in terms of trade, and the fall in wage share from reduced worker organization. However, in the 2010s, following the financial crisis, the profit rate either declined or remained relatively stable in most countries.

During the mid-1990s, one notable characteristic of the region was the low profit rate. This reduced capital profitability was a legacy of the centrally planned years and the economic crisis stemming from the disintegration. In 2019, many Central and Eastern European countries saw their profit rates return to similar or slightly higher 1990 levels, with Bulgaria and Poland exhibiting the highest profitability in the 2010s. However, it remained lower in the Czech Republic, Belarus, Latvia, the Republic of Moldova, Ukraine, and the Russian Federation. Notably, the last five countries were former Soviet republics.

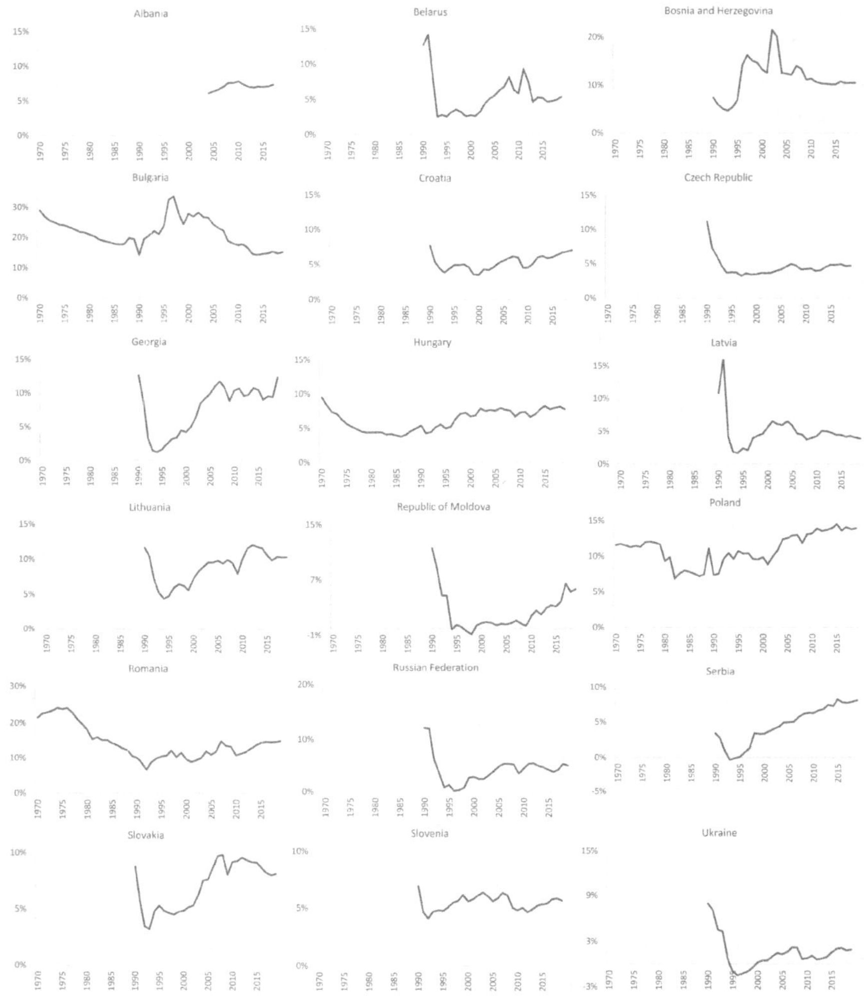

Figure 6.6 Rate of profit in Central and Eastern European countries, 1970–2019.
Source: EPWT 7.0.

Capital accumulation in the Central and Eastern European countries

A necessary condition for catching up is that the follower country's capital accumulation exceeds that of the leader country. As suggested by the Cambridge equation, capital accumulation is determined by profit and savings and investment rates. Before we investigate the capital accumulation in the Central Eastern European economies compared to the United States, let us first examine their net investment rates.

Figure 6.7 depicts the net investment rates in Central and Eastern European countries from 1970 to 2019. Notably, the data for the five centrally planned

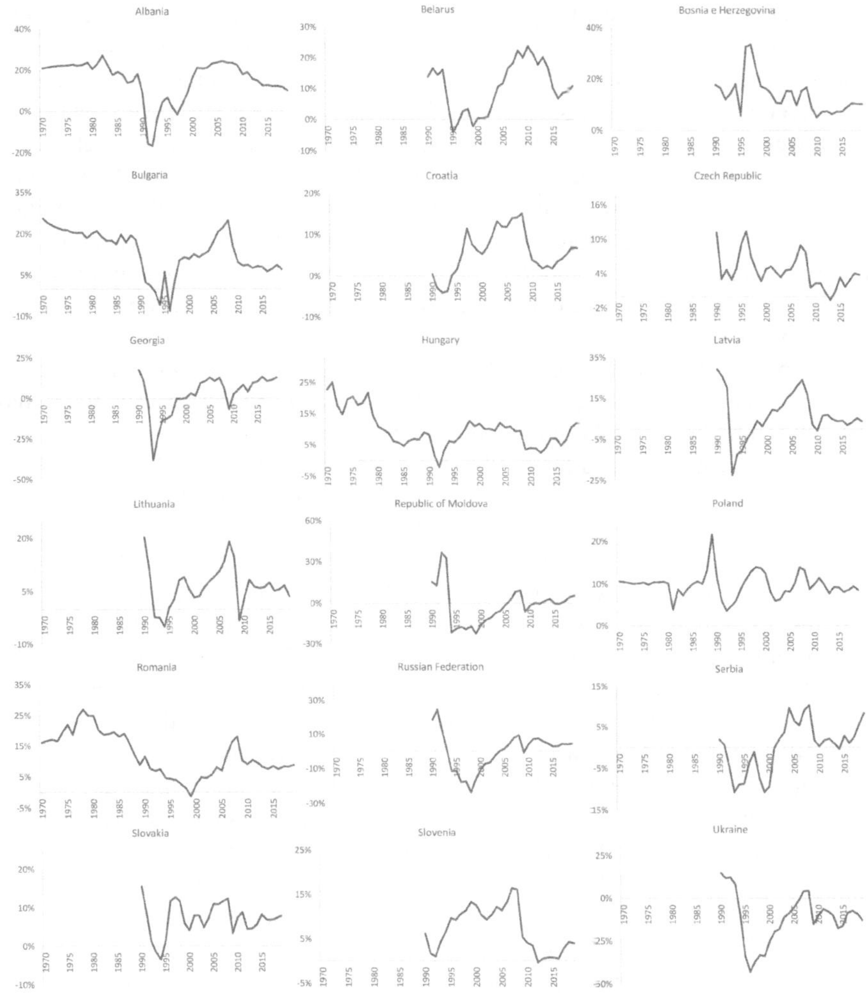

Figure 6.7 The net investment rate in Central and Eastern European countries, 1970–2019.
Source: EPWT 7.0.

economies with information available from 1970 to 1990 reveal high net investment rates and remarkable stability during that period. Hungary, however, experienced a decline in its net investment rate during the 1980s.

After 1990, the net investment rate saw a sharp decline, reaching negative or near-zero values for most countries, except for Bosnia and Herzegovina, the Czech Republic, and Poland. In the late 1990s, there was an overall increase in net investment rates. The countries that emerged from the Soviet Union, as well as Serbia, experienced more pronounced and prolonged declines in net investment rates compared to other nations. In the Republic of Moldova, Ukraine, and the Russian Federation, the net investment turned positive in the mid-2000s.

The assessment in the EU appears to have had a positive impact on net investment. These countries gained access to a range of benefits provided by the EU for its poorest partners, including subsidies, financing funds, and infrastructure investments. Moreover, these countries also received a large amount of external investment.

However, after the 2007 financial crises, there was a decline in the net investment rate for most countries in the region. Poland, perhaps the most successful country in catching up with the United States in the region, was able to maintain a positive net investment rate similar to its years of central planned economy. On the other hand, Ukraine the country with the worst economic trajectory displayed a negative net investment rate after the transition to a capitalist economy, with the exception of a few years.

The profit rate plays a crucial role in determining capital accumulation in capitalist economies. A higher profit rate in a follower country is a central factor contributing to higher capital accumulation compared to a leader country. Figure 6.8 displays the scatterplot and linear fit between the difference in profit rates (r^i-r^{USA}) and capital accumulation ($g_K{}^i$-$g_K{}^{USA}$) for eighteen Central and Eastern European countries in comparison with the United States.

A positive correlation is evident between the difference in profit rates and capital accumulation, signifying that as the difference in profit rates increases, the difference in capital accumulation also rises. However, most Central and Eastern European countries displayed lower capital productivity and profit rates than the United States, despite having a higher profit share. While many countries in the region aimed to increase profitability and competitiveness by reducing the wage share, there are limits to how much real wages can be reduced.

In the region, Bulgaria, Poland, Romania had higher profit rates and capital accumulation through almost all the years under study. Bosnia and Herzegovina, Georgia, Lithuania, and Slovakia exhibited higher profitability and capital accumulation in the 2000s and 2010s. These countries also exhibited profit rates greater than the largest EU economies, Germany, France, Italy, Spain, and the Netherlands, in 2019 following the EPWT 7.0.

Other countries generally exhibited lower profitability and capital accumulation for all or most of the period under investigation, including the Czech Republic, Serbia, Slovenia, the Republic of Moldova, the Russian Federation, and Ukraine. Despite having lower profit rates and capital accumulation, the Czech Republic, Serbia, and Slovenia maintained their relative distance in labor productivity in relation to the US economy, while the Republic of Moldova, the Russian Federation, and Ukraine fell behind.

The accession to the EU, which was an important factor in resuming growth through increased trade and external investments, did not clearly impact profitability. However, most countries that became full members of the EU usually displayed greater profit rates than the other nations in the region.

Our findings align with the model presented in Chapter 2, highlighting the critical role of increased capital accumulation in the process of catching up. Net investment, acting as a proxy for the net savings rate, measures the ratio of the net social surplus allocated to fixed capital in GDP. Countries that maintained their borders

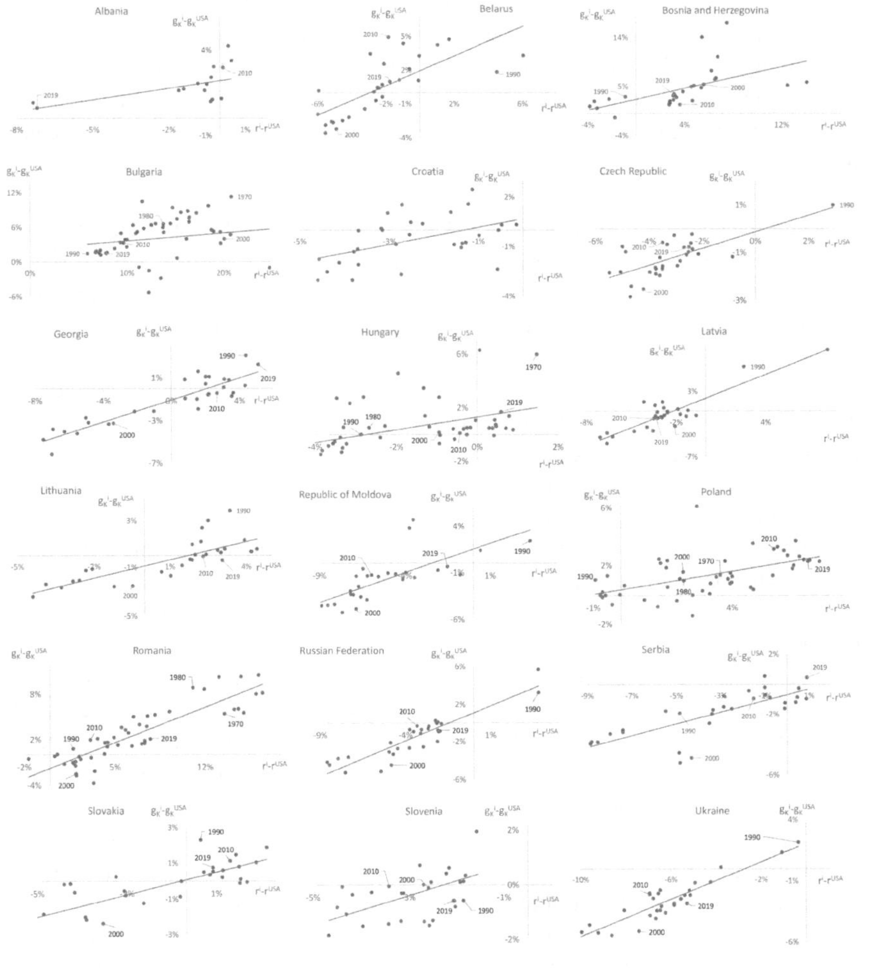

Figure 6.8 The scatterplot between the differences in capital accumulation rates, g_K^i-g_K^{USA}, and profit rates, r^i-r^{USA} for Central and Eastern European countries and the United States: 1970–2019.

Source: EPWT 7.0.

and joined the EU quickly raised their net investment rate and their profit rate. In contrast, countries which emerged from the dissolution of Yugoslavia, which also experienced armed conflicts, and those that succeeded the Soviet Union did not recover their previous net investment rate and profitability.

Restarting capitalism and unequal development: Winners and losers

The transition from former central planned economies to capitalism was tumultuous. The neoliberal shock focused on privatization and restoring rapidly the entire functioning of the price mechanism. However, price deregulation resulted in high inflation that caused a fast decline in real wages, leading to a fall in demand and output. The disintegration of the Soviet Union and Yugoslavia led to the emergence of new nations without functional states and the disruption of existing economic connections between firms, workers, and internal and external markets. In countries where existing states and borders were maintained or where the emergence of new nations was the result of negotiation and mutual agreement, the severity of the crisis was less dramatic.

In the late 1990s and early 2000s, Central and Eastern European countries experienced positive growth as countries transitioned to capitalism. Unsurprisingly, countries that joined the EU and benefited from membership achieved superior economic outcomes. Poland, Bulgaria, Hungary, and Romania had the dual advantage of maintaining their borders and functioning state, and also became EU members.

The integration of Central and Eastern European countries into the capitalist economy can be categorized into two groups. The first entered as special EU partners, aligning with developed capitalist nations. They were able to better capitalize on their skilled labor force and income equality as assets for the new role in the capitalist economy. The second entered as international competitors, a similar condition with other developing countries, relying on commodities export for growth, particularly raw materials and energy. Interestingly, the Republic of Moldova and Ukraine, which belong to the second group, are among the poorest countries in Europe.

The neoliberal integration in the capitalist economy of the Central and Eastern European countries are typical example of combined and uneven development. The specific conditions under which each country transitioned and integrated into the capitalist economy led to significantly different outcomes. It became evident that the mere transition to capitalism was insufficient for achieving growth and catching up, contrary to conventional expectations. Those countries that became members of the EU were able to catch up, benefiting from a special invitation, while many countries that remained outside the EU fell behind.

One remarkable feature of the trajectory in Central and Eastern Europe was a significant decline in the number of workers. Immigration provided labor for the developed countries in the EU. Membership drove higher investments that promoted labor productivity growth. There was a successful complementarity between the new members and the established EU nations. Interesting, most countries that did not join the EU experienced an even stronger trend of declining workforce, coupled with reduced success in boosting labor productivity and increasing wages.

The Russian Federation, the largest economy in the region, managed to recover in the 2000s. Nevertheless, it faces the challenge of having one of the lowest profit rates in the region. Its economy depends on gas and oil exports, despite having high-technology sectors like military equipment and aerospace industries. The country's ability to sustain a stable growth trajectory under these conditions remains uncertain. However, there is a noticeable inclination to shift away from Europe and explore a more complementary arrangement with China. This involves providing energy resources and receiving goods and investments in industrial activities, potentially accelerating the process of catching up.

In a broader context, the ongoing catching-up process in Central and Eastern Europe relies on the ability to foster industrialization and high-value-added services. As most countries experience a decrease in their workforce, the significance of industrial activities in driving labor productivity growth becomes more pronounced. Such growth can support the rise in wages and potentially stem the emigration of labor to other countries.

The role of the state is pivotal in driving the development of the region, as it must formulate policies that support capital accumulation and ensure the provision of infrastructure and public goods. However, the distinct trajectories impose different conditions for an active state role. Countries outside the EU have fallen behind but appear to possess more leeway in implementing policies aimed at fostering catching up through industrialization, despite their lower level of labor productivity. On the other hand, EU members exhibit higher labor productivity and appear well-equipped to adopt new techniques. Nevertheless, EU membership may reduce the autonomy of these countries in designing policies geared towards industrialization. In this context, the Central and Eastern European economies seem to exhibit a bifurcation in their trajectory, some with Western-oriented tendencies and others, under Russian leadership, oriented toward Asia. The question of which economies will be successful in catching up remains to be seen.

Bibliography

Amsden, A., Kochanowicz, J., and Taylor, L. (1998). *The Market Meets Its Match: Restructuring the Economies of Eastern Europe*. Cambridge: Harvard University Press.

Cockshott, P., and Cottrell, A. (1993). *Towards a New Socialism*. London: Coronet Books.

Foley, D., and Marquetti, A. (1999). Productivity, employment and growth in European integration. *Metroeconomica*, 50, pp. 277–300.

Foley, D., Michl, T., and Tavani, D. (2018). *Growth and Distribution*, 2nd edition. Cambridge: Harvard University Press.

Hobsbawm, E. (1996). *The Age of Extremes: A History of the World, 1914-1991*. London: Knopf Doubleday Publishing Group.

Kotz, D. (2023). Imperialism and the Ukraine war. *Review of Radical Political Economics*, 55(4), pp. 568–576.

Scheiring, B., and Lawrence, K. (2023). Deindustrialization, social disintegration, and health: A neoclassical sociological approach. *Theory and Society*, 52, pp. 145–178.

7 The forgotten continent

Falling behind in Africa

European colonialism profoundly affected Africa's economic development under capitalism, particularly during the 19th and 20th Centuries. After World War II, the decolonization began. In 1945, Africa had only four independent states: Liberia, South Africa, Egypt, and Ethiopia. During the 1950s and 1960s, the number of independent nations in the region grew, and by the middle 1970s, most African states had achieved independence. This newfound self-determination gave rise to expectations of an economic upturn that would accelerate development and promote living standards.

With few exceptions, African economies under European rule relied on large subsistence sector and the exploitation of natural resources. After gaining independence, many countries adopted an import substitution industrialization strategy, which helped spur economic growth. As the nation-states attempted to solidify their power, internal conflicts erupted, fueled by ethnic animosities and territorial border disputes. The late 1970s and 1980s witnessed a surge of violence and civil wars in many countries as Cold War alignment replaced colonialism. The conflicts expanded as the Golden Age ended and the economic growth declined.

In the 1980s, Africa faced a severe setback in its social and economic development as declining commodity prices, combined with the debt crisis, led to increasing reliance on foreign loans and aid. With the end of the Cold War and the rise of neoliberalism, international institutions such as the International Monetary Fund and the World Bank imposed adjustment policies and loan conditionalities on countries, generically known as Structural Adjustment Programs. The primary goal was to reform the state, combat corruption, and stimulate growth. However, the results were disappointing, as neoliberalism failed to generate economic growth. Instead, it heightened poverty, inequality, and social unrest in numerous African nations.

In the early XXI century, Africa's economic growth has improved, primarily due to better terms of trade and a positive outlook on development. However, many challenges still need to be addressed, particularly regarding countries' ability to expand capital accumulation and incorporate technical changes to achieve sustainable growth.

This chapter investigates catching up and falling behind in African countries between 1970 and 2019. However, the study of African countries' economic performances presents notable challenges due to limitations in the dataset. The availability of reliable data is limited, and the quality of the information requires careful

DOI: 10.4324/9781003223382-8

consideration when interpreting findings. The current chapter is an exploratory study, providing an essential starting point for future research to enhance the understanding of African economies.

The chapter is divided into four sections. The first section provides a brief economic history of African countries following their independence. It examines regional features and addresses key factors that impact economic development, including political instability and integration with the global economy. The second section outlines the impact of technical change on the profit rate in African economies. The third section discusses the linkages among natural resources, the profit rate, and capital accumulation. The final section investigates how the African countries, the ones with the lowest labor productivity globally, can catch up with the leading country.

A brief history of African countries after independence

The analysis of Africa's economic growth must start with acknowledging a distinction between the regions of North Africa and sub-Saharan Africa. Since ancient times, the Northern region has had strong ties to Western Asia and Southern Europe. Sub-Saharan Africa had fewer contacts, mostly in coastal regions. It experienced a slave trade associated with plantations on the American continent at the early years of capitalism in the XV and XVI Centuries.

In the XIX Century, European countries began penetrating the continent in a process known as "the scramble of Africa." During European colonialism, the dominant colonial powers in Africa were France and Great Britain, backed by secondary colonial players including Portugal, Spain, Belgium, Italy, and Germany. European rule remained dominant until the second half of the 20th Century, exploiting African populations and resources. Notice that distinctive characteristics and consequences marked European colonial rule. Germany was forced to relinquish its African colonies after World War I.

Colonial powers pursued policies aimed at extracting profits from their colonies. However, these policies also increased investments in commodities production and transportation. They further led to the establishment of administrative structures in these regions, which encountered varying degrees of resistance or collaboration from the African peoples and the local population. These interactions led to subordinate capitalist development and the emergence of a local elite.

European colonialism resulted in minimal benefits for the African population. It tactically exploited ethnic divisions to strengthen European dominance over the territories. Furthermore, racist ideologies were employed to deny political power to indigenous people.

The political struggle toward self-determination and independence gained momentum after World War II. The Fifth Pan-African Congress held in Manchester in October 1945 was a relevant sign of a new stage in the struggle for decolonization. The African countries' independence combined external and internal factors. The main external factors were the fragility of the former colonial powers after the World War II, combined with the economic difficulties and the emergence of the Cold War.

The internal factors driving decolonization movements included increase nationalism, revolt against colonial exploitation and expanded literacy and education in certain countries. North African countries achieved independence through nationalist movements against European rule, as exemplified by the War of Independence of Algeria. Egypt formally gained independence in 1922, reduced ties with Western powers, and pursued national policies after the 1952 revolution.

In sub-Saharan Africa, nationalist movements also played a role in the struggle for independence. These movements were directly related to the dissolution of the former colonial territories controlled by the United Kingdom, France, Portugal, Belgium, and Spain. The colonial regions were ruled by Europeans and had little resemblance to the cultural and historical heritage of the African people. As the imperial powers crumbled, former colonial territories pursued independence, in some cases with the collaboration of the European powers, in others against them, but always under the sight of the Cold War alignment.

The independence movements faced obstacles in their early stages. Initially, the European countries responded with a combination of repression and concessions to delay or prevent independence. The effectiveness of these responses varied, leading to differing levels of violence. In former British colonies, transitions were peaceful in some cases, while in others, there was violent repression.

The 1956 Suez Crisis was a landmark in the independence process of African countries. The crisis was triggered by the invasion of Egypt by Israeli forces, with the support of Great Britain and France. European countries aimed to reverse the nationalization of the Suez Channel promoted by the Egyptian government. The three allies defeated the Egyptian army. After intense pressure from the United States and the Soviet Union, the invaders withdrew. The aftermath of the Suez Crisis exposed the limitations of Great Britain and France's power.

British colonies faced different independence processes. For instance, in 1949, Gold Coast (later known as Ghana) experienced a period of repression and ultimately emerged as the first British African colony to gain independence in 1957. There was a long fight in Kenya with the Mau-Mau uprising. Moreover, there were relatively peaceful transitions in other territories, as in the cases of Sudan (1956), Nigeria (1960), Uganda (1960), Sierra Leone (1961), Gambia (1965), Botswana and Lesotho (1966), and Swaziland (rename Eswatini in 2018) gained independence in 1968.

Political complexities and social turbulence emerged in the independence of Libya in 1951, and Somalia in 1960. Social tensions also occurred in the dissolution of the former Federation of Rhodesia and Nyasaland, also known as Central Africa Federation, leading to the independence of Malawi and Zambia in 1964, and Rhodesia in 1965, later becoming Zimbabwe in 1980. Zimbabwe's journey to independence was marked by a civil war, opposing the white minority rule and the local opposition. Tanzania obtained independence in 1961 amid political unrest, particularly associated with the Zanzibar revolution. The archipelagos of Mauritius and Seychelles achieved independence in 1968 and 1976. Eritrea's independence was finally obtained in 1991 after a prolonged war.

The French empire which was declining before the Second World War was further destabilized with conflicts between Axis-aligned Vichy France and the Allies.

Concessions were made to the colonial territories to maintain its empire. However, protests demanding self-rule began in Algeria as early as 1945. The French military crushed the Malagasy Uprising in Madagascar in 1947 and repressed the insurrection in Cameroon in 1955. France granted independence to Morocco and Tunisia in 1956. The French Fifth Republic and a new constitution were established as Algeria's conflicts escalated to war. The new constitution created the French Community in 1958, replacing the former French Union. The colonial territories held a referendum where only French citizens could vote. While most of them approved the new constitution, Guinea rejected it, becoming independent in 1958.

In 1960, several African countries proclaimed independence from France. Madagascar, Chad, Congo (Congo-Brazzaville), Gabon, and the Central African Republic became independent within the French Community. Dahomey (later renamed Benin), Niger, Upper Volta (later renamed Burkina Faso), Côte d'Ivoire, Senegal, Mali, and Mauritania chose to withdraw from the community. Cameroon (with the integration of the British-administered Southern Cameroons in 1961) and Togo, both United Nations Trust Territories under French mandate, became independent in the same year. Algeria achieved independence in 1962 after a brutal war. In addition, there were political turbulence and conflicts in the Comoros, which gained independence in 1975, and in Djibouti, which became independent in 1977.

Other newly independent countries included the then-named Republic of Congo in 1960, formerly a personal possession of King Leopold of Belgium and one of the most violent colonial regimes in the continent, it later became the Republic of Zaire. Since 1997, it has been known as Democratic Republic of the Congo (D. R. Congo), established in a turbulent process. Rwanda and Burundi, whose former colonial ruler was Belgium, became independent in 1962. Equatorial Guinea gained independence from Spain in 1968. The former Portuguese colonies achieved independence through long wars of national liberation. The 1974 Carnation Revolution in Portugal accelerated the process, resulting in the independence of Guinea-Bissau in 1974 and Angola, Cabo Verde, Mozambique, and São Tomé and Príncipe in 1975.

South Africa presented the specificity of adopting Apartheid, an institutionalized system of racial segregation. It also acted as a source of instability to its neighbors by trying to influence regional political outcomes, with Namibia being a primary example. Namibia gained its independence from South Africa in 1990, as Apartheid was approaching its demise.

During the 1960s, as the independence process progressed, African countries faced the challenge of building their states. Several countries experienced political instability in the years following their independence, with many of their governments being overthrown. Initially, African governments relied on the former political and economic structures inherited from the colonial period. The reliance on primary exports and foreign aid persisted despite the hopes of adopting an import substitution strategy after independence. One of the central dilemmas the new African states encountered was how to pursue a development strategy with often faulty and ineffective institutions.

In the 1970s, North African countries experienced higher growth rates than their counterparts in Sub-Saharan Africa. One reason was that North African states were more stable and structured than their sub-Saharan counterparts, leading to fewer internal conflicts. Between 1971 and 1980, the annual average growth rate in North Africa was 5.9 percent compared to 3.2 percent in sub-Saharan Africa, as shown in Figure 7.1.

Commodity prices, especially oil, influenced those higher average growth rates. While some countries benefited from price increases, others suffered the consequences of declining terms of trade. The fluctuation in commodity prices explained the volatility in growth rates. Furthermore, this volatility was also associated with conflicts in the continent, including civil wars in Ethiopia, Angola, and Burundi, wars between African nations, such as Libya-Egypt, Uganda-Tanzania, Chad-Libya, and battles involving non-African countries such as the Yom Kippur War between Egypt and Israel.

After the oil shocks of the 1970s, African countries turned to foreign debt and recycled petrodollars. When the Federal Reserve raised interest rates in 1979, the region was hit by a debt crisis similar to that experienced by Latin America. Growth rates declined with the consolidation of neoliberalism. Between 1980 and 2000, the annual average growth rate in North Africa was 4.3 percent. Growth rates in sub-Saharan countries experienced a sharp fall, with the region's annual average growth rate dropping to 1.7 percent. One of the main causes of this decline was falling commodity prices in the 1980s and 1990s. Despite previous efforts to industrialize, the sources of economic dynamism remained unchanged, leading to economic hardships. These difficulties were further compounded by institutional limitations and ethnic rivalries, resulting in a crisis in sub-Saharan Africa.

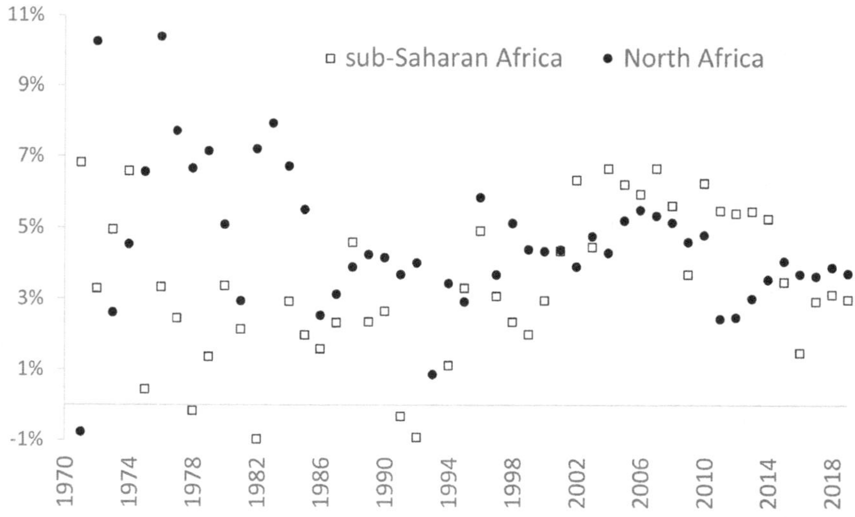

Figure 7.1 Contrasting the GDP growth rates of North and sub-Saharan Africa: 1971–2019.
Source: EPWT 7.0.

North Africa's lower growth rates derived primarily from the falling oil prices in the 1980s. The economic slowdown, coupled with the authoritarian nature of the political regime in these countries, gave rise to political unrest during the period. The resulting political turmoil was often associated with religious insurgency and escalated throughout the 1990s. It resulted in a civil war in Algeria in 1991 and political conflicts in Egypt and Tunisia, while international sanctions affected Libya. However, the regimes managed to remain in power.

The situation in sub-Saharan Africa was difficult. The region's notably lower economic growth contributed to the emergence of several armed conflicts and acute political changes during the 1980s and 1990s. The end of the Cold War and the absence of the previous support provided by the Soviet Union further complicated the matter. The conflicts in the region ranged from civil wars in Uganda (1980–1986) and Rwanda (1990–1994) to the First and Second Congo Wars (1996–2003), which involved various nations and resulted in the loss of millions of lives.

In South Africa, the compound effects of international pressure and sanctions with the economic slowdown led to the fall of Apartheid and the establishment of a democratic regime. The HIV/AIDS epidemic further destabilized the region. In this context, the World Bank and the International Monetary Fund pushed neoliberal policies in the continent. The usual toolkit of pro-market reforms was proposed and selectively adopted by countries.

The states' capacities to implement public policies were constrained in many countries. The state's roll-back significantly impacted the poor, who were already vulnerable due to economic and social inequalities (Rempel, 2008). The incapacity of neoliberal policies to change economic structures further compounded African countries' challenges.

At the turn of the XXI Century, institutional reforms took place in several countries aimed at reducing the authoritarian nature of the African states. The growing Chinese demand for commodities benefited the region, especially sub-Saharan Africa, whose annual average growth rate between 2001 and 2010 jumped to 5.6 percent. North Africa also saw a rise in growth; the average growth rate was 4.7 percent, slightly higher than the preceding period. Foreign investment related to commodity production returned, further boosting output growth.

The countries on the east coast of Africa increased their industrial output, receiving some investment in activities previously carried out in Southeast Asia. Although the 2008 neoliberal crisis did not immediately impact the region, the average growth rates between 2011 and 2019 were lower than the previous decade. The average growth in sub-Saharan Africa was 3.9 percent, while it fell to 3.3 percent in North Africa.

A political crisis erupted in several North African countries in 2011, resulting in the overthrow of several authoritarian governments from power. After 2015, political stability returned to the region. The average growth rates of sub-Saharan countries surpassed those of North Africa from 2004 to 2014, marking a distinct pattern from previous decades. However, the neoliberal crisis impacted the sub-Saharan economies as commodity prices fell and the previous pattern of sluggish growth returned.

Technical regress and the profit rate in African countries

Despite the distinct trajectories of African countries, the leading economies remained the same from 1970 to 2019. Four countries, namely, Nigeria, Egypt, South Africa, and Algeria, accounted for between fifty and sixty percent of the continent's GDP when measured in purchase power parity. Although their ranking positions occasionally changed, the relevance of these countries in the African economy remained relatively stable over time.

During the study period, the labor productivity gap expanded in most African countries. Figure 7.2 shows the labor productivity for 47 countries relative to the United States between 1970 and 2019. The labor productivity gap increased for 30 economies and narrowed for 17 countries. Throughout the period, 20 countries exhibited labor productivity levels inferior to 10 percent of those observed in the United States. By 2019, 19 out of 47 countries had labor productivity below six percent of that observed in the US economy. Africa remains the continent with the largest labor productivity gap worldwide. Among the four largest economies, only Egypt was able to catch up with the United States. Botswana, Egypt, and Mauritius were the most successful countries in reducing their labor productivity gap.

We can identify three distinct phases in analyzing catching up and falling behind in African economies. The first phase, spanning from the 1970s to the early 1980s, coincided with the crisis of the Golden Age. During this period, one group of countries experienced a decline or maintained a stable gap in labor productivity. This group primarily consisted of oil-exporting nations and countries that avoided major political conflicts. In contrast, a second group of countries saw an expansion in their labor productivity gap. This expansion was closely associated with conflicts related to decolonization or military coups, exemplified by countries like Angola, Ethiopia, and Uganda. By the end of the 1970s, some of these nations also suffered a decline in their terms of trade, as was the case with Ghana.

The second phase, from the 1980s to the early XXI Century, corresponded to neoliberalism. was marked by the debt crisis and declining commodity prices. During this phase, the labor productivity gap increased, with most African countries falling behind. Just a few, such as Egypt, Lesotho, Mauritius, and Botswana, managed to reduce the gap. The second phase was characterized by various social and political challenges, including crises and wars, particularly in sub-Saharan Africa.

Between the early 2000s and 2019, the third phase was marked by a catching up in labor productivity in most countries, while others maintained the previous gap. There was an increase in commodity prices, benefiting exporting countries. The improvement in terms of trade gave some room to pursue economic growth strategies.

The overall pattern reveals that many African countries made progress in catching up during the 1970s but experienced falling behind from the 1980s to the early 2000s. Subsequently, some countries made gains in the early XXI century, particularly during the commodity boom. However, their labor productivity still exhibited a large gap compared to the United States.

Phases of catching up tend to exhibit a Marx-biased pattern of technical change, with declining capital productivity and rising labor productivity. Figure 7.3 graphs

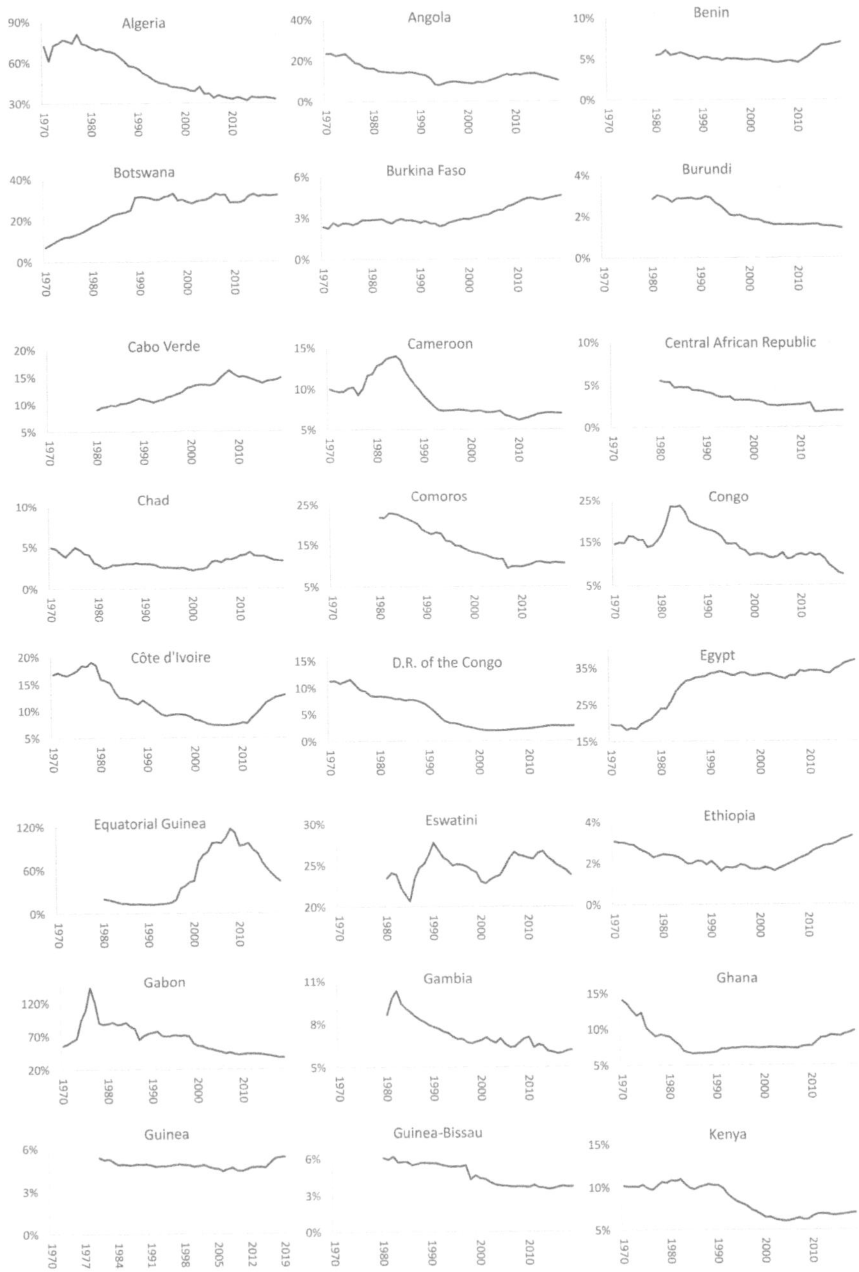

Figure 7.2 Labor productivity in African countries relative to the United States, 1970–2019 (*Continued*)

Source: EPWT 7.0.

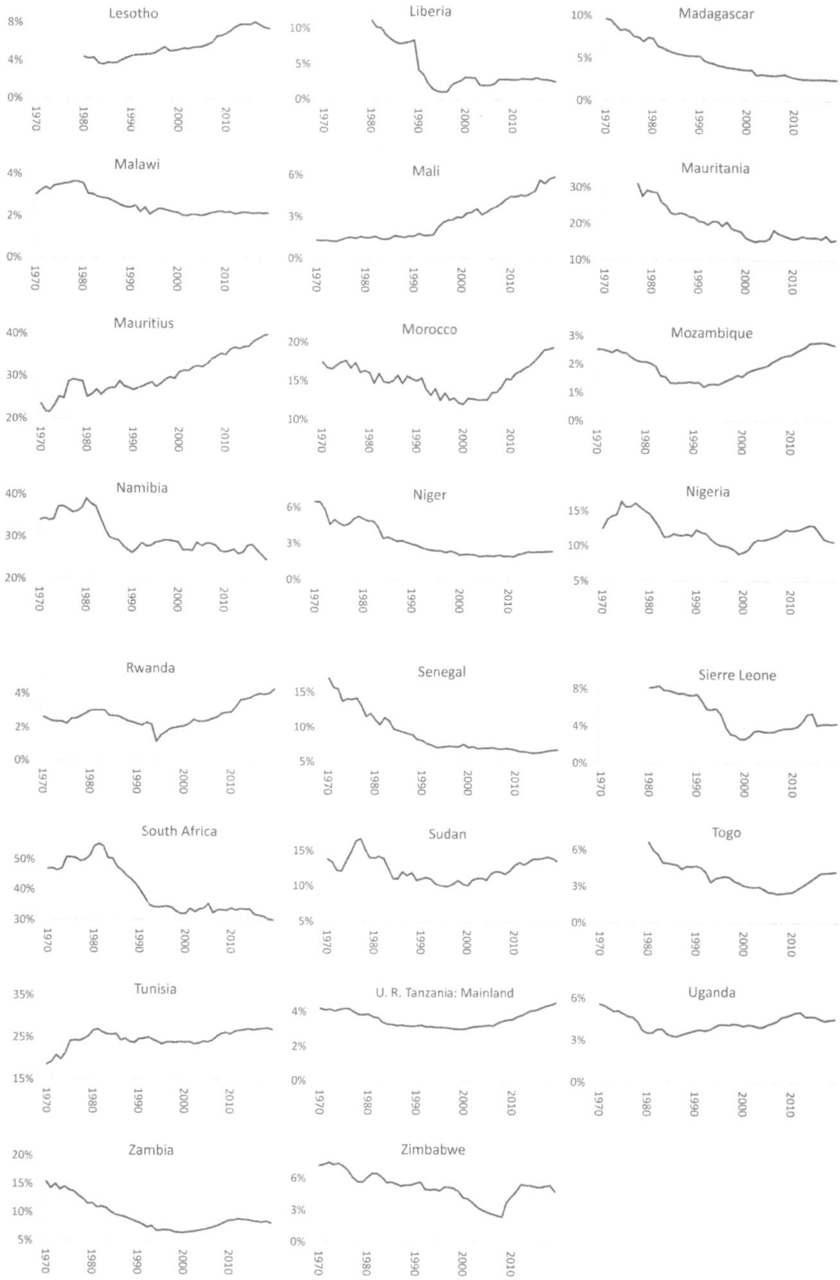

Figure 7.2 (Continued)

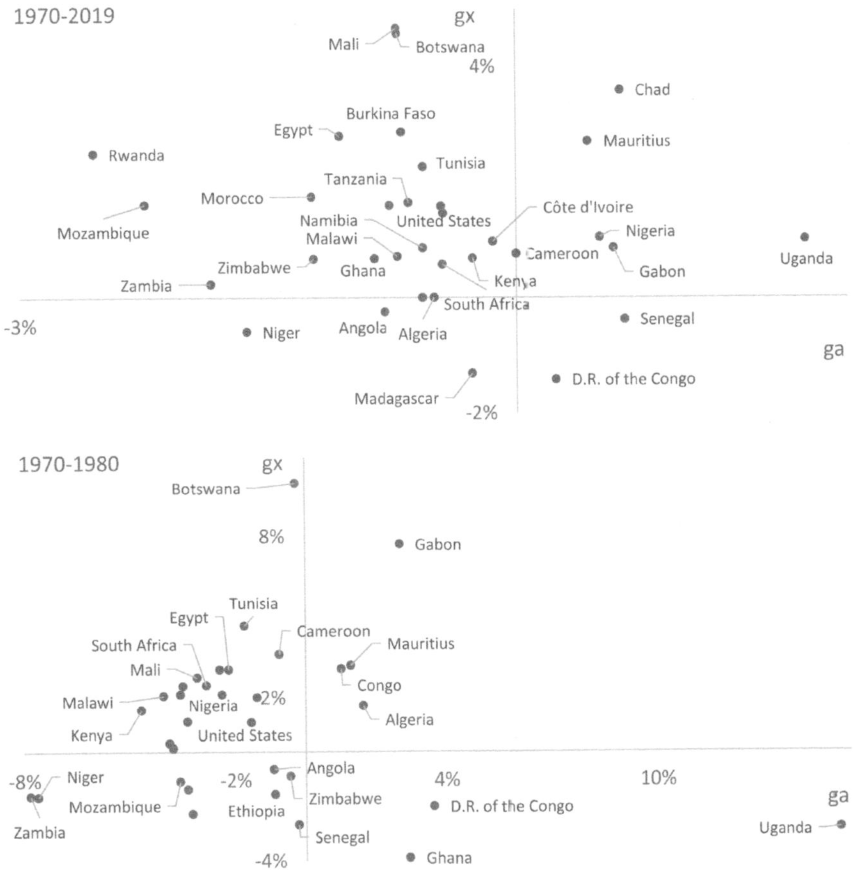

Figure 7.3 The (ga, gx) points for African countries and the United States: 1970–2019 and 1970–1980.

Source: EPWT 7.0.

the rates of change in capital productivity and labor productivity, the pair (ga, gx), for the periods 1970–2019 and 1970–1980, and Figure 7.4 displays the same information for the periods 1980–2000, and 2000–2019. Information for Burundi, Benin, Central African Republic, Comoros, Cabo Verde, Guinea, Gambia, Guinea-Bissau, Equatorial Guinea, Liberia, Lesotho, Mauritania, Sierra Leone, Eswatini, and Togo starts in 1980. For simplicity, we consider growth rates in the open range -0.1% to 0.1% equal to zero.

The technical change in the 1970–2019 period was consistent with labor-saving, capital-using Marx bias in 19 African countries, Burkina Faso, Botswana, Côte d'Ivoire, Egypt, Ethiopia, Ghana, Kenya, Morocco, Mali, Mozambique, Malawi, Namibia, Rwanda, Sudan, Tunisia, Tanzania, South Africa, Zambia, and Zimbabwe;

Figure 7.4 The (ga, gx) points for African countries and the United States: 1980–2000 and 2000–2019.

Source: EPWT 7.0.

with input-saving technical change for five countries, Gabon, Mauritius, Nigeria, Chad, and Uganda; with a technical regress in three countries, Angola, Madagascar, and Niger. Moreover, we detected the Harrod-neutral technical change in Cameroon, the inverse Marx-biased technical change in the D. R. of Congo and Senegal, and the Solow-neutral technical regress in Algeria and Congo-Brazzaville.

In the 1980–2019 period, the technical change was Marx-biased for Guinea, Gambia, Equatorial Guinea, Lesotho, and Eswatini; it displayed an input-saving technical change for Benin, Cabo Verde, Guinea-Bissau, and Togo; it presented a technical regress in Burundi, Central African Republic, Liberia, and Sierra Leone; it was Harrod-neutral technical regress in Comoros and Solow-neutral technical change in Mauritania.

There were three phases of technical change, consistent with the catching-up and falling behind phases observed between 1970 and 2019. First, between 1970 and 1980, half of the 32 countries with available data displayed a Marx-biased technical change. Four economies presented an input-saving technical change, while nine countries showed technical regress. In three economies, an inverse Marx-biased technical change was observed. This phase coincided with increased terms of trade and the implementation of debt-based ISI development strategies in some countries. Technical regress occurred in countries with internal conflicts, such as Ethiopia and Zimbabwe, or undergoing late independence processes, like Angola and Mozambique.

In the second phase, from 1980 to 2000, 16 countries presented technical regress, 10 had input-input saving technical change, 17 displayed Marx-biased technical change, and four showed an inverse Marx-biased pattern. The debt crisis, which followed the second oil shock and the hike in US interest rates, marked this phase and was a central factor in boosting neoliberalism in developing countries. The decline in terms of trade and the adverse conditions to service the debt had a strong negative impact on the economic performance of African countries.

With the end of the Cold War, many African countries lost access to international aid from the socialist bloc. This and the emergence of regional armed conflicts significantly impacted their economic performance. Institutional failures and limitations of the industrialization strategy also contributed to the decline in capital productivity. This can be seen in the examples of Nigeria, which suffered from worsening terms of trade and political conflict, resulting in a succession of coups d'état. Algeria followed a similar path, resulting in a civil war in the 1990s. South Africa faced the end of Apartheid and the effects of capital flight before the regime change. Labor productivity declined in these three countries.

In the third phase, from 2000 to 2019, growth rates in the continent recovered due to the commodity boom. In this phase, 25 countries showed an input-saving technical change, 14 exhibited a Marx-biased technical change and two showing Harrod-neutral technical change. Only four countries experienced technical regress, one exhibited an inversed Marx-biased technical change, and one a Solow-neutral technical regress. The terms of trade and capacity utilization expansions and falling capital goods prices were key drivers of the input-saving technical change observed in most countries.

As discussed previously, technical change is critical in determining the profit rate. Figure 7.5 shows the net profit rate for 31 countries with data available since 1970. Among them, 22 countries exhibit a U-shaped curve pattern. They experienced a decline in profitability between the 1970s and the end of the 1980s or early 1990s, followed by an increase in profitability. These countries include South Africa, Nigeria, Egypt, Kenya, and Tanzania. However, some countries experienced a decline in profitability at the beginning of the XXI century, such as Botswana and Cabo Verde, which displayed an inverted U-shaped curve. There was a decline in profitability in Morocco, while Senegal and Mauritius exhibited a positive trend. Capital productivity changes were the main driver of profit rate movements in the long run.

Capital productivity and profit rate exhibited similar phases in the period of study. Between 1970 and 1990, 25 countries experienced falling profit rates, while six saw an increase. Botswana, Mauritius, and Senegal, countries recognized as

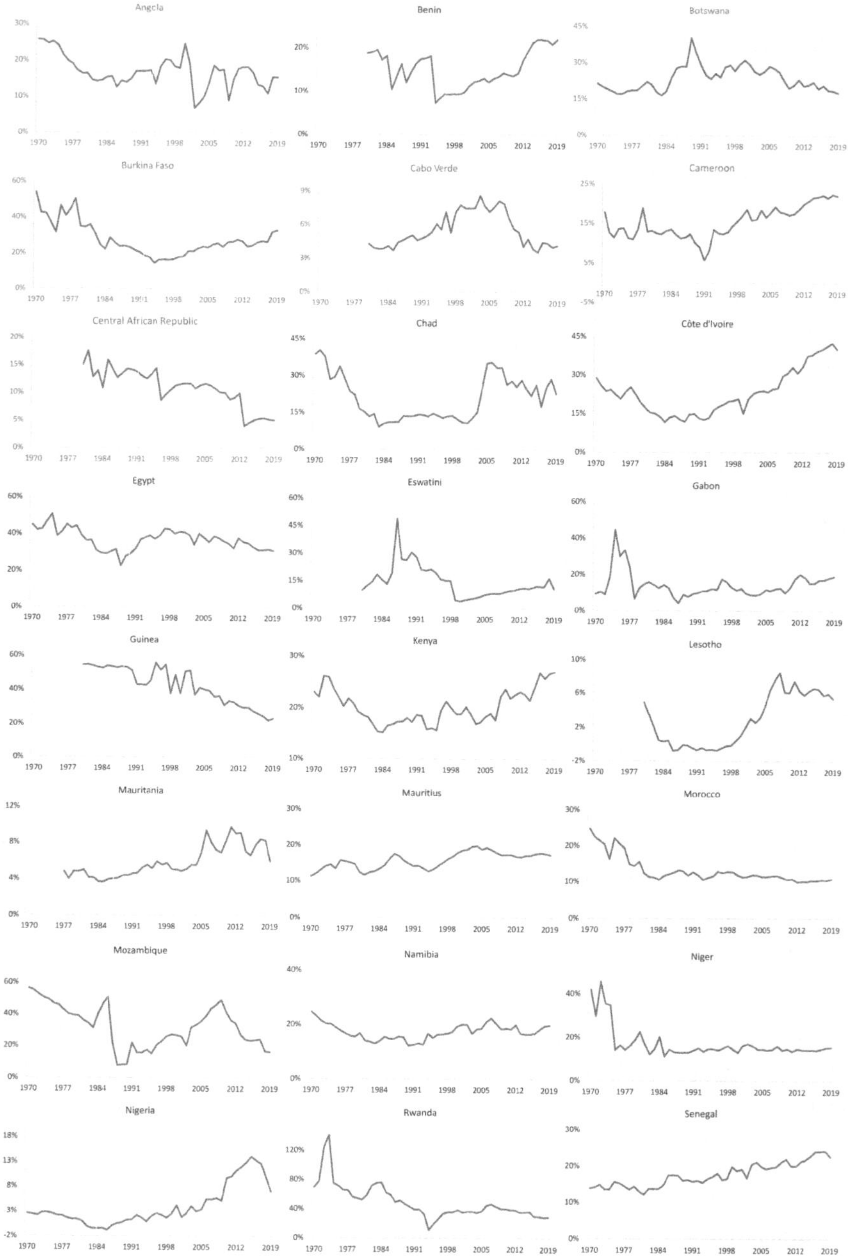

Figure 7.5 The net profit rate for 31 African countries (1970–2019). (*Continued*)

Source: EPWT 7.0.

Figure 7.5 (Continued)

successful cases of African economic growth (Ndulo, 2008), showed increased profitability in the period. During the 1970s, favorable terms of trade and high liquidity in the international financial markets allowed for investments in capital goods and infrastructures. These investments were associated with attempts to promote structural change and enhance the capabilities of the state. However, these investments led to a decrease in capital productivity.

The high investment rates that characterized the 1970s were short lived. The interest rate rise that marked the beginning of the neoliberalism and the global recession of the early 1980s led to a decline in commodity prices and investment rates. As a result, export revenues fell, and profit rates declined. Many countries experienced acute economic and political crises. The 1980s was a decade of economic regression in Africa, with few exceptions. Unlike the 1970s, the fall in profit rates in the 1980s was not the result of policy efforts to enhance production capabilities and labor productivity. Low or negative growth in both labor and capital productivity resulted in severe technical regression across the continent.

In the 1990s, Africa witnessed a resurgence in profit rates driven by increased capital productivity. Initially, this recovery was uneven, with numerous nations grappling with civil wars, political conflicts, and institutional challenges. Gradually, as commodity demand expanded and institutional crises were overcome, the profit rates rebounded across the continent with rising terms of trade. Between 1990 and the middle 2000s, profit rates increased in many countries, including South Africa, Nigeria, Egypt, Mauritius, Senegal, and Kenya. In some cases, profit rates remained stagnant until 2019, as in Morocco and Niger, declining in Botswana, the Central African Republic, Guinea, Rwanda, and Cabo Verde. While poor countries like Niger, Central African Republic, and Rwanda could not resume the former profitability associated with commodities exports, others with higher capital accumulation in the previous period also did not increase their profitability.

Profitability expanded until the global financial crisis of 2007. Following the crisis, the decline in the terms of trade led to a fall in the profit rate. African economies heavily rely on commodities exports, making terms of trade a crucial determinant of their economic trajectories and a source of volatility in their growth rates. Another pivotal factor affecting growth is political conflicts. During the 2000s, the region witnessed a comparatively more stable political environment, marked by reduced conflicts and civil wars compared to preceding years. In Africa, there existed a mutual reinforcement between improving economic growth conditions and enhanced political stability. Nonetheless, some significant political challenges persisted in certain countries, such as the Boko Haram insurgency in Nigeria, civil wars in South Sudan and Libya, and conflicts in Mali and the Central African Republic.

Natural resources, profit rate, and accumulation

As previously discussed, exports of natural resources are the primary source of demand and hard currency for African countries. The increase in commodity demand improves the terms of trade, resulting in higher capital productivity, which in turn induces rising profits and investments. It also provides policy space to apply countercyclical policies.

African countries relying heavily on commodity exports are vulnerable to severe crises when international demand and terms of trade experience a downturn. The consequences of such crises include a decline in economic growth resulting from falling profit rates and reduced access to hard currencies. This phenomenon elucidates, at least partially, the recurring cycles of catching up and falling behind observed in many African countries.

Figure 7.6 shows the difference in capital accumulation between African countries and the United States between 1970 and 2019. The dotted line is the actual difference, and the solid line is the three-year moving average. It reveals that only Burkina Faso, Botswana, Cabo Verde, Guinea, Egypt, and Morocco presented higher capital accumulation rates relative to the United States during the study period. Most African countries exhibited phases of lower accumulation rates than the United States.

Between 1970 and 2019, we observed a cyclical pattern in capital accumulation with respect to the United States. Overall, there was higher accumulation rate in the 1970s. It fell in the 1980s and 1990s with the debt crises, the neoliberal turn, and regional political conflicts, reaching negative numbers in several countries. These shifts were also intertwined with changes in terms of trade. Accumulation rates recovered after 2000, albeit with some exceptions. In general, the capital accumulation rate in the region declined compared to the United States, especially between 1980 and 2000, leading to a higher labor productivity gap and falling behind.

Capital accumulation experienced a resurgence at the onset of the XXI Century, driven by a rise in commodity demand. Notice that this rebound was not uniform across all economies. In particular, Egypt, Nigeria, and South Africa did not witness this resurgence; instead, they grappled with stagnant accumulation.

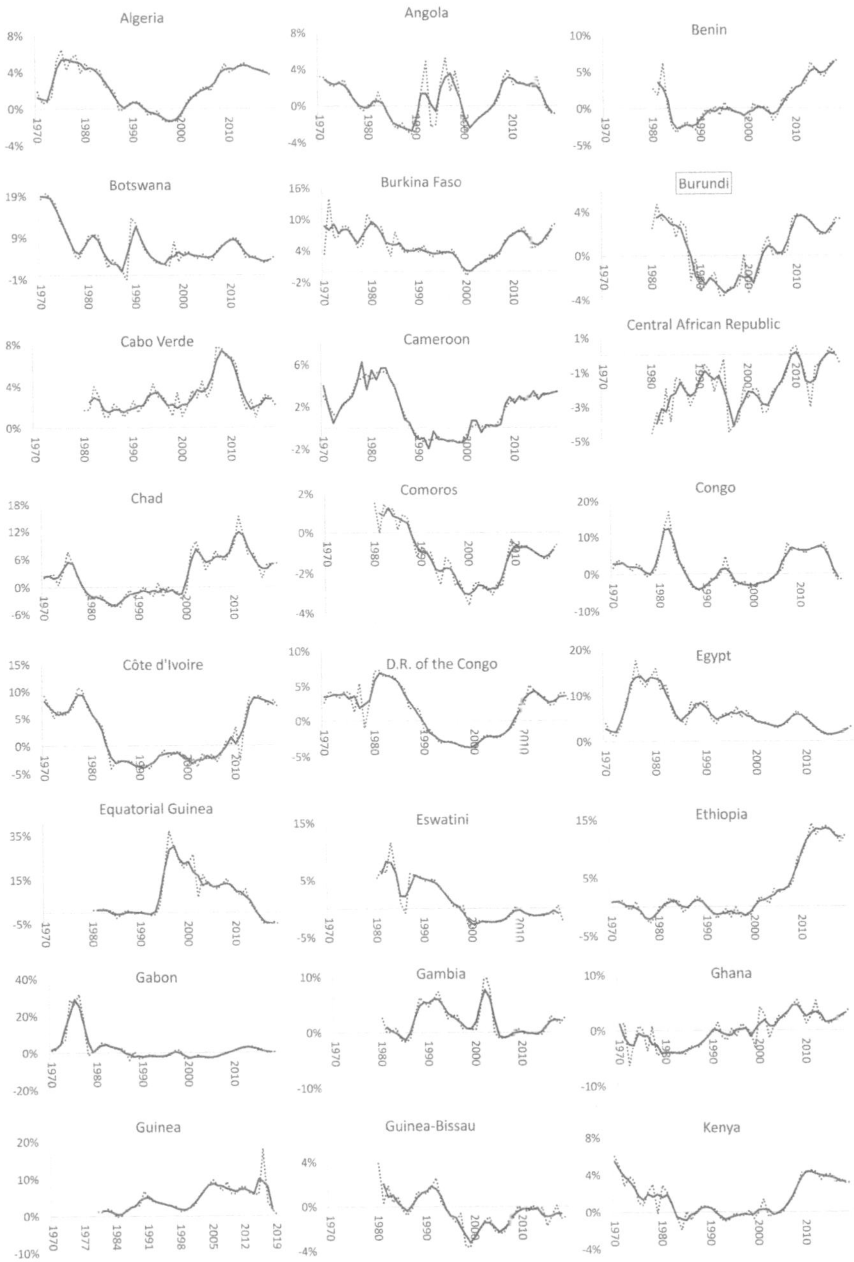

Figure 7.6 The difference in capital accumulation between African countries and the United States: 1970–2019. (*Continued*)

Source: EPWT 7.0.

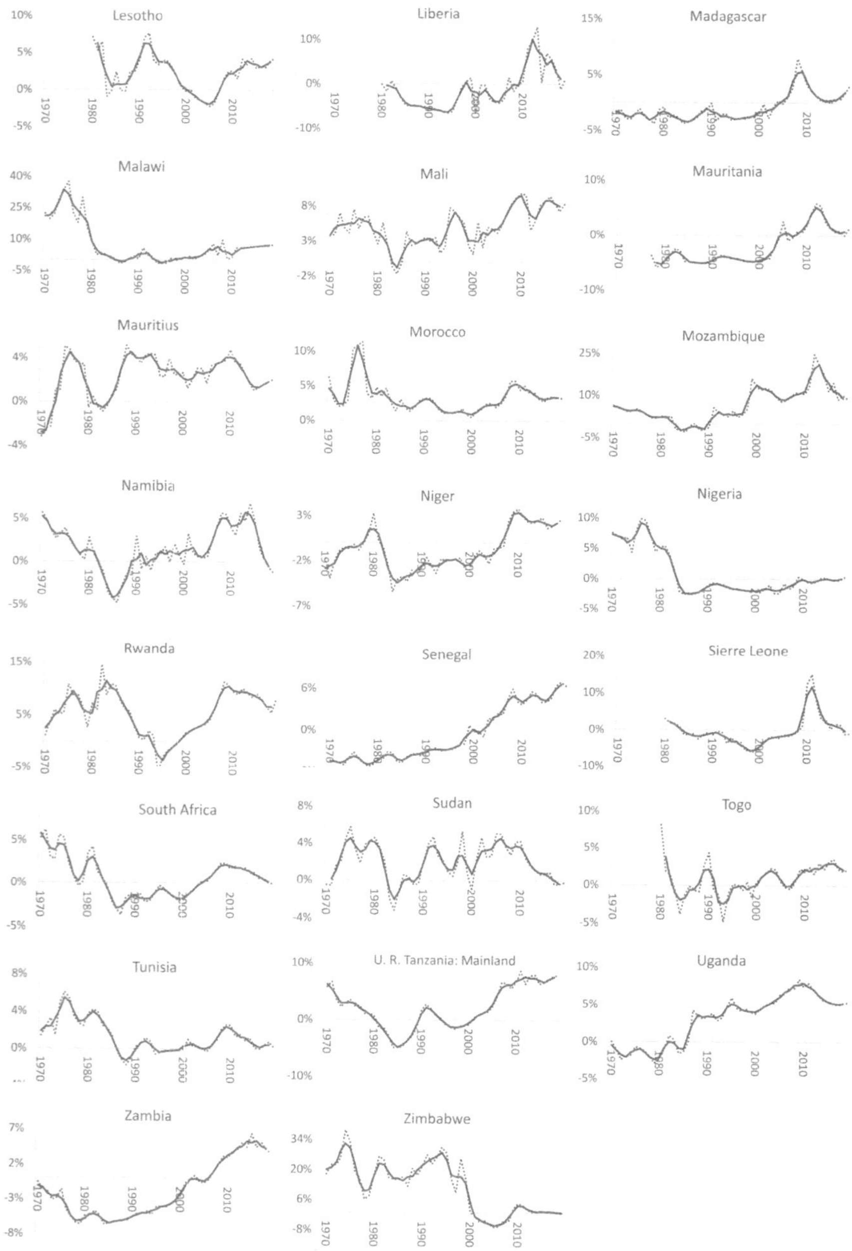

Figure 7.6 (Continued)

These results are consistent with the model of Chapter Two, especially when considering the effects of terms of trade on capital productivity. The rise in terms of trade facilitated increased capital productivity, which led to a higher profit rate, ultimately driving up capital accumulation. Catching up requires higher capital accumulation in the follower than in the leader country, which was the African case in periods of rising terms of trade.

The main driver for capital accumulation is the profit rate. The higher the difference in the profit rates between the follower and the leader, the greater the capital accumulation in comparison with the leader. Figure 7.7 displays the scatterplot

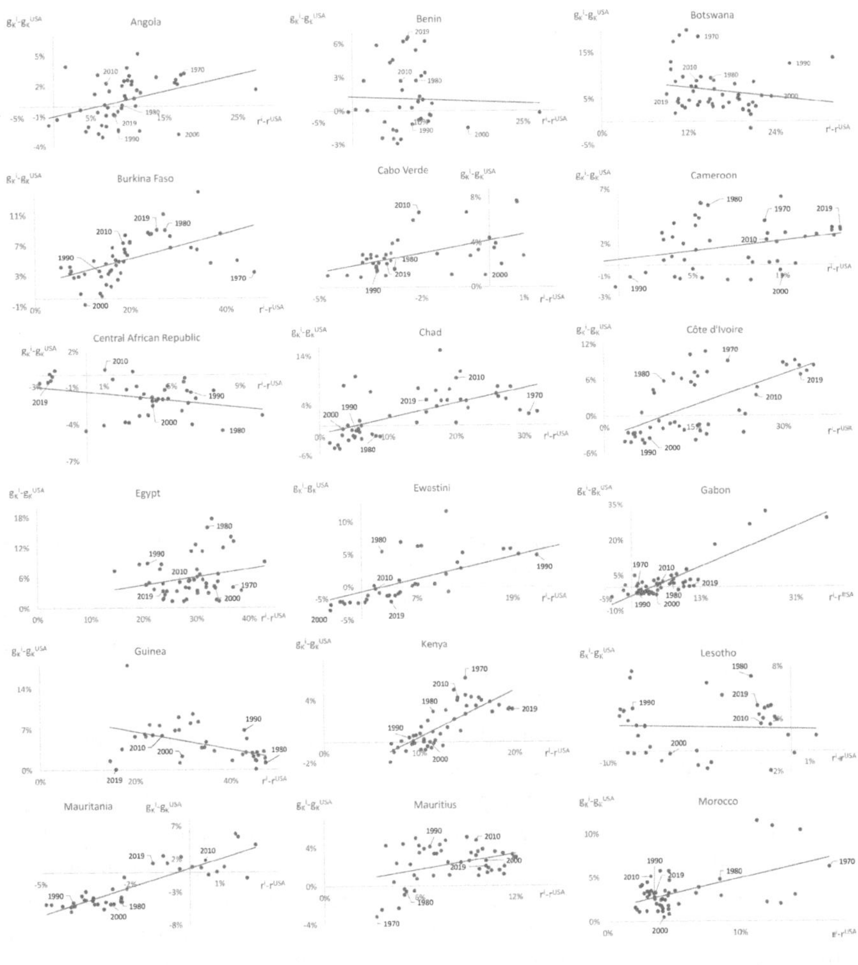

Figure 7.7 The scatterplot between the differences in the profit rate, r^i-r^{USA}, and capital accumulation, $g_K{}^i$-$g_K{}^{USA}$, for 32 African and the United States: 1970–2019. (*Continued*)

Source: EPWT 7.0.

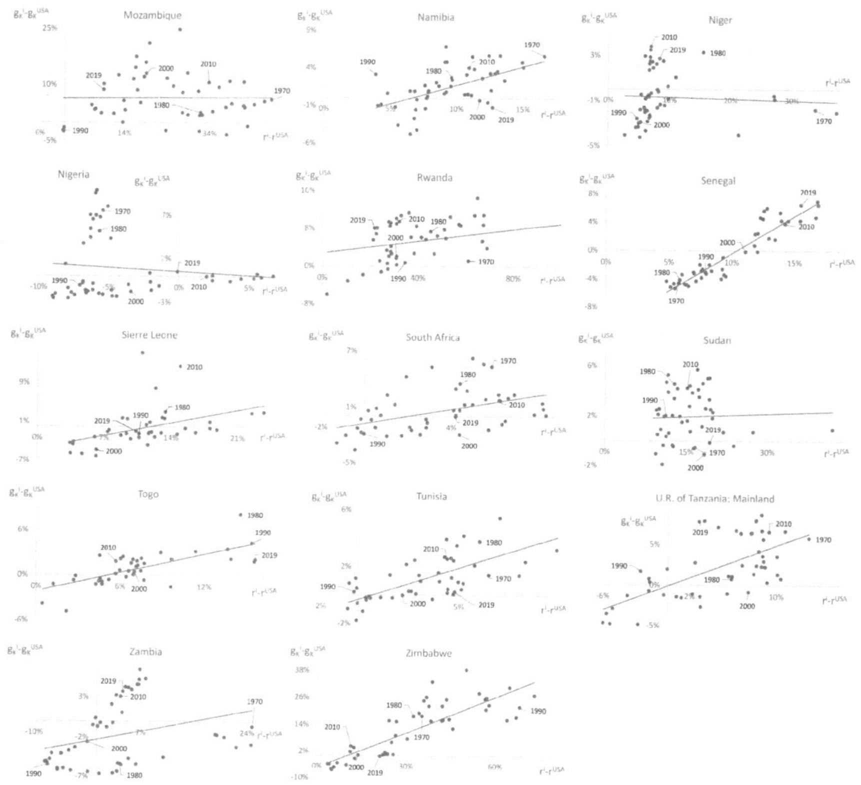

Figure 7.7 (Continued)

between the differences in the profit rate, r^i-r^{USA}, and in capital accumulation, $g_K{}^i$-$g_K{}^{USA}$, and their linear fit for 32 African countries and the United States. There was a positive correlation between the variables for two-thirds of the sample. Political conflicts, institutional limitations, and commodity price fluctuations help explain negative relationships between accumulation and profit rates, as observed in countries like Algeria, Morocco, Niger, and Nigeria.

The other determinant of capital accumulation is the investment rate. In Africa, the investment rates were high in the 1970s, followed by a decline in the 1980s and 1990s due to neoliberal policies and internal conflicts. The debt crisis resulted in rising debt services and reduced access to external resources, which, combined with neoliberal economic policies, led to lower public investment. However, in the early 2000s, there was a resurgence in investment rates driven by China's growing demand for commodities. This trend was particularly notable in resource-rich countries, such as DR of Congo, Rwanda, Senegal, Tanzania, and Zambia. Despite this, most African countries face significant challenges in raising and attracting investment due to political instability and underdeveloped infrastructure.

The new frontier in the making

In the XXI century, Africa has partially recaptured some growth dynamics lost during the 1980s and 1990s. This resurgence in growth has primarily been fueled by the rising demand for commodities from Asia. Additionally, after two decades of political upheavals, many African nations have achieved greater political stability. However, the historical pattern of subordination to external economic dynamics has persisted. While the blend of stability and growth has fostered positive expectations for the future, the current trajectory appears insufficient to overcome the historical underdevelopment of the region. Countries that remain predominantly reliant on commodities and focused mainly on an outward-oriented approach will likely face challenges catching up with major global economies.

Africa, with its relatively younger population compared to other continents, holds the promise of being a source of labor, capable of producing and consuming industrialized goods. However, the continent faces several limitations that impede further progress. Firstly, many of its countries still lack a well-defined national development project. Moreover, the capitalist segments within these nations often pursue a primitive accumulation approach, focusing on the extensive exploitation of natural resources, with the resulting profits primarily flowing into international financial markets. This dynamic is exacerbated by the institutional weaknesses in the region, including issues like weak governance, limited access to finance, inadequate infrastructure, and persistent conflict in some areas. Addressing these issues is fundamental for ensuring the sustained growth and development of the continent.

Africa may require foreign investments to boost its investment rate, capital accumulation, and labor productivity. While China and India have emerged as potential partners in the XXI Century, historical ties with the United States, the United Kingdom, and France remain significant. As international competition for foreign investment intensifies among old and new global powers, African nations can capitalize on their resources and benefit from the growing demand for commodities.

Nonetheless, national development strategies are necessary to accelerate productivity and growth. In this sense, it is essential to prioritize industrialization and its associated services to enhance labor productivity and access higher-value sectors within global value chains. Furthermore, improving Africa's infrastructure is crucial to stimulate economic development. Adopting the usual recipes of Western multilateral organizations like the World Bank will fail to enhance African living standards. Countries with larger populations can follow the path of some Southeast Asian nations and undergo industrialization. However, to sustain larger urban populations and achieve sustainable growth, higher levels of education and agricultural productivity are necessary.

The challenge for Africa lies in achieving economic growth and channeling it toward improving living standards. Sustaining the advance of democracy and overcoming divisive politics is central for the continent to achieve those aims. However, persistent economic growth is essential to ensuring long-term political stability.

It can generate positive feedback, helping to promote the necessary institutional changes for economic and social development.

The region holds substantial prospects for economic growth, with numerous opportunities on the horizon. However, sustaining economic growth and enhancing labor productivity remains a pressing challenge. Drivers for accelerating capital accumulation must be found and put in place to ensure sustained and equitable development. The new century has brought new possibilities for the continent, as emerging markets like China and India offer prospects for partnerships and investment opportunities.

To fully capitalize on the benefits of these opportunities, African countries must adopt new development paradigms, set well-defined objectives, and learn from past successful experiences. Through these initiatives, the region can overcome enduring obstacles, such as income inequality and political instability. Ultimately, the success of Africa's development hinges on the ability of its nations to harness the abundant resources and potential of the continent for economic and social development.

Bibliography

Ndulo, B., ed. (2008). *The Political Economy of Economic Growth in Africa: 1960 – 2000*. New York: Cambridge University Press.

Rempel, R. (2008). Periodizing African development history. *African Economic History*, 36, pp. 125–128.

Conclusion

Worldwide lessons for catching-up

The book explores the dynamics of catching up and falling behind in developing economies from a global perspective. It investigated the diverse trajectories of catching up and falling behind of 40 Asian countries, 20 Latin American countries, 47 African countries, and 18 Central and Eastern European countries spanning the 50 years from 1970 to 2019, utilizing empirical data, the classical Marxian growth model, and insights from economic history. While catching up is possible, history has shown it to be challenging.

The empirical and historical analyses offer valuable lessons into the regularities related to catching up and falling behind in economic development processes and help illuminate country-specific circumstances. While they may not offer a definitive roadmap for successful catching up, when combined with the model, they can provide an understanding of the necessary conditions for countries to expand their labor productivity rapidly. The analyses also highlight the problems that have blocked the progress of nations that fell behind.

The economic model aligns with Marx's view that underdeveloped countries should follow the path of technical change set by developed capitalist nations. Economic growth and catching up involves raising labor productivity and reducing capital productivity through industrialization of the productive system and infrastructure building. However, this trajectory often leads to a decline in the profit rate and, therefore, a decrease in the incentives for investment and capital accumulation. How to circumvent this problem is one of the central issues that a national development plan must face.

The period from 1970 to 2019 witnessed important structural changes in the global economy, spanning from the crisis of the Golden Age to the rise and eventual crisis of neoliberalism. Regarding economic policies, this era transitioned from developmentalism, in which the state played a determinant role in industrialization, to a neoliberal approach, where the state's function shifted towards ensuring markets "proper" functioning.

Neoliberalism led to financialization, with finance increasingly shaping the countries' productive structure. This, coupled with free trade rhetoric, drove the liberalization of cross-border capital and merchandise movements. Globalization profoundly impacted the concentration and centralization of capital across economic sectors and countries, influencing where production was located. Many

DOI: 10.4324/9781003223382-9

developing countries experienced premature deindustrialization and a shift toward primary economic activities. However, some nations took advantage of neoliberalism to bolster their catching up. China serves as the primary illustration, yet other nations also have capitalized on the offshoring of industrial activities.

The process of decolonization in Africa and Asia, which gave rise to numerous developing nations, continued during the period of study. Economic growth became a primary objective of the newly formed countries, as it potentially expands employment, reduces political disputes, and plays a central role in alleviating poverty. While in Asia, decolonization led to the establishment of strong nation-states, in Africa, it often resulted in weaker states marked by enduring internal disputes, with some persisting to the present day.

The period also witnessed the USSR's dissolution and the end of the Cold War. The result was the demise of the Soviet model as an alternative to capitalism and the emergence of transitional economies in Central and Eastern Europe and Asia, including the Russian Federation. Neoliberal capitalism integrated most world regions under its dominance, fostering interdependence among countries.

The United States strengthened its position as a hegemonic imperialist country during the 1980s and 1990s, imposing neoliberalism across numerous countries worldwide. It used its imperialist power to reward aligned nations and exert pressure on those opposing its interests, employing various methods, including military, economic, financial, and political forces.

While the United States and its partners still hold economic dominance worldwide, neoliberalism has created a contradiction between the interests of large financial and productive capitals and the nation-state. There are differences between the wealth and power of a nation and the wealth of its wealthiest individuals, who profit within a globalized economy. Deindustrialization, persistent trade deficits, and lower economic growth have reshaped the hegemonic role of the United States in the global economy.

In recent decades, developing countries, both in terms of production and population growth, have expanded in importance, which may represent a profound and enduring change in the global landscape. This transformation spans economic, political, and military dimensions, representing a possible power transition from Western and Northern regions to Eastern and Southern parts of the world. Whether these trends persist and whether a developing country will catch up and eventually leapfrog the developed nations are complex questions that only time can adequately address.

The conclusion is organized into four sections. The first explores lessons for catching up on historical experiences. The second assesses the role of (re)-industrialization in rising labor productivity. The third considers the relationship between neoliberalism and unequal development. The last section calls for a new perspective on backwardness, acknowledging it as a pressing international problem.

The necessary conditions for catching up

Raising labor productivity and ensuring its equitable redistribution are fundamental for development and promoting human development. However, as the historical experience during neoliberalism showed, sustaining long-term labor productivity growth is challenging for most countries. The interplay between institutional organization, on one side, and how technical change and income distribution affect the profit rates, which is a key determinant of capital accumulation and growth, on the other, is crucial in addressing the fundamental question of how developing countries can initiate and maintain rapid labor productivity growth over time.

The critical first institutional innovation is establishing a well-functioning national state free from external interference, a task impossible in colonial contexts. Maintaining internal stability by mitigating intense disputes and civil conflicts is also important. These foundational conditions are essential for undertaking a national development project, which may foster a unified sense of identity and purpose across different segments of society. Such initiative can generate a shared vision of the future, helping to reduce the distributive conflicts between and within social classes.

The state plays a leading role in establishing a national development project, defining the industrial policy and essential elements during the catching up. Among the central definitions are how the labor market will be organized; what sectors will be industrialized initially; how the tax system will be organized; which economic sectors will be taxed; which ones will be subsidized; how capital accumulation will be financed; what will be the interest rate and the exchange rate; how production will be shared between public enterprises, private firms, and external partners; how technical knowledge is transferred and produced nationally, defining the policies of research and development; how the judicial system will work, enforcing contracts and establishing property rights. A capable state bureaucracy is required to address these fundamental issues effectively.

A well-defined industrial policy is a mechanism for gradually building competitive advantages by artificially boosting sectoral profitability. As developing economies create competitive advantages and diversify their production and exports, they are better positioned to address the problems associated with catching up. An industrial policy that facilitates adopting energy-saving technological changes will expedite the transition toward achieving net-zero greenhouse gas emissions.

The successful historical experiences of the catching-up indicated that the follower countries displayed a Marx-biased technical change. Mechanization of production through industrialization is central to raising labor productivity. In many cases, the rapid mechanization led to a decline in capital productivity and, therefore, in the profit rate, reaching a level comparable to or even lower than that of the United States. There was a faster catching up in capital productivity than labor productivity. Disparities in velocity of catching up in labor and capital productivities could be attributed to differences in scale of production and workers' capacity to learn. External factors such as public infrastructure, education, innovation capacity, and the institutional framework within which firms operate might also play a role.

A high-profit rate is pivotal in driving robust mechanization during the early stages of catching up. However, as rapid capital accumulation reduces capital productivity and the profit rate, the success of catching up in a second moment may hinge on elevating saving and investment rates. It might potentially further erode capital productivity and the profit rate, thereby jeopardizing the process. This issue is observed in many middle-income trap countries. In these cases, state intervention becomes essential, expanding investment even as the profit rate declines, as in China. This concept aligns with the Keynesian proposition of socialization of investment, contrasting sharply with the policies pursued by most Latin American countries during neoliberalism, when there was a decline in investments by the state and public enterprises.

Various factors can lead to falling behind, as illustrated by numerous experiences considered in previous chapters. As discussed above, the decrease in capital accumulation often results from a falling profit rate, which, in turn, is typically linked to declining capital productivity. Consequently, countries must implement policies to maintain capital productivity while promoting labor productivity growth. One effective countermeasure against declining capital productivity and profit rates is reducing the cost of capital goods through a comprehensive industrial policy. In the early stages of catching up, importing capital goods and associated techniques can often be cheaper. However, as a country approaches the technological frontier, shifting toward local production and entering sectors with greater technological intensity, as South Korea exemplifies, may prove to be the most strategic path forward.

The decline of terms of trade also reduces the profitability and capital accumulation of countries dependent on natural resources, as exemplified by African and Latin American countries, and the former URRS republics. Moreover, the volatility of the terms of trade intensifies the movements of the business cycle with important effects on capital accumulation, a phenomenon observed worldwide. Capital accumulation in oil-exporting Western Asian nations reflected the movements of petroleum prices.

Another crucial aspect is the state's role in addressing infrastructure and production in capital-intensive sectors, which often yield lower profit rates than the average. Additionally, achieving balanced growth is essential to prevent a crisis of disproportion, ensuring that supply and demand for the different industrial and agricultural sectors remain in balance. This challenge is connected to maintaining appropriate fiscal and monetary policies to avoid the declining capacity utilization usually associated with cyclical movements.

A rise in the profit rate can also be driven by a decrease in the wage share, as shown by the experience in India. However, maintaining the stability of labor share while preventing the decline in the profit rate also ensures that workers benefit from increased labor productivity, easing the distributive and social conflicts. This stability further facilitates the expansion of household consumption, simplifying the effective management of aggregate demand.

A central issue is associated with how to finance industrialization and the process of catching up. Taxing the sector responsible for generating foreign exchange conflicts with established interests, which is one of the main reasons explaining why resource-rich countries often delay their industrialization process. Moreover, sectors with comparative advantages typically enjoy higher profitability than the others, giving rises to problems associated with Dutch disease.

Developing countries often turn to external debt to finance their development. However, historical experience has revealed the inherent limitations of such financial strategies. The financial crises stemming from external debt in Latin America and Africa in the 1980s illustrate that debt can function as a form of external dominance over national economies. This external debt burden can undermine the development process, as the concerns of the debtor country are often relegated to a secondary position. Similarly, external aggression through military actions and economic sanctions can also derail national development.

The United States and its developed partners exert significant influence over the processes of catching up. Mere industrial expansion by followers, as seen in Import Substitution Industrialization, may not lead to a successful outcome as production is often confined to internal markets without being integrated into the capitalist economy. Instead, a more effective approach, as seen in Asian experiences, involves integrating into a leading country and its partners, pursuing industrial production based on a developmental strategy. This strategy allows peripheral nations to participate in the economic framework established by the leading country and its allies, offering a pragmatic and promising path to catching up.

The last paragraphs addressed external factors, considering the existence of a national development project. However, there is the possibility that segments of the capitalist classes and state bureaucracy may abandon the national project development. In neoliberalism, a contradiction emerged between national interest and the concerns of financial capitalist classes. As countries integrated into the globalized financial economy, a disconnection arose between the nation and the location where profits are generated. The transformation of local capital into international financial capital eroded the ties between the big bourgeoisie and national development.

While adopting national development and industrialization projects does not guarantee that a country will catch up, opting for a free-market approach is highly likely to lead to failure.

Is (re)industrialization synonymous with catching up and reducing backwardness?

A fundamental question is whether (re)industrialization is necessary for catching up in the present day. Historical experiences have shown that successful catch-ups were accompanied by industrialization. Recent examples include Japan, South Korea, and China. Conversely, countries with premature deindustrialization, such as Brazil, have fallen behind. Some African nations did not even start their industrialization. However, in a few cases, such as in Mexico, industrialization during neoliberalism did not result in catching up. Most high-income, nonindustrialized countries in Western Asia depend on oil rents. Therefore, while industrialization is not necessarily synonymous with catching up and reducing backwardness, it is a critical component of economic development.

During neoliberalism, there was a premature deindustrialization in numerous countries in Latin America, Central and Eastern Europe, and Africa. Deindustrialization typically involves shifting from manufacturing production and employment toward sectors usually characterized by lower capital intensity and higher profitability. Many of these countries experienced regressive technical change, marked by relatively stagnant labor productivity as workers moved to sectors with lower labor productivity and higher capital productivity.

The manufacturing production was relocated to Asia, particularly to China. The rapid expansion in labor productivity in Chinese manufacturing led to a decline in industrial prices in relation to the prices of natural resources. The countries with abundant natural resources further deindustrialized as they exploited their comparative advantages. The process of deindustrialization was accompanied by reduced capital accumulation, despite some expansion in the profit rate.

Traditionally, the manufacturing sector is characterized by higher labor productivity and better-paid jobs. Moreover, transforming products through manufacturing generates demand for goods and services, diversifying the productive structure. This expansion necessitates technological advancements and an increase in labor knowledge and skills. Additionally, it contributes to urbanization, which, in turn, may expand infrastructure and reduce the cost of providing essential public services such as education, housing, and health care, ultimately boosting the economic well-being of a nation.

Manufacturing amplifies the division of labor and the productive complexity of an economy, offering opportunities for the emergence of new industries, particularly when integrated with existing activities. In a diversified economy, dealing with the problems associated with terms of trade becomes easier.

In recent decades, manufacturing has experienced a profound transformation. Communication and information technology advances have led to a convergence between manufacturing and service sectors. Boundaries between services and manufacturing are becoming blurred, giving rise to a phenomenon known as the "servicification of manufacturing." The process involves a combination of higher technological sophistication and the advantages of economies of scale and scope.

The volume of investments required for industrialization is a challenge and often surpasses the resource mobilization capacity of many developing countries, even for nations with national development banks, such as Brazil. The developing countries have relied on various methods to mobilize domestic resources for industrialization. The mobilization of national resources involves two strategies. The first is using the tax system, which includes raising taxes or expanding the tax base. The second is inflationary financing, which extends the government's resources and transfers income from labor to capital. Both approaches may lead to distributive conflicts and inflation.

Developing countries have also employed external resources to finance industrialization, including loans, foreign aid, and foreign direct investment. While these resources provide capital, they also pose problems related to external debt payments and the lack of foreign currencies. These problems may culminate in exchange rate devaluations, resulting in distributive conflicts and inflationary pressures.

(Re)industrialization usually involves investment in capital-intensive sectors, particularly as the process advances beyond its initial phases. As discussed previously, it may lead to a decline in capital productivity and, consequently, a fall in the profit rate, which can reduce capital accumulation. Successful (re)industrialization requires rapid economic growth to maintain profitability.

Another problem arises from the dependency on specific industries or sectors, leaving the country vulnerable to economic downturns when those sectors face difficulties. This vulnerability is acute for small countries which specialize in particular products. One hypothetical solution is a coalition of developing countries cooperating on collective industrialization. This arrangement could benefit many countries, particularly those with limited local populations and scale of production. However, the feasibility of this approach depends on high level of political and social cooperation.

Many questions remain regarding the role of manufacturing in promoting catching up and development. Industrialization can sometimes exacerbate income inequality within a country, as the benefits may be distributed unevenly, favoring specific social groups over others. Inequality can also occur in the geographical distribution within the country. Furthermore, the increased demand for a skilled labor force associated with manufacturing growth can contribute to inequalities, especially in countries with uneven access to education.

(Re)industrialization, if not managed sustainably, can result in environmental problems, such as pollution and resource depletion. Developing countries may be tempted to follow the historical path of industrialization of the Western countries and dismiss environmental restrictions, at least in its initial stages. As ecological impact mitigation involves costs, an important point is how to fund the necessary investment to avoid those impacts. On the other hand, environmentally friendly products can represent an opportunity to take advantage of the backwardness and promote industrialization.

Indeed, (re)industrialization can be a fundamental tool for catching up and reducing backwardness by modernizing and expanding the productive capacity of a country. Industrialization tends to incorporate technical progress and remains a powerful vehicle to promote labor productivity growth. Green industrialization may also be a tool for reducing greenhouse gas emissions.

However, its success in achieving these goals depends on various factors. It starts with reaching a minimal political and social consensus that allows for building a national development project. The national development project must consider the level of backwardness of each country, as well as its vocations and possibilities in terms of available resources, labor force education and skills, possible energy sources, and the set of techniques that can be adopted.

The success of (re)industrialization must also include how it is managed, the policies in place, and the inclusiveness of development efforts. The capacity to arbitrage social disputes is also fundamental since industrialization tends to alter the power correlations among social groups. In this vein, a comprehensive approach to development, beyond just economic growth, is essential to ensure the long-term benefits of industrialization. Furthermore, one must consider the international scenario and the opportunities and restrictions presented by the asymmetric relations between nations. Industrialization can face difficulties or facilities depending on the relative position of the developing country in the international context. Geopolitical disputes can simultaneously open some opportunities while others are closed.

Ultimately, the aspects discussed above point to the fundamental relevance of state capacities as the primary locus where strategies and conditions for industrialization are conceived and implemented. Unlike the market, which allocates resources primarily to maximize profits without guaranteeing national development, the state remains, in the XXI Century, the political and economic entity capable of intentionally driving industrialization.

Neoliberal capitalism and uneven development

Asia, Latin America, Africa, and Central and Eastern Europe were subject to the same general principles of neoliberal capitalism. Yet, these principles operated within different national contexts, shaped by varying economic, political, and social structures and distinct ways which those structures interact with the international economic system. In each nation, these structures determine income distribution, which, coupled with the technique in use, define the profit rate, subsequently influencing capital accumulation and the potential for catching up. Although these structures evolve over time, they are path-dependent, resulting in diverse trajectories of development.

While the neoliberal globalization of the capitalist economy spurred growth in some Asian economies, it had detrimental effects in Latin America and Africa. In Central and Eastern Europe, the countries that joined the European Union benefited from the transition by integrating their economies into the neoliberal order, while those that remained outside the EU fell behind. Neoliberal capitalism had contradictory effects on developing countries, resulting in uneven capitalist development.

The most successful catching-up has been observed in Asian regions. Over the past decades, many countries in Eastern, Southeastern, and Southern Asia have made progress in catching up in labor and capital productivities. These results have been driven by comprehensive development strategies, bolstered by factors such as national sovereignty, stability, and financial robustness. Besides adopting state-led growth strategies, these nations have benefited from offshoring industrial activities and the free trade policies adopted by Western countries during neoliberalism.

The Asian countries that emerged after the dissolution of the USSR faced complex challenges in establishing national identities, building coherent state structures, and transitioning to market-oriented economies. Many oil-dependent nations in Western Asia also grappled with identity and state-building, often complicated by wars and internal conflicts.

During the catching-up, Asian countries experienced the Marx-biased pattern of technical change, with rising labor productivity and declining capital productivity, resulting in a falling profit rate. The countries responded to this decline in different ways. Japan embraced neoliberalism, channeling profits into the financial system and reducing investments. In contrast, China increased its investment rate, even in the face of declining profitability. India adopted neoliberalism to reduce the wage share, boosting profits, and facilitating capital accumulation.

Large Asian nations such as China, India, and Indonesia appear increasingly capable of fostering their technical development, reducing reliance on foreign technology. However, these countries may face increased competition as the process of globalization recedes. The ascent of China as a global competitor has prompted increasing restrictions from the United States, reshaping the dynamics of globalization and economic integration. Nevertheless, China has demonstrated a capacity to adapt to developmental challenges, suggesting that the labor productivity gap between both countries, even if at a lower velocity, will continue to decline.

In the process of catching up, Asian countries rapidly expanded their carbon dioxide emissions. There is a pressing need for a shift toward environmentally sustainable technical change to absolute decouple economic growth from greenhouse gas emissions. This transformation could potentially spur additional growth but necessitates a thoughtful balance between capital accumulation and environmental sustainability.

Most Latin American countries fell behind during neoliberalism. The decline in the profit rate during the 1970s and the subsequent adoption of neoliberalism in the 1980s led to a fall in the investment rate, lower capital accumulation, and reduced economic growth. This stands in contrast to the response to the crisis of 1930s, when many Latin American nations adopted a developmentalist model, resulting in industrialization, less dependence on commodity exports, and catching up with the United States.

The crisis of developmentalism in Latin America paralleled the Golden Age crisis in developed nations. International financial institutions, especially the International Monetary Fund, gained regional influence during the debt crisis, advocating neoliberal reforms. The local business elites endorsed neoliberalism as profit rates declined, leading to the dismantling of the developmentalist state.

In the early 1990s, Latin American countries reintegrated into global financial markets, pegging currencies to the dollar, which controlled inflation and facilitated further neoliberal reforms, reinforcing their role as commodity producers, and causing deindustrialization. The 1997 Asian financial crisis spread to Latin America, fueling political resistance against neoliberalism.

Around 2000, left-wing parties came to power, known as Pink Tide wave. The surge in commodity prices enhanced profitability, and the adoption of a pragmatic economic policy that combine elements of both neoliberalism and developmentalism resulted in modest increase in capital accumulation, facilitating the catching up.

As the terms of trade declined following the 2007 financial crisis and the wage share increased, the profit rate plunged, leading to a fall in political support of Pink Tide governments. Subsequently, many Latin American countries fully adopted a late neoliberal policy framework.

The adoption of neoliberalism by Central and Eastern European countries during the transition to capitalism resulted in mixed outcomes. These nations embraced neoliberal principles, neglecting to leverage their economies in the existing industrial capabilities, skilled labor force, and income equality. The neoliberal shift prioritized privatization and market deregulation, which led to declining output, high inflation, and increased poverty during the 1990s.

The Central and Eastern European nations that joined the EU have generally experienced better economic outcomes, benefiting from the technological transfers and the special financial conditions established in the accession treaties. These countries also benefit from integration in the EU single market, allowing them access to a larger consumer base, becoming deeply intertwined with the developed capitalist nations.

However, the other Central and Eastern European economies have exhibited volatile economic performances and reduced economic growth. These economies rely on commodities production, particularly raw materials, and energy, contributing to their economic instability. While these countries have higher possibilities to move away from neoliberalism, the available resources for development of its productive forces are limited. The alternative is to search for partnerships with the Asian countries that are contesting neoliberalism or to integrate into the European Union.

In the XXI Century, Africa experienced a partial resurgence in economic growth after a profound regression during neoliberalism. The economic revival was driven by increased demand for its commodities from Asian markets. It was not associated with changes in its productive structure. Additionally, many African nations have achieved greater political stability after decades of political upheaval. However, some countries still grapple with establishing a well-functioning state machinery.

Neoliberalism emerged in the early 1980s in the context of debt crisis and falling commodity prices. It was compounded by the institutional limitations of the new African states and internal conflicts, leading to a period of economic regression. Similarly, to Latin America, the International Monetary Fund and the World Bank imposed conditionalities on loans to foster neoliberal reforms in African societies, reducing state structures and establishing marked-friendly institutional arrangements.

During neoliberalism, most African countries fell behind. A new upturn began only after commodities prices soared at the beginning of the 2000s. The economic growth of most African countries is still largely dependent on foreign dynamics. A lack of the state capabilities to promote well-defined national development projects remains in most African countries. In many cases, the national states have reduced capacity to provide infrastructure and public goods, in extreme cases, even they cannot enforce state authority over parts of their territory.

Africa could benefit from international cooperation to raise capital accumulation and catch up. The emergence of projects like the Belt and Road Initiative, promoted by China, and the relevance of emergent powers like the BRICS group may represent new opportunities for cooperation for African countries. However, the challenge is taking advantage of these opportunities while avoiding repeating the patterns of foreign impositions seen in the XX Century.

Thus, structural crises drove significant institutional shifts in capitalism, profoundly impacting the dynamics of catching up and falling behind. The capitalist changes resulting from the neoliberal crisis will bring new implications for developing countries. The key questions involve how developing countries will be influenced by these changes, what these changes will entail, and how developing nations will respond to them.

A new world ahead

In 2019, the average worker in the Central African Republic, one of the poorest countries worldwide, produced 6.8 dollars per day when measured at 2017 purchasing power parity. In India, the average worker produces 50.4 dollars daily, while in the United States, the average worker produces 355.9 dollars. The rapid expansion of labor productivity is a fundamental step in reducing poverty and improving the well-being of the poor population. However, it has been an enormous challenge for backward nations to achieve high growth rates in labor productivity and catch up with the developed countries.

Historically, and as discussed in this book, backwardness has primarily been viewed as a national problem. Nevertheless, individuals living in the Central African Republic, India, or any other less developed nation aspire to and have the right to enjoy a similar level of well-being as a US citizen. There are three possible ways for this to happen.

The first approach involves rapidly increasing labor productivity in less developed countries, leading to a process of catching up. However, this necessitates infrastructure, industrialization, and the employment of energy based on fossil fuels. While most of the money generated in production stays within national borders, the greenhouse gases spread globally. Promoting rapid expansion of labor productivity is a complex task, and often is challenging for most developing countries.

The second option is an individual solution through immigration to a developed country. While some immigration may bring mutual benefits, massive populational movements can negatively impact both nations. The third option involves the stagnation or reduction in labor productivity in developed countries and an increase in labor productivity in developing countries. This solution shares some similarities with the propositions made by the degrowth movement. Therefore, backwardness must be viewed as an international problem, and its solution requires coordinated and collaborative action and a new global order.

During neoliberalism, the established international order, led by the United States, imposed restrictions on the economic growth of most developing countries. The main exceptions were the Asian nations that either did not follow or implement a mild version of neoliberalism and the Central and Eastern European nations that joined the European Union. However, neoliberalism has contradictions and has weakened the hegemonic position of the United States. The crisis of neoliberalism also represents the crisis of the US hegemony and the prevalent international order.

The ongoing struggle for global hegemony between the established order, led by the United States and its developed allies, and the emerging order, captained by China and its developing nation partners, raises the potential for a new cold war. The competition and geopolitical tensions carry the risk of negative consequences for addressing critical global issues that demand international cooperation. Poverty, inequality, demographics, and the environment are among the pressing concerns. These complex problems require global cooperation, innovative solutions, and substantial investment.

A global, large-scale investment in sustainable energy infrastructure, aimed at significantly reducing greenhouse gas emissions while fostering green production of essential goods and services for the world's population, could mark the initial crucial step. Most of these investments should prioritize environmental and social goals over profit motives, allowing developing countries to catch up and reduce poverty.

Addressing the pressing challenges facing humanity requires a departure from neoliberalism. The pivotal question is whether capitalism, driven by profit motive, can provide a viable path toward environmental sustainability and equitable economic development for humanity. Alternatively, it may require the demise of capitalism and the transition to a new framework to effectively address the complex problems of the XXI Century.

Index

Note: Pages numbers in *italics* refer figures and **bold** tables in the text.

For Product Safety Concerns and Information please contact our EU representative GPSR@taylorandfrancis.com Taylor & Francis Verlag GmbH, Kaufingerstraße 24, 80331 München, Germany